MOSQUITO THUNDER

No. 105 SQUADRON RAF AT WAR 1942–5

STUART R. SCOTT

FOREWORD BY

AIR MARSHAL SIR IVOR BROOM
KCB CBE DSO DFC** AFC RAF (RET'D)

SUTTON PUBLISHING

First published in the United Kingdom in 1999 by
Sutton Publishing Limited · Phoenix Mill · Thrupp · Stroud · Gloucestershire GL5 2BU

First published in paperback in 2001

British Library Cataloguing in Publication Data
A catalogue record for this book is available from the British Library.

ISBN 0-7509-2691-0

Typeset in 10/12pt Times.
Typesetting and origination by
Sutton Publishing Limited.
Printed and bound in England by
J.H. Haynes & Co. Ltd, Sparkford.

Contents

F/L Peter Rowland with his other form of transport when not flying Mosquitos. (Via Keith Rowland)

In memory of the late
Captain Peter Wilton Townsend Rowland DFC, RAF
and his son, Keith.

Captain Keith Rowland with the author.

Foreword

AIR MARSHAL SIR IVOR BROOM
KCB CBE DSO DFC✳✳ AFC RAF (RET'D)

Stuart Scott's passionate interest in the history of No. 105 Squadron was first seen in his splendid book *Battle-Axe Blenheims* which covered the squadron's history during that early devastating period of the Second World War for daylight bomber aircraft.

In December 1941 No. 105 became the first squadron to re-equip with the Mosquito bomber aircraft – a version of this all-wooden multi-role aircraft, which produced a quantum leap in performance over all other twin-engined aircraft. This book embraces several years' further research into official records and the first-hand recollections of survivors in order to produce the graphic story of No. 105 Squadron while equipped with Mosquitos.

Throughout 1942 the squadron operated in the daylight bomber role, mostly at very low level. Daring daylight raids, many of which received great publicity at the time, are described in fascinating detail.

In 1943 No. 105 Squadron was transferred to the newly formed Path Finder Force. Flying at very low level in daylight was replaced by flying at very high level at night. The squadron, in company with No. 109 Squadron, was equipped with Oboe – the most accurate blind bombing marker used in the war. The book contains an excellent description of how that aid worked, the accuracy it achieved and its overall effect on the day-to-day activities of the squadron. The raids led by No. 105 Squadron before and following the D-Day invasion of Europe illustrate vividly the part which bomber aircraft – and the rest of the Path Finder Force – played in the invasion and successful advance by Allied land forces across Europe.

This is a fascinating book. We owe a debt of gratitude to Stuart Scott for carrying out the tremendous amount of research which was necessary to produce it.

Pilot Ivor G. Broom (left) and his observer, Tommy Broom, both as flight lieutenants, in front of their Mosquito. Although unrelated, they were known as 'The Flying Brooms' as depicted by the crossed broomsticks below the observation window on the nose of their aircraft.(Via Sir Ivor Broom)

Preface

'UK four-niner-niner, continue climb Flight Level one-zero-zero, turn left heading three-four-one.' 'Climb Flight Level one-zero-zero, and three-four-one the heading, UK four-niner-niner' came the immediate reply. This brought us 'east-abeam' RAF Biggin Hill. It was summer 1993, and I was on board an Air UK BAe 146 'whisper jet' leaving London's Gatwick Airport. After a long, tiring week working in Kent during the construction of the Channel Tunnel as a Chartered electrical consulting engineer, I was going home. It was a bright Friday summer's evening and I was in 'the office', the aviation term for the flight deck. I had been given the most privileged seat of all – the 'jump seat'; a spare seat which swings out to the rear of and between the captain and the first officer. The fact that I had identification and was learning to fly light aircraft must have influenced the captain's decision to permit me to enter the aircrew's world. The captain that day was Keith Rowland, and his first officer was Tim Hall. Both made me very welcome and after a detailed safety briefing and enthralling take-off along runway 26L, we were bound for Glasgow.

Captain Rowland glanced down at Biggin Hill, the old RAF aerodrome which, among others, was famous for its vital contribution to the winning of the Battle of Britain. He drew my attention to the spectacle, which I viewed with enthusiasm through the rear of the flight deck's port window. The captain remarked how interested he was in both Formula One motor racing and RAF aircraft of the Second World War, before proceeding to tell me a story of an RAF bomber coming in to land at a Second World War aerodrome. Returning from an operation, the pilot had found that there were several other aircraft waiting to gain permission to land. With an impatient plea to the tower, he advised of his predicament. Having just returned from a flight over enemy territory, and coming in on only two engines, he desperately required to land. With some sympathy, the tower responded to the pilot's urgent request and the green light was given for an emergency approach and landing. The pilot duly brought his aircraft on to final approach, lined up and touched the bomber down safely, much to the relief of all concerned. On arrival, however, there was much consternation on the ground, as the stricken aircraft turned out to be a Vickers Wellington which, as any air-minded person would recall, was only ever equipped with two engines!

Keith and I chatted further, between interruptions for air traffic control, and it transpired that he was particularly interested in twin-engined aircraft. I mentioned that I too had a similar interest, and that my particular passion at the time was for the Bristol Blenheim medium bomber. I explained that I was engaged in writing a book in memory of my uncle, Stuart George Bastin, who had been a sergeant WOp/AG on Blenheims, and who had been killed attacking shipping at low level in the Mediterranean, while flying from Malta in 1941. Keith replied that his interest lay particularly with the de Havilland Mosquito, as his father had flown many during the war, and had thankfully survived. Imagine my surprise when it turned out that both of our relations had been members of 105 Squadron. Both were initially sergeants, based, albeit at different times, at RAF Swanton Morley in Norfolk where the squadron was an integral part of No 2 Group, Bomber Command.

Subsequently, Keith and I became the best of friends, and I met his charming wife Anne and their two lovely little children, Hannah and Sarah. Keith and I often discussed in depth the wartime exploits of our respective relatives. I soon perceived the great depth of feeling Keith had for his father, who had progressed from the RAF to become an airline pilot, but had unfortunately passed away from cancer a few years before. Keith's intense admiration for the courage of his late father's wartime exploits on 105 Squadron was much the same as I hold for my late uncle. Consequently, when the opportunity arose, I decided to extend my researches from the Blenheim era of 105 Squadron to its Mosquito era and record their deeds in the form of a book. Hence *Mosquito Thunder* came into being. Sadly, shortly before publication, Keith was prematurely taken from us. Consequently, *Mosquito Thunder* is to be a tribute to Keith as well as his father, Captain Peter Rowland DFC, and those like him who bravely defended our country, often against very severe odds.

Acknowledgements

My most sincere thanks go to Air Marshal Sir Ivor Broom for his generous contributions and untiring support in my endeavours to produce this book. Much of his valuable time was spent reading my manuscript, providing his editorial comments and, in particular, writing the Foreword, for which I offer my deep appreciation.

I would particularly like to express my heartfelt thanks and gratitude to the following individuals, who also spent much of their time corresponding with me, providing personal recollections and anecdotes, copies of their log books, and an abundance of photographs, all of which add considerably to the accuracy and general interest in a factual study such as this: S/L W.R. Ball RAF (Ret'd); Donald C. Boa DFC, RAF (Ret'd); the late Dennis Bolesworth RAF (Ret'd); W/C R.W. Bray DFC, RAF (Ret'd); Phillip H. Brown DFC*, RAF (Ret'd); Thomas J. Broom DFC*, RAF (Ret'd); Mike Carreck DFC, RAF (Ret'd); W/C Peter J. Channer DSO, DFC, RAF (Ret'd); Ron 'Bill' Channon RAF (Ret'd); G/C H.J.'Peter' Cundall CBE, DSO, DFC, AFC, pfc, psa, RAF (Ret'd); Eric Dick RAF (Ret'd); A. Cecil Dunlop RAF (Ret'd); Grenville Eaton DFC*, RAF (Ret'd); S/L Tony W. Farrell DFC, AFC, RAF (Ret'd); Wally Fennell RAF (Ret'd); Geoffrey H. Gilbert DFC*, RAF (Ret'd); H.C. 'Gary' Herbert DFC, RAF (Ret'd); S/L W.E.G. Humphrey DFC*, RAF (Ret'd); Kenneth H. Kiely RAF (Ret'd); Jim Lang RAF (Ret'd); The late Tomas P. Lawrenson DFC, RAF (Ret'd); the late Cyril F. Muller DFC, DFM, AE, RAF (Ret'd); Geoffrey Parker DFC, RAF (Ret'd); the late W/C D.A. George Parry MBE, DSO, DFC*, AE, RAF (Ret'd); Air Commodore Graham R. Pitchfork MBE, BA, FRAeS, RAF (Ret'd); Ronald W. Plunkett DFC, RAF (Ret'd); H.D. 'Bill' Riley DFC*, RAF (Ret'd); A/Cdr Edward B. 'Ted' Sismore DSO, DFC**, AFC, AE, RD (Danish), RAF (Ret'd); Captain Peter Sleight DFC, RAF (Ret'd); G/C Keith Somerville DSO, DFC, AFC, RAF (Ret'd); the late Tony E.A. Spong Army (Air Liaison Team) (Ret'd); the late Richard A. 'Dick' Strachan DFC*, RAF (Ret'd); Cliff H. Streeter RAF (Ret'd); Patricia Tennison WRAF (Ret'd); Frank Templeton RAF (Ret'd); Robin P. Thomas DFC, RIBA, RAF (Ret'd); the late Stan Twigg RAF (Ret'd); the late Trevor C. Walmsley DFC, RAF (Ret'd); Brigadier General Jack V. Watts DSO, DFC*, CD, RCAF (Ret'd); S. Tom Wingham DFC, RAF (Ret'd); The late R.J. 'Bob' Woodhouse RAF (Ret'd); Tommy Williams RAF (Ret'd), Lord Lieutenant of Derbyshire.

In addition, I would like to thank the following for their kind assistance, provision of photographs and/or permission to reproduce excerpts from their and/or their families' texts of their manuscripts and/or details from their RAF log books: Dutch author Henk F. van Baaren; author Chaz Bowyer; Anthony Edwards, son to the late Air Commodore Sir Hughie Idwal Edwards VC, KCMG, CB, DSO, OBE, DFC, KStJ, RAF (Ret'd); author Jonathan Falconer; Norwegian author Cato Guhnfeldt; author James J. Halley; Australian author Arthur Hoyle RAAF (Ret'd); Mrs Pauline F. Kirby, widow to F/L N.H. Kirby DFC*, RAF (Ret'd); Dutch author Aad Neeven; S/L Charles Patterson DSO, DFC, RAF (Ret'd); Mrs Betty Ralston and Mr D. Ralston, widow and son respectively to the late W/C Roy Ralston DSO*, AFC, DFM, RAF (Ret'd); the late Captain Keith Rowland, son to the late Captain Peter W.T. Rowland DFC, RAF (Ret'd); Brigadier General Jack V. Watts DSO, DFC*, CD, RCAF (Ret'd); Hugh de Lacy Wooldridge, son of the late W/C John de Lacy Wooldridge DFC*, DFM, AE; and the Wooldridge Estate/Crécy Books.

Thanks also go to the following: Commonwealth War Graves Commission Internet Website; Deutsches Historisches Institut (German Historical Institute), particularly Andre Bastisch and

Mrs Cameron; Craig S. Goldie BA, FIHT, FIMgt; Charles P. John; The Mosquito Aircrew Association, particularly Archivist/Editor, Barry Blunt BA (Hons); General Secretary Gordon Hinds; Membership Secretary Tony Wilson; The Air Crew Association, particularly the Editor of *Intercom*, W/C A.R. Watkins BA, FRSA, RAF (Ret'd), and Branch Secretary, John Sampson DFC*; RAF Station Marham, particularly S/L Ed Bulpett RAF (Ret'd), CRO and F/Sgt Ray Biddle RAF, Station Historian; RAF Museum, particularly Andrew Whitmarsh; Lionel D.A. 'Rusty' Russell RAF (Ret'd); Captain Roger Stanley.

Last but not least, I would like to put on record my love and appreciation for my wife, Catherine, who throughout this project has encouraged me and sacrificed her personal time with me, so that those who fought with and many of whom died with 105 Squadron should not be forgotten. If I have missed anyone from the above I can only apologize, and thank them for their contribution.

It should be noted that all ranks and decorations mentioned in the text are those applicable at that time; where 'acting' ranks were applicable, the full substantive rank has been used. Also, brackets thus [ ] have been used by the writer to insert supplementary information.

Glossary of Terms and Abbreviations

AA	Anti-Aircraft
AASF	Advanced Air Striking Force
A/Cdr	Air Commodore
ACHU	Aircrew Holding Unit
Ack-Ack	Anti-Aircraft Fire
ACM	Air Chief-Marshal
AE	Air Efficiency award
A/F	Airfield
AFC	Air Force Cross
AOC	Air Officer Commanding
AOC-in-C	Air Officer Commanding-in-Chief
A/P	Aiming Point
ATC	Air Training Corps
AVM	Air Vice-Marshal
B	Bomber
BATF	Blind Approach Training Flight
BEM	British Empire Medal
BOAC	British Overseas Airways Corporation
BSc	Bachelor of Science
Bt	Baronet
CB	Companion of the Order of the Bath
CBE	Commander of the Order of the British Empire
CFI	Chief Flying Instructor
CMG	Companion of the Order of St Michael and St George
CO	Commanding Officer
Crack	Forces slang meaning 'of highest quality'
CRT	Cathode Ray Tube (like a TV screen)
CSBS	Course Setting bomb sight
DBF	Destroyed By Fire
DBR	Damaged Beyond Repair
D/F	Direction Finding
DFC	Distinguished Flying Cross (Officers only)
DFM	Distinguished Flying Medal (NCOs only)
DR	Dead Reckoning (navigation technique)
DSO	Companion of the Distinguished Service Order (Officers only)
DTs	Delirium Tremens (illusions brought on by alcohol abuse)
ENSA	Entertainments National Services Association
ETA	Estimated Time of Arrival
F/C	Flight Commander
FIDO	Fuel burning fog dispersal system for aerodromes
Flak	German Anti-Aircraft Fire
F/O	Flying Officer
FPU	Film Production Unit
FW	Focke-Wulf
F/Sgt	Flight Sergeant
G	Gravity
G-Force	Gravity Force
G/C	Group Captain
Gen	Air Force slang for 'General Information'
GP	General Purpose (Bomb)
GPLD	General Purpose Long (Time) Delay (Bomb)
GPSD	General Purpose Short (Time) Delay (Bomb)
GST	German Standard Time
Hangar	A storage shelter for aircraft
HE	High Explosive
H/F	High Frequency (Radar) or Heavy Flak
IAS	Indicated Air Speed
IFF	Identification Friend or Foe: a device on aircraft to allow radar stations to determine if the aircraft was 'friendly' or an enemy
INT/OPS	Intelligence / Operations
JG	Jagd Geschwader (German Day Fighter Wing)
KCB	Knight Commander of the Order of the Bath
KT	Knight of the Thistle
LAC	Leading Aircraftsman
lb	Pound(s) weight
LB	Long burn

LD	Long delay
Liechtenstein	German airborne radar
LMF	Lack of Moral Fibre (cowardice)
Lorenz	Beam approach radar
Lt	Lieutenant
Luftwaffe	German Air Force
Mae West	Life Jacket
MC	Military Cross (Award) or Medium Casing (Bomb)
MCU	Mosquito Conversion Unit
Merlin	Rolls Royce 'Merlin' engine
Mess	Communal Relaxation Quarters
Met.	Meteorological
MiD	Mentioned in Despatches
MO	Medical Officer
Morse	Morse Code – a sequence of dots and dashes which represent letters of the alphabet in groups which can be assembled to form text
MT	Motor Transport
MTU	Mosquito Training Unit
NAAFI	Navy Army & Air Force Institutes
Nav	Navigator
NCO	Non-Commissioned Officer
NFT	Navigation Flight Test / Night Flying Test
NTU	Night Training Unit
OBE	Order of the British Empire
Oboe	Blind bombing aid controlled by radar
OC	Officer Commanding
Op(s)	Operational sortie(s)
ORB	Operations Record Book
OTU	Operational Training Unit
Panzer	Tank (German)
pfc	RAF Flying College symbol
PFF	Path Finder Force
Photo-Freddie	Photographic Reconnaissance Aircraft
P/O	Pilot Officer
Pongo	Royal Air Force slang term for an Army Officer
PoWs	Prisoners of War
PR	Photo Reconnaissance
Prang	Royal Air Force slang term for 'crash'
PRU	Photo Reconnaissance Unit
psa	RAF Staff College symbol
PWD	Petroleum Warfare Department

Q-Code	Form of Morse Shorthand, e.g. QDM: Course to Base
RAAF	Royal Australian Air Force
RAF	Royal Air Force
RAFVR	Royal Air Force Volunteer Reserve
Recce	Reconnaissance
RNAF	Royal Norwegian Air Force
RNZAF	Royal New Zealand Air Force
SASO	Senior Air Staff Officer
SBA	Standard Beam Approach (radar)
SD	Short Delay
Sgt	Sergeant
SIO	Station Intelligence Officer
S/L	Squadron Leader (rank) or Searchlight
Sortie	Aerial Excursion
Sperrbracher	Merchant vessel converted to a gun platform
Stalag	German Prisoner of War camp
Stalag Luft	German Prisoner of War camp for airmen
TAS	True air speed
TI	Target Indicator
TRE	Telecommunications Research Establishment
u /s	Unserviceable
USA	United States of America
USAAF	United States Army Air Force
VC	Victoria Cross
VE	Victory in Europe
Verey pistol	A pistol which shot an illuminating ball into the air for recognition purposes
Vic	V-shaped aerial aircraft formation
WAAF	Women's Auxiliary Air Force
W/C	Wing Commander
WO	Warrant Officer
WRAC	Women's Royal Army Corps
W/T	Wireless Telegraphy
Würzburg	German ground mounted radar system to control anti-aircraft guns, searchlights and night-fighter aircraft
WOp/AG	Wireless Operator/Air Gunner
*	Bar to an award (i.e. a repeat of the same award)
**	Second bar to an award (i.e. a second repeat of the same award)

Introduction

No. 105 Squadron began life on 3 October 1917 at Andover, flying RE8 aircraft and later the two-seat Bristol F.2b biplane fighter. After the First World War was over in 1919 it disbanded, to be re-formed in April 1937 to operate Hawker Harts, Audaxes and latterly, before the Second World War, the Fairey Battle. The squadron fought bravely as part of the AASF, but was soon decimated. Having returned from its French base to RAF Honington in Suffolk, it was re-equipped with the very much 'state-of-the-art' Bristol Blenheim MkIV medium bomber.

The new bomber was faster than many of the front-line fighters of the time and, for defence, was equipped with a turret in the upper part of the fuselage. It was contemporary thinking that in a tight box formation and with mutual machine-gun defensive cover, the bombers would be quite a match for the opposing fighters. Sadly, this was to prove not nearly as effective as was thought. The Blenheim suffered grievously at the hands of the enemy, and soon became obsolete. It had been thrust into roles for which it was not designed, having been the best hope the RAF had at the time. The Blenheims of 105 and other squadrons fought courageously, and the highest award for valour, the VC, was issued to three airmen, each flying a different mark of Blenheim – W/C Hughie Idwal Edwards, CO of 105 Squadron, being one of them. He received this great distinction having flown a Blenheim MkIV while leading the squadron on a daring low-level daylight attack on the town of Bremen on 4 July 1941.

At the end of that month the squadron was detached to Malta to sink Axis shipping sailing from Italy to supply Rommel's Afrika Korps. Here in the seething Mediterranean heat and under cloudless skies, they flew at sea-level to attack their quarry. They acquitted themselves very well, committing thousands of tons of enemy supplies to the deep, though suffering severe losses in the process. Their detachment to Malta was to have lasted about three weeks, but it was after some three months that 107 Squadron eventually relieved them. This allowed those of 105 Squadron left alive to start their eventful journey back to England, courtesy of the Royal Navy.

On 11 October 1941, the remnants of 105 Squadron returned to RAF Swanton Morley in Norfolk, from where they had departed on the first stage of their journey to Malta. Some then went on to OTUs 'on rest' as instructors; others went on to other squadrons. For the observers and WOp/AGs, the options available included re-training as pilots or navigators.

At Swanton Morley the daily routine continued. The Spitfire MkIIas of 152 (Hyderabad) Squadron flew operationally, and apart from the gentle purr of Merlin engines delighting the ears, the sights were mainly of the odd Blenheim MkIV, the Blenheim MkV (known as a 'Bisley') and the No. 15 Blind Approach Training Flight (BATF) Airspeed Oxfords taking off and landing. During this time, many crews were brought in from 13 OTU at RAF Bicester in Oxfordshire, and from 17 OTU at RAF Upwood in Huntingdonshire (now in Cambridgeshire). More Blenheims were ferried in for training use. W/C Peter H.A. Simmons DFC came from RAF Wattisham, having officially taken over command of 105 Squadron on 1 October 1941.

On 10 November 1941 the observers of the squadron began a wireless course. They were placed under the instruction of P/O Wilson DFM, the station navigation officer, and the instructor in charge of observers, P/O Gerry Quinn DFM, both of whom had been decorated by King George VI at Buckingham Palace only days before. This course, and the engineering officer P/O W.C. Brennan's return from a course at Hatfield, was the prelude to the squadron being equipped with a new aircraft which, like its predecessor the Blenheim, was reputed to be the fastest aircraft available at the time, and of revolutionary construction. No. 105 was about to have the great distinction of becoming the RAF's first ever Mosquito Bomber squadron!

Part One – 2 GROUP

CHAPTER I

The de Havilland Mosquito

The history of the Mosquito or 'Wooden Wonder' has been well described elsewhere; however it is worth considering its unique construction and the salient features of this most successful twin-engined bomber.

The Mosquito's fuselage was constructed in two longitudinal sections on a mahogany mould, on which the inner beech skin was mounted along with the structural members. The structure was then cemented together and flexible steel clamps held it securely onto the mould, to give the necessary adherence under pressure to maintain bonding. A balsa wood filling was then added and smoothed, to give a clean surface prior to the outer skin being applied, which was again constructed of beech. The other half of the fuselage was constructed in a similar manner. Each half was then fitted with a significant amount of internal equipment before both halves were clamped together or 'boxed-up', as it was termed. To permit the two halves to bond together, they were held in place by wooden laminate bands. The whole assembly was then covered with Mandapolam, a fabric which was subsequently doped to provide tension, and then painted.

There was a large cut-out at the base section of the fuselage, aft of the cockpit, which was ultimately joined on to the wings at four large pick-up points. The wings were constructed in one section to fit neatly and simply into the fuselage cut-out, the lower part of which was replaced after the procedure was complete. The wings were built with front and rear Canadian spruce spars of box section, separated by spruce ribs and plywood webs. The upper surfaces were made of beech plywood, constructed separately as two skins. Along the wing, throughout its length, ran square-section spruce stringers. Underneath, the wing was skinned in only one layer of beech plywood, which ran from the wing-tip back to the central wing-tank area, where stressed balsa wood panels were fitted as fuel tank doors. Laminated plywood strips were moulded to form the wing leading edges each supported by several wooden nose ribs. The leading edges, which from their position outboard of the engines formed a taper as they neared the tip of the wing, were constructed of nose rib formers with a D-skin, and were attached to the front spar. Flaps were slotted and formed in wood, whereas the ailerons were of a light alloy frame and skinned. The whole wing assembly was glued together and supported where necessary by metal screws.

Before mating with the fuselage section, the wings were fitted with as much equipment as possible, such as fuel tanks, undercarriage assemblies and welded steel tube engine mountings, wing radiators which had flap-controlled outlets ahead of the front spar on the underside, as well as hydraulic piping, engine controls and electrical wiring. The tail fin was also constructed of wood, with a covering plywood skin. Attached to the fin was a rudder, this time formed in aluminium with trim tabs and a fabric covering, as were the elevators, initially. Below the tail fin was a retractable tail wheel and beneath the engines were the undercarriage units, again with retractable wheel assemblies supported by rubber blocks, held under compression. This was

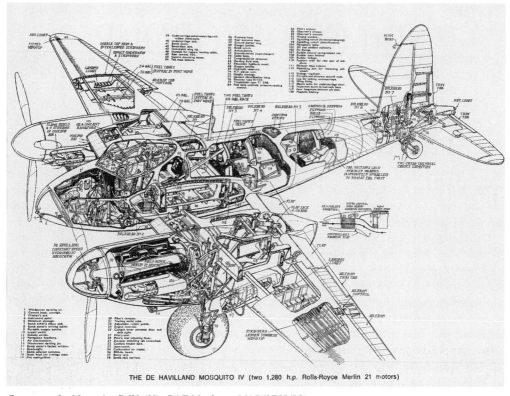

THE DE HAVILLAND MOSQUITO IV (two 1,280 h.p. Rolls-Royce Merlin 21 motors)

Cutaway of a Mosquito B.IV. (Via RAF Marham: MAR/0768/98)

unusual, as oleo-pneumatic shock absorbers were the norm; however rubber block construction had the operational benefit of a lesser maintenance requirement.

The Mosquito was equipped with two Rolls-Royce Merlin engines, each of which was in turn equipped with de Havilland metal three-bladed propellers, which had fully variable pitch and could be feathered if necessary.

Following many minor adjustments to consolidate the design of the prototypes, the last 10 PR Mosquitos from a batch of 19 ordered were converted to the unarmed bomber variant and would be referred to as B.IV Series i Mosquitos. The aircraft were serial-numbered W4064 to W4072 and each could carry four 250lb bombs in a bomb bay in the bottom of the fuselage. Subsequently, the Series ii Mosquito would have a larger bomb capacity, allowing transportation of four 500lb bombs in the bomb bays, albeit with specially designed shorter tail fins to adapt to the space available in the aircraft, which was at a premium. Observer, Mike Carreck describes the Mosquito's cramped interior:

To get in you had to climb a thin rickety red metal ladder; telescopic, it folded in on itself. At any given moment it would detelescope and you would have to stand around looking a right twerp in the intrepid bird-man kit while an embarrassed LAC tried to disentangle himself and it. There was a navigation table that slid out from the panel at the front of the cockpit. As you slid it out, ha-ha, it fell on the floor. All Mosquito navigators ignored it and clipped their Mercator charts to a piece of board that rested on their knees like a tea-tray. In fact, navigating a Mosquito was like being at a nightmare party for afternoon tea as you juggled not with cup, saucer, plate and cucumber sandwich but with dividers, protractors and maps from the jumble in the canvas satchel at your feet.

The Mosquito was a very good-tempered aircraft. It kept you nice and warm – not too hot, not too cold – just how you liked it. No question of red-hot knees while the rest of you froze as in some aircraft I could mention. No need for bulky Irvin jackets, clumsy flying boots; suede shoes and yellow socks quite acceptable [a reference to the socks Geoffrey de Havilland Jnr was wearing when delivering the first Mosquito]. In a wooden Mosquito there were no sticking out bits of metal to rip your battledress. Yet another delightful feature of the Mosquito was that it always smelt new – that indefinable 'new car' scent.

After the knockabout nonsense of the ladder, you would watch your pilot going up through the hatch like a five-year-old sweep up a Victorian chimney. A tight fit, it always looked odds-on against his chances of squirming through with parachute and dinghy banging below his knees. You would give him a moment or two to get settled, and then up you would go, wriggling through. The Mosquito cockpit was about the size of one of those old red telephone kiosks, cosy if not intimate. Your pilot would now be sitting in gentlemanly ease in his armchair, everything to hand, controls just so. You squirm around, there isn't an inch to spare and you take your seat beside him and a trifle behind. There is another great advantage of the Mosquito, the side-by-side seats, as you are in instant communication if

S/L Reggie Reynolds accompanied by his observer P/O E.B. 'Ted' Sismore address workers at de Havilland Aircraft Co. at Hatfield, on 25 February 1943. Standing at a table patriotically draped in the Union Jack flag, they extol the virtues of the 'Wooden Wonder' bomber they were waging war in, courtesy of the labours of those assembled before them. (Via E.B. Sismore)

somebody needs a tourniquet, and you are there to twist it on, and in the case of oxygen failure and bird collision. The only trouble is, the navigator doesn't have a seat. He is expected to make himself comfortable on the bare wooden spar across the cockpit.

Near the IFF set is a reel of wire. When you unwind it with its handle, the wire streams out behind the Mosquito: the aerial for long wave radio. You are always very sure indeed that the aerial has been wound back in before landing; its whiplash can kill! Above you is the Verey pistol and a horizontal wheel, about 9 inches in diameter and marked in compass degrees, which you turn to rotate the direction aerial for loop bearings; a dial opposite you has two needles that cross at a central line to show correct bearing. Behind you, left to right, are the Morse key, the black box of the radio receiver, with a big glass semi-circle for the tuning dial and the transmitter with coloured knobs and cut-outs for your fingers. A contortionist's job using the radio equipment; you have to twist around with your left arm aching over your right shoulder to get to the Morse key, with your oxygen tube and intercom cable probably doing their best to strangle you; not that your pilot doesn't have his moments of agony, reaching arm-breakingly behind and groping for the taps to change between outer and main fuel tanks.

In front of the navigator, in the Perspex nose of the Mosquito, is your 'office' with the MkIX bombsight, an undignified crawl away. There is a pad to kneel on, a box with the four fusing switches and the bomb-release button on its cable. A clear vision panel was set in the forward dome for aiming. Just before the 'office', on the floor, there was the circular switch for the camera. To avoid bomb hang-ups, there was a pull-out lever very clearly marked JETTISON. You yanked it after the 'bombs gone' before the bomb doors were closed. Above it, on the instrument panel in its slot was the compass deviation card with a graph to show the effect of the individual Mosquito's magnetism on all compass headings, established when the Mosquito was 'swung'.

This then, was the unarmed Mosquito MkIV bomber type, which initially went into service with 105 Squadron. The aircraft came to be loved by all who flew her, as Mike Carreck further explains: 'My pilot, Pete Rowland, once said of us flying the Mosquito that we were like a couple of extraordinarily wealthy chaps out for a spin in the world's most expensive sports car. Like all pilots, he adored the Mosquito, a dream to fly. I loved it too, the pair of us sitting so comfortably together, side by side between those two glorious Merlins, magnificent views of ground and sky, flying so fast and so high, faster and higher than almost anyone had flown before – lords of creation. There will always be just one aircraft for me – the Mosquito!'

CHAPTER 2

And in the Beginning . . .

Construction of RAF Swanton Morley had begun early in 1939, and it had opened in September 1940, sporting only a 'K'-type hangar and a convex grass runway. The base is situated in the countryside just north-west of the village of Swanton Morley, which is only a few miles from the nearest town of East Dereham, itself about 16 miles west of Norwich. On opening, RAF Swanton Morley was immediately home to 105 Squadron and its Blenheims; however, those days were now over and a new era was about to dawn.

For the new aircrew who were being posted in to join 105, the surroundings for some were acceptable and for others less so, depending on where lady luck (or rank) would have one billeted. No 152 Squadron had taken up residence on 31 August 1941, and consequently accommodation on the base was at a premium.

There were, however, those who had a fairly enjoyable start to life at RAF Swanton Morley, such as F/O Robin Thomas who was billeted nearby in a large country house named Bylaugh Hall, where he had a room he shared with a pilot officer. Robin recalls in his memoirs *Student to Stalag*:

Up till now I had never resided in an Officers' Mess, and although the hall was in no way 'the Mess', it was entirely taken over by the RAF and therefore was a sort of country annexe fully equipped with batmen and a staff of administrators. The room I shared with Titch [F/O V.F.E. Treherne DFM] was large with a beautiful open roaring coal fire, attended to exclusively by our batman who also brought hot water, in a china ewer, as well as tea, coffee and cocoa last thing at night. He woke us in the mornings with a cup of tea, cleaned our shoes and polished our buttons. I am all in favour of batmen! The aircrew sergeants were also billeted in the hall but the space they occupied was more crowded than ours and they did not have batmen to attend to their comforts.

One of the new arrivals, a sergeant not provided with the luxury of Bylaugh Hall, was Michael Carreck. Subsequently, he described life at the new base in a slightly different manner: 'By no means our favourite RAF station. We slept in Nissen huts – half a tube of corrugated tin. It was unbelievably cold in the Norfolk winter, in spite of coke stoves glowing cherry-red. We had mud up to our ankles when we

F/O Robin P. Thomas. (Via Robin Thomas)

walked, frozen, across to the ablutions – not that many of us washed much. We all slept under greatcoats and anything else we could pile on our beds. Some of the frostier among us slept in their uniforms.'

However, recreation was fairly typical of any high-spirited RAF station in the earlier days of the war, as Robin Thomas recalls: 'Our stay at Swanton Morley was long enough to discover that sharing a mess with a fighter squadron did not produce many quiet evenings to sit comfortably in an armchair enjoying a well-earned drink. The armchairs were usually moved to one side to make room for a game of no-rules rugger with a cushion as a ball, or employed to crouch behind when a handful of machine-gun bullets had been thrown on the fire. There always seemed to be plenty to drink, either in the Mess or in East Dereham where a pub with a heating system in the bar, consisting of an enormous open hearth upon which a sackful of coke burned in a pile some 2ft high, caused the customers gradually to retreat to the other end of the room.'

In contrast, however, Sgt Carreck remembers East Dereham as: 'Swanton Morley's haven of rest and relaxation. Lorries took us there in the evenings to enjoy the fun. Lively it was not. Never mind the wartime blackout, I was there a few peacetime years later – at 9 p.m. it was utterly silent, completely deserted, dark and lonely.' In conclusion, he summed up his experiences of 'fun' in East Dereham as having: '. . . no recollection of any frolic, of anybody friendly, and as for popsies [the wartime expression for young ladies], forget it! I think it is reasonable to comment on East Dereham's effect on us that none of us even knew it should be pronounced "East Derrum".'

However, irrespective of how life was perceived at the station, there was work to be done and much speculation and activity was going on while the squadron was working up to receiving the first of its new steeds. At last, on the morning of 15 November 1941, there was a new sound in the air and those on the station gathered to see a beautiful sight. A sleek new aircraft had appeared from the north-west and passed overhead at customary low level. It was knocking on 300 miles per hour; an incredible speed to those used to the comparatively slow Blenheims. The audience watched in awe as the aircraft went up to about 3,000ft, banked vertically and turned tightly with vapour trails streaming off the wing tips – the Mosquito had arrived and a new era was about to begin. It would be an era that would bring further courageous deeds synonymous with the name of 105 Squadron. The Mosquito or 'Mossie' as it was to become affectionately known, was to prove a 'crack' aircraft, assigned to a 'crack' squadron.

Sgt Carreck, among others, witnessed the arrival of the B.IV series i Mosquito, and observed that: '. . . the squadron's first Mosquito, W4064, came storming in a few feet above the hangars, and we heard that marvellous crackle of the Merlins as it came in to land. Moments later, it taxied up to were we all waited, agog. The hatch was opened; a ladder positioned and down came suede shoes and yellow socks, followed by Geoffrey de Havilland Jnr. They say of an aircraft, as it looks, so it flies. There's never been an aircraft as beautiful as a Mosquito. It wasn't just its clean, streamlined, gracious profile; it was much more than a picture-book aircraft – the Mosquito was alive! On the ground, with its slender fuselage, tail cocked high, and those two mighty engines, it looked as if it was holding itself back from leaping into the air. Flying . . . here it comes, it's gone . . . you heard the thundering authority of those Merlins, caught a glimpse of it flashing past, chin high, job to do, get out of my way.'

The station commander, Group Captain Battle OBE, DFC was on hand, along with the squadron commanding officer, W/C Peter H.A. Simmons DFC, to greet de Havilland as he emerged from under the nose of the Mosquito. All who had witnessed the dramatic display on arrival were ecstatic, and it was noted in the squadron ORB that 'Even the Spitfire pilots of 152 Squadron were impressed'. W/C Simmons was subsequently taken up for a flight and apart from having been reported as being a little green about the gills, when subsequently relaxing in the Officers' Mess he could not stop extolling the virtues of this new top secret wonder bomber.

In preparation for things to come, there began a series of 'bends' tests for potential Mosquito airmen, which started the next day. The tests were to simulate flight up to 35,000ft for four hours and were conducted by S/L Bright of 90 Squadron, the only squadron in Bomber Command operating the high-flying Fortress Is. It was essential that the effects of high-altitude flying were fully understood, and even the MO, F/O T.B. Russell, was despatched to Farnborough on a course to learn the medical intricacies of such flights. Despite this, some pilots very nearly came to grief from the effects of lack of oxygen [now known as 'hypoxia'] at altitudes in excess of 10,000ft, examples of which we shall see later.

On 17 November 1941 S/L Alan R. 'Jesse' Oakeshott arrived on the squadron, having been posted in from No. 4 BATF. He was to take over command of A-Flight from S/L Bryan W. Smithers DFC, who had been posted for a tour on Stirling bombers to 149 Squadron at RAF Mildenhall, 12 miles north-west of Bury St Edmunds. Smithers was well known and respected, having served on Malta with the squadron's Blenheims and was to be sadly missed. However, S/L Oakeshott ably filled the post. One who was there remembered Oakeshott as being, 'tall, well over six foot, and well built. A serious man with grave expression who made no attempt to be liked, but we were all tremendously fond of him.'

That same day, the squadron received its second Mosquito, W4066, and as usual Geoffrey de Havilland Jnr was at the controls for the arrival. Interest in the new aircraft had become intense and that day the AOC, Air Vice-Marshal Donald F. Stevenson DSO, OBE, MC, and a group of officers visited the station. With W4064 having been returned to Hatfield by Geoffrey de Havilland Jnr, this was to be the first Mosquito bomber to be left on charge of 105 Squadron. W4064 was nevertheless to return to the squadron days later.

The next Mosquito, W4068, arrived on 25 November 1941 and the CO, W/C Peter Simmons, took S/L Darwen, the CO of 152 Spitfire Squadron, up to show off its capabilities. This was to prove a lasting memory for him before his squadron departed on 1 December, bound for their new base at RAF Coltishall.

At this time, it was decided that a representative of 105 Squadron would be sent to Boscombe Down to consider how the Mosquito would perform in squadron service and F/L D.A. 'George' Parry DFC was given the job. He recalls his trip to see the experimental B.IV in action: 'W4057 – at first, when the aircraft arrived, flying was limited so it was arranged that F/L Jack Houlston and myself go down to Boscombe Down where it was on test. I flew it first and then Jack took over. We then went up to the mess for lunch where we met the OC Test Flight and Geoffrey de Havilland. We were asked for our opinion and said we were very impressed. I mentioned some buffeting on the tail, which Geoffrey said would be cured by extending the engine nacelles. I also said it was tail-heavy coming in to land. The OC Test Flight solved the problem by suddenly remembering that 1,000lb ballast had been put into the aircraft to check the C of G [centre of gravity].'

For the next week or so there was little flying owing to inclement weather, and activities were restricted to a lecture to all aircrew on the use of the constant speed propeller and to practise evacuations of the camp. Mike Carreck recalls the incident on 7/8 December 1941 when the latter was in progress and all aircrew had allegedly made good their escape from the enemy who had 'captured' the aerodrome: 'One night Swanton Morley held an exercise and the station was attacked by "German paratroops". We slept on the floor of the Sergeants' Mess, warm, best sleep I'd had in weeks. At some unearthly hour, somebody came in and woke us – "The Japs have bombed Pearl Harbour!" – I turned over and slept even more blissfully, knowing the war was won.'

On 8 December, the four Mosquitos and three Blenheims left, bound for another aerodrome which had been constructed in 1939, and which had been extensively used by 2 Group. It had seen many valiant Blenheim operations, attacking the enemy on land and at sea in those suicidal anti-shipping operations in the North Sea (or 'Stevenson's Sea of Carnage' as it was commonly known, due to the horrendous losses inflicted by the anti-shipping operations ordered by AVM Stevenson). One of the most notable sorties was by 18 Squadron to drop a replacement leg to Douglas Bader when he was a 'guest' of Hitler. The aerodrome was RAF Horsham St Faith, near Norwich, and it was to this location that the whole of 105 Squadron departed in convoy, at 09.00 hours on the 10th. Their arrival was marked by a parade that afternoon ordered by the CO, W/C Peter Simmons.

RAF Horsham St Faith offered a standard of living much suited to the standards aspired to by the aircrew. Robin Thomas described their new location as: 'a permanent station with proper hangars, messes and administrative building. It had existed for some time, and the airfield was grass, with no runways (at that time) and not very large. There were considerable attractions; ten minutes on a bicycle would suffice to get from the Officers' Mess to the Bell Hotel in the centre of Norwich. The villages of Spixworth, Wroxham, Horning and Sprowston, complete with pubs, were equally accessible though a little further away.'

The nearest large town was Norwich. Mike Carreck noted:

After East Dereham – paradise. You could pick up a bus just outside Horsham St Faith airfield and in ten or fifteen minutes be in a city full of pubs, attractive shops, cinemas, friendly people and if you were on the hunt for crumpet, a promising palais de dance called Samson and Hercules, otherwise known as Sodom and Gomorrah. When the time came round for leave, there were plenty of direct trains to London from Norwich Thorpe station. Norwich is, of course, a beautiful city. However, I don't think any of us visited the cathedral with its Norman tower and fifteenth-century spire. Just to be in the market place and to be surrounded by the Guildhall, the Maddermarket theatre and the Church of St Peter Mancroft was a soothing reminder that there was a civilization outside the briefing room at Horsham St Faith.

Of the pubs I can only name The Castle. This is where a fighter pilot, top button undone [it was customary for those fighter pilots who had fought in the Battle of Britain to leave the top button of their tunic undone in recognition], came stamping in. 'Bring me a whisky', he bellowed at the barman, 'I've been chasing the Hun all day!' Astonished silence followed, only broken by the quiet voice of a Blenheim air-gunner asking 'could I have a double please, *I've* been chasing the Hun all day.'

After Swanton Morley – heaven! It was a permanent station with radiators, bathroom opposite one's own room (shared with another sergeant, in my case Pete Rowland). We had every comfort and we all came to life once more. Pete and I were commissioned at Horsham St Faith, and how we relished the food in the Officers' Mess, the cook being out of this world. However, soon he was gone as the NAAFI took over and gone were those memorable meals. We had a civilian batman between us in those early days of 1942 – the life of Riley, but not for long. We soon lost him and a WAAF batwoman to RAF austerity.

The station had other luxuries that Robin Thomas describes: 'The dining room downstairs was adjacent to a large ante-room, well furnished with a grand piano, radiogram, dartsboard and lots of comfortable, well-upholstered armchairs. Nearby was a billiards room, a writing room and a guests' sitting room used by the WAAF officers.'

There was some entertainment to break the operational monotony, and mess parties, known as 'thrashes', were the order of the day whenever possible. Beery sing-songs often erupted around

*F/L Michael Carreck (observer) and F/L
Peter Rowland (pilot). (Via Keith Rowland)*

the 'old Joanna', rather like the modern 'rugby song', sung with much youthful exuberance. References were often made in the songs to the genitalia of one Mr Banglestein, the nocturnal habits of the feline species and occasionally to the sexual prowess of the elephant. Party games were also popular, and often centred around the ability to balance a tankard of beer on one's head, accompanied by the rapturous singing of 'does "so-and-so" know the Muffin Man, Muffin Man, Muffin Man', etc. Just before the bar closed, enamel jugs of beer would be ordered containing the only drink generally consumed and referred to as 'Harpic', following which the thrash might well end with the imprints of sooty feet across the ceiling. As Mike Carreck explains: 'It helped us to let off steam; helped us to forget operations were costing us one Mosquito in every six' – a reference to the heavy losses initially incurred by the squadron, as we shall see.

Robin Thomas describes operational life with a significantly small number of Mosquitos, which was largely due to delivery delays incurred, due to the necessity of designing a shorter 500lb bomb to increase the bomb-load of the Mosquito:

There were various other aircraft to which we had access for training, fetching and carrying, visiting, going on leave and simply for enjoyment. There were a couple of Masters – single-engined, two-seat fighter-trainers – an Anson, at least two Blenheims, a Tiger Moth, at one time a Puss Moth, and the use of Airspeed Oxfords belonging to the Blind Approach School who also used the airfield. [In fact one of the Mosquitos was fitted at this time with 'Lorenz' (beam approach equipment).] It was to be some time before sufficient Mosquitos arrived to make operations possible, but in the interim, although there was considerable frustration, there was seldom tedium.

The Anson was used as a general workhorse, and on one occasion I was in it on a journey to Hatfield, the birthplace of the Mosquito, to fetch some engine cowlings for the few Mosquitos we did have. The opportunity was taken to look over the factory and see the fuselages being moulded from birch plywood and balsa wood. At the end of the factory tour, having been told the entire neighbourhood was by now devoid of dog kennels, garden sheds, rabbit hutches and any other timber structure easily removed during the blackout, we returned to face the problem of getting four aluminium engine cowlings into the Anson. Each cowling was some 7 or 8ft long, 2ft wide and quite substantial. It was soon apparent that the pilot and navigator (me) would have to get in first and the rest of the crew, two groundcrew fitters, would have to get the cowlings in with a minimum of assistance from us, which I didn't mind, but with almost no possibility of us at the front ever getting out of the door at the back without the prior removal of the cowlings. This I did mind, but fortunately the necessity did not arise. The Anson rattled noisily into a take-off, even more noisily into the landing at the other end, following a flight of happy rattling heard easily above the noise of the engines.

Life continued with several training flights, allowing those who had flown the Mosquito to pass on their new-found skills to those with whom they served. After all, nobody else had any experience of this new top-secret aeroplane, although security seemed to be a little lacking, as

No. 105 Squadron's Airspeed Oxford 'taxi': groundcrew group with WAAF MT 'driver' relaxing. (Via Cliff Streeter)

Mike Carreck points out: 'One side of Horsham St Faith airfield was bounded by a busy public road. Odd, considering Mosquitos were highly secret. The most amateur spy could click a shutter any time.'

W/C Peter Channer DFC (who had received his DFC for an attack with 18 Squadron on Knapsack power station at Köln (Cologne)) recently corroborated this perception. He remembers an RAF sergeant who, so incensed by the apparent lack of security on RAF bases, chose RAF Horsham St Faith to prove his point. The young, blond-haired airman had been shot down previously, and escaped before approaching the Air Ministry. With their backing, he was allegedly provided with a German officer's uniform, which he wore when he arrived at the station, claiming he was Swedish. He then bluffed his way into the mess for lunch as well as the operations room before it was realized that the swastika on his uniform just might not be of Swedish insignia! The Intelligence Officer, S/L Victor Brookes, who had previously detained two German escapees from a Magister aircraft, had recognized the uniform immediately he had clapped eyes on it and the young 'German officer' was arrested before he could subsequently tell captors who he really was. It was perhaps not coincidental that on 12 January 1942 all flying crews were to attend a lecture by the SIO, S/L Vaughan – the subject matter being 'security'.

Flying continued, and navigators were given the opportunity to practise their navigation skills. Despite being frustrated by bad weather, cross-country flights were carried out and fuel consumption tests completed at various altitudes, and W/C Simmons reached 30,000ft without problems.

Christmas was now looming and on Christmas Eve, seasonal supplies were flown in from Dishforth in a dual-controlled Blenheim. However, one pilot nearly missed the festivities – Sgt Pete Rowland, who had only joined the squadron at the beginning of the month, had been taken by S/L Jesse Oakeshott on a 15-minute hop to Coltishall in Anson N9717. Some time later that day, for his return journey, Sgt Rowland was given DH82A Tiger Moth T5812, but managed to get lost during the flight. As it was getting dark, he considered it prudent to force-land in a field at Bungay 17 miles north-east of RAF Horsham St Faith, which he successfully did, having flown for one hour. He arrived safely home and a guard was mounted on the aircraft. On Christmas Day, S/L Oakeshott's festivities were interrupted as he returned after lunch to Bungay to retrieve the Tiger Moth from the field.

As was the tradition in the RAF, Christmas Day was the day when the senior NCOs and officers served dinner to the other ranks, a situation which Mike Carreck remembers when this happened previously and he was with his Blenheim crew: '. . . my pilot and WOp/AG were both officers. I've never felt so humiliated.' Nevertheless, this year the event was a great success and the officers held their dinner in the evening. The next day some local residents were entertained in the Officers' Mess for a cocktail party.

CHAPTER 3

Working Up

The new year started as 1941 had ended, except that 1 January saw the station on 'stand-down', possibly to ensure recovery from the excesses of the party the night before. The weather was still inclement but some flying continued. One noteworthy occasion was the visit paid to the squadron on 4 January by a well-known officer, W/C Hughie Idwal Edwards VC, DFC, who had returned from his publicity tour of the USA, and was now CFI at Wellesbourne Mountford, a few miles east of Stratford-upon-Avon. His visit was to prove a foretaste of things to come.

There was some excitement on the 5th, as an engine of the CO's Mosquito failed when flying over the Irish Sea. Consequently, he had to do an emergency landing at RAF Portreath in Cornwall, where he left the aircraft and returned to RAF Horsham St Faith by train. Sgt Swan was sent to retrieve it the next day once the engine fitters had repaired the fault. It was to be rather a dramatic return for Sgt Swan however, as on the 7th he departed RAF Portreath, where the runway suddenly drops away to reveal the sea below at the bottom of the cliff-face. In the event the departure was uneventful, but on coming in to land back at RAF Horsham St Faith, he added insult to injury and overshot, demolishing part of the boundary fence before coming to a halt, no doubt red faced and a bit shaken but safe and sound nevertheless. Given that this was the first 'prang' in a Mosquito bomber, and that another was grounded because the leader tanks were cracked, there was much interest shown by the manufacturer – so much so that Major de Havilland and his engineers came in person to view the damaged aircraft in the hangar.

Perhaps not insignificantly, only seven days later, the Station Commander at RAF Horsham St Faith, Group Captain G.R.C. 'Cockie' Spencer OBE, gave a lecture to the aircrew on 'the shortage of spares in the RAF and the necessity of avoiding unnecessary damage to aircraft through negligence'. A General Staff Air Liaison Officer Grade 3, responsible to the Station Commanding Officer, was Tony E.A. Spong, who described Cockie Spencer as: 'A very pleasant man. We called him "Uncle"! He was near retirement; I think he had a leg injury dating back to the previous war. I remember him with affection as he always sought me out whenever he took to the air in his Tiger Moth.'

Shortly thereafter, six army officers were taken up in an Anson for experience of flying and to gain an insight into the RAF's capabilities. Army officers were often cruelly referred to in RAF circles as 'pongos', allegedly named after a Victorian anthropological dictionary's definition of an African turtle, characterized by large feet and limited intelligence. Many 'pongo' sorties followed, as pilot Jim Lang remembers: 'There was a lot of spare time to put in, due to the scarcity of aeroplanes. De Havilland were only able to produce about one [Mosquito] a week to RAF Horsham St Faith. So it was decided to send a group of aircrew to Yarmouth, where the South Staffs Regiment was established, in an effort to learn something about the Army's training methods. A couple of days with them included an assault course – some fun!'

Robin Thomas, Jim Lang's navigator, also remembers the event and in *Student to Stalag*, he recalls the trip when they were met by a couple of 'Officer "brown jobs" complete with a large covered truck.' Accommodation was in a three or four storey local workhouse building which he describes as an 'elderly brick building, long since condemned as an unsafe structure' which was 'the only time my camp kit was ever used for the purpose it was intended. It proved

In front of an army truck at Great Yarmouth at the start of a week of army 'appreciation' in 1942 are, left to right: P/O Jim Lang; F/L A.E. 'Skelly' Skelton; South Staffordshire Regiment soldier; P/O P.W. Kerry; W/O D. Jobson; F/Sgt L.G. Collins, RCAF. (Via Jim Lang)

adequate and comfortable. No one was allowed into the building after midnight, so we were shown how to scale the garden wall at a place where foot-holes had been formed in the brickwork. This is when you discover the real reason why the Army wear khaki, it does not show brick stains so badly as Air Force blue.'

Many events ensued, such as riding in Bren gun carriers, taking part in street fight simulations, and driving tanks in Thetford forest. On one occasion: 'A bridge was built across a ravine in the face of "enemy" fire and when complete, soldiers with nothing more sophisticated than a bayonet went over and, wriggling along on their stomachs, prodded the ground ahead to discover and remove mines. One of them crawled into a shell hole and for a moment disappeared from view, before coming out again on the other side. After going forward about 10ft, there was a sharp bang and bits of soldier flew in all directions. A gasp of horror came from the audience, followed by nervous laughter when the soldier in the shell hole stood up with a happy smile at the success of his little trick. He had, of course, used a rope in the hole, looped around a stake, to pull a very realistic dummy out over a real mine.' Some time later, there was a reciprocal arrangement and 105 Squadron were to host a visit by the 'brown jobs'. The main aim was to return the hospitality shown as well as to familiarize the Army officers with flying as well as life in the RAF. This was accomplished by providing copious quantities of alcohol from the local hostelries, and taking them up flying. Robin Thomas writes: 'It was obligatory, when taking them for a flight, to get them worried by flying dangerously, just above the trees and chimneypots. In their ignorance, they tended to associate the ground with normality and safety, not in the least being concerned that it was flashing by just beneath them at around 200 mph. One chap literally pleaded with the pilot to go back down again as he did not at all like being up at 2,000ft.'

On 20 January 1942, S/L Peter Channer DFC tested out a Magister, which had been recovered from a field near Caister. Two German escapees had apparently been thwarted as their fuel had run out and had chosen a field to put the stolen aircraft down in. Sadly, the same day, the Tiger Moth crashed. F/L Woods was killed and P/O Olney suffered severe injuries.

Thereafter, life consisted of flying practice when the spares situation and weather allowed. Many trips were made to Hatfield to pick up Mosquito spares, and Mosquito compasses were swung. Soon it was to snow and when the weather prevented flying, instruction was given to crews on the link trainer (the forebear of the modern flight simulator), as well as instructional films shown on such topics as 'course and bearings and compasses' and 'air reconnaissance and "G-forces"'. Lectures were also given on 'first aid', 'Mosquito hydraulic system', 'W/T procedure', 'oxygen and its uses in high flying' and 'night flying procedure'. Even the Station Dramatic Society got their chance on 26 January to perform to the squadron *The Case of the Frightened Lady*. Snow was a problem and dogged attempts to fly. On 3 February, following a station parade and inspection, the squadron was dismissed to carry out snow-clearing duties which were organized into morning and afternoon shifts, with the result that a flare path was cleared by the end of the day. The bad weather continued, and it was not until four days later that flying could resume. On 11 February the 90 Squadron base at RAF Polebrook, home of the high-flying Fortress I bombers was visited, significantly to pick up oxygen equipment. Much training in the use of Mosquitos followed and soon came the day, on 17 February, when F/L Parry took to the skies with a 1,000lb bomb-load to see how the Mosquito handled bombed-up, particularly on take-off and landing.

March started with poor weather conditions yet again, but the squadron managed to extend the experience of flying with a war-load, by attempting bombing runs from high and low level at West Raynham's range. On the 17th and the 26th, a Spitfire MkV took to the air from RAF Duxford to give the Mosquitos climbing and evasive action practice against 'enemy' interception. Mosquito cross-country sorties using beacons and the H/F D/F facilities were carried out, as well as further decompression tests. Mike Carreck remembers these tests: 'Horsham St Faith had a decompression chamber. They used to put us in it and bleed out the oxygen. The idea was to let us know what happened if our Mosquito's oxygen failed. In fact we had no memory of how oxygen lack made us behave, but the rest of the squadron did. The chamber had windows so they could watch our antics like people used to spend a holiday watching the lunatics at Bedlam. Hardly politically correct, but it was a hoot to see someone trying to whack a pencil against a French letter hanging by a string!' The month of March had drawn to a close and lessons about oxygen starvation were soon to be most pertinent.

April 1942 started in tragic fashion, with the crash of a Blenheim MkIV, T1828, flown by Sgt P.H. Swan, RAAF. At 3,000ft, just below the cloud base, he collided with Sgt D.E.A. Welsh's 25 Squadron Beaufighter MkI, R2056, flying out of RAF Wittering. The Beaufighter crash-landed, but the Blenheim fell to the ground, both aircraft coming to earth near Thrapston, a village 8 miles east of Kettering in Northamptonshire. Sgt Swan managed to bale out on his parachute, and was rescued from a river by two Land Army girls. He had suffered a broken arm and leg, but sadly his observer, Sgt George Yorke Larmour, was killed in the accident.

Back at RAF Horsham St Faith there was nearly another tragedy, as during a high-level cross-country flight in Mosquito W4072: GB-D, a fault occurred in Sgt Pete Rowland's oxygen economizer. His sergeant navigator, Mike Carreck, remembers the incident: 'Height 27,000ft.

As high altitude flying was to become necessary, aircrews were given carefully supervised simulated altitude training in a decompression chamber such as this one at RAF Marham. (Via RAF Marham: MAR/0754/98)

Suddenly Pete starts roaring with laughter and great hoots of merriment. "Down! Down!" I shrieked at him but he laughs all the more; funniest thing he's ever heard. I hammered his shoulders with my clenched fists shouting "Down! Down!"; funniest thing he's ever seen; never laughed so much in his life. I'm pointing "Down! Down!" and to Pete, this is the most marvellous fun. It would be even more fun to do what Mike says, and Pete dips the nose of our Mosquito and height reeled off the altimeter. He came to and we went home.'

On 8 April, F/L Houlston delivered a Mosquito from RAF St Athan in South Wales, south-west of Cardiff. It was a little different from the previous ones delivered, as it was a Fighter Mosquito, type F MkII, converted to a trainer by the fitting of dual controls. Later versions were referred to as the Type T MkIII. W4075 had served with 1655 MTU as aircraft 'W' but was now given the 105 Squadron aircraft code letter 'T' (for 'Trainer', presumably). Training continued apace, with new crews being given cross-country flights at 15,000ft, before progressing to the 10,000ft, 20,000ft and 27,000ft sortie altitudes at which the rest of the 'experienced' members of the squadron were operating.

On the night of 27 April 1942, the Luftwaffe bombed Norwich, which brought the short-lived training to an abrupt end. The raids had started three days earlier when Exeter was bombed, as was Bath on the 26th. These attacks were seen as the start of Hitler's reprisal raids on historic towns. He was said to have selected the choice of targets from his Baedeker tourist guide. The influence of raids on Norwich affected the squadron until 1 May 1942, with air and groundcrews despatched to Norwich on demolition and rescue work. Mrs Patricia Tennison, then Patricia Capel, Sergeant Watchkeeper, INT/OPS, remembers the attacks on Norwich: 'I was at Horsham St Faith when Norwich was bombed. It was an old, furnished, and properly built station. When the raids were on we could watch Norwich burning from the camp. The operations room was partly sandbagged up, and on one occasion in the operations room, when the group captain and everybody else was there, we were on duty and told to "get down!" as we heard the rattle of machine-gun bullets along the roof'. Following the attack, allegedly by a German aircraft inspecting the damage to Norwich from the night before, Patricia recalls how nerves were steadied: 'We were all given a tot of rum. As the sergeant, I was in charge of issuing the rum, which had to be logged in a book, which made more work for me.'

However, May continued with much flying training, including numerous dual cross-country flights. Spares were again picked up from Hatfield to keep the Mosquitos flying. Additionally, a large bombing programme was to start at 05.30 hours on the 18th, which was hampered by the weather closing in by breakfast time. Undaunted, simulated bombing runs were attempted on the 21st, and finally, on the 28th, 105 Squadron was at last put on standby. Spare Mosquitos were also standing by for air-sea rescue work and the squadron held its breath, as crews were called to briefing for operations. At last, after months of working up, 105 Squadron was again to become operational with its new 'Wooden Wonder' bomber – the Mosquito!

CHAPTER 4

The Mosquito Bites

The Cabinet Secretariat's D.M. Butt produced a report in August 1941 which recognized that Bomber Command's offensive thus far had suffered from a severe lack of bombing accuracy. Its Directive No. 22 was also to recognise this fact, and pave the way for concentrated attacks, not just on precision industrial targets. St Valentine's Day, 14 February 1942, was to herald a change of policy within Bomber Command that would ultimately, and fundamentally, change the *modus operandi* for its squadrons; 105 was to be no exception. From this point on, the emphasis was to be on 'area bombing', largely on urban areas of Germany.

One man in particular was to be its champion – ACM (later Marshal of the RAF) Sir Arthur Travers Harris KCB, OBE, AFC. On 22 February 1942 he was appointed successor to AVM J.E.A. Baldwin, who was acting in the position of the departed Air Marshal Sir Richard E.C. Peirse KCB, DSO, AFC as AOC-in-C, RAF Bomber Command. Harris, who was born in 1892, was the son of a member of the Indian Civil Service and was of singularly determined stock. He took up his appointment at RAF Headquarters at High Wycombe in Buckinghamshire at once, and was rarely to be seen outside this location for the remainder of the war. His second-in-command was SASO AVM R.H.M.S. Saundby, and together they had command over eight Groups: Nos 1, 2, 3, 4, 5, 26, 91 and 92.

The accuracy of the subsequent area bombing was largely due to a radar position fixing system, which until the middle of 1942 was known as TR 1335. Thereafter, it became known as Gee. It had been developed by the TRE, and employed three ground stations. A 'master' and two 'slave' stations located in England transmitted electronic pulses to the bomber. The pulses could be plotted on the navigator's Gee chart, a grid system which gave a triangulated fix of position, accurate to a mile or less but which had a limited range of around 350 miles. This restriction was due to the radar pulses only being receivable in line-of-sight over the earth's curvature. Its other vulnerability was radar jamming, which it was considered might only give the initial type of Gee a six-month life. Consequently, the introduction of Gee was delayed until May 1941. Until the provision of Gee, the observer (or navigator as they later became known) had to rely on DR or astro-navigation to locate their position over enemy territory. Gee, however, proved a much more accurate method, not only of finding targets but also of following the correct track back home to base after the bombing run.

An initial approach to area bombing was to employ the use of marker flares, and subsequently incendiaries, to illuminate the target upon which the main force would drop their bomb-loads. Proving attacks followed. The Renault factory at Billaincourt west of the centre of Paris was hit on the night of 3/4 March 1942, which proved without doubt the effectiveness of marking by flares. The town of Lübeck was next, on the night of 28 March 1942, when ten Gee-equipped Wellingtons led a separate force of bombers, setting alight great fires with their incendiaries and high explosives, burning many of the town's medieval wooden buildings in the process.

Following these successful raids, Bomber Command attacked other towns such as Rostock, to be followed by the largest raid yet. The objective was to destroy the port and city of Hamburg, but should weather conditions dictate otherwise, then Köln was to suffer instead. If this was to prove impossible, then Essen was to be the target. Consequently, on the night of

The Electrical Section groundcrew at RAF Marham. Left to right: Cliff Streeter; Cpl Len Hunt; Danny Cooper; George Morby; Cpl Len Ellis; F/Sgt Smith (wireless); Cpl Bob Woodhouse; 'Ginger' Parker; Bob Binley. (Cliff Streeter)

30/31 May 1942, a force of 1,047 aircraft successfully attacked Köln. At the time, it was the largest number of aircraft ever assembled for one operation, aircraft being taken from squadrons and OTUs alike. Fifty-five Bomber Command airfields contributed from all over the east of England. Aircraft were despatched from Middleton St George in the north, 6 miles east of Darlington, to Hampstead Norris in the south, and from Pershore in the west to Horsham St Faith in the east. Armstrong Whitworth Whitleys, Avro Lancasters and Manchesters, Bristol Blenheims, Douglas Bostons and Havocs, Handley Page Halifaxes and Hampdens, Short Stirlings and Vickers Armstrong Wellingtons took part, all supported by night-fighting Hawker Hurricanes. High explosive and incendiaries rained down on the city, leaving Köln a fiery inferno – Harris was elated.

Cliff Streeter arrived on the squadron in early 1942, having completed an electrical course at Melksham. He remembers that on the night of the thousand-bomber raid, the 105 Squadron groundcrew Electrical Section was out on the town: 'The electrical section paid a visit to the Black Bull pub, just outside Norwich. One of the lads, George Thornley, was a very good accordion player but, unusually, had not taken it with him. We talked him into returning for it, and he and I cycled back to Horsham. We were very surprised, on arrival, to see some loaded bomb trolleys being towed out to the dispersal area. We duly returned to the pub with the accordion and had a rather boisterous night. Later, on arrival back at the main gate, all in various degrees of sobriety, the police had a list of names. Those of us who were on it were told to report to our flights forthwith, to find to our great elation that the squadron was once again operational. Our elation was dampened though when one of our aircraft failed to return.'

This first operational sortie for 105 Squadron's Mosquitos had commenced on 31 May 1942. Two sets of exhaust stubs spat blue flame and smoke as the first of the Merlin engines of Mosquito W4072, GB:D sprang into life. The other engine was started up similarly and at 04.00 hours S/L Oakeshott and his navigator F/O Hayden taxied out for take-off: target – Köln. As the aircraft lifted off from RAF Horsham St Faith another chapter in 105's history was about to unfold. Armed with four 500lb bombs, it was an hour before Oakeshott was over the city and dropping his bombs to add insult to the injury of the previous night's activities. So dense was the smoke that it was not possible to take photographs and 'D' for Dog returned to base, to land two hours from departure, at 06.00 hours.

Half an hour later, P/O William Deryck Kennard and P/O Eric Raymond Johnson were to take off in W4064:C, heading for the same location, but when 08.30 hours arrived, the Mosquito did not reappear. Tragically, on only the second operation for the squadron's Mosquitos, the first aircraft had failed to return. Their machine had fallen victim to German flak. Ten km south-west of Antwerp, at Bazel on the west bank of the Schelde river, they had tried to crash-land but ultimately ditched. Both were killed. The bodies of the crew members were washed ashore and were subsequently laid to rest in Antwerp's Schoonselhof Cemetery.

The next to search out the city were P/O E.A. Costello-Bowen and observer W/O Tommy Broom in W4065:N who left at 11.40 hours, followed five minutes later by F/L Houlston with his observer, F/Sgt Armitage in W4071:L. Once more, both aircraft were able to drop their bombs on Köln, but once again were prevented from taking photographs due to the dense smoke. One final attempt was made at 17.10 hours, when S/L Peter Channer DFC and his

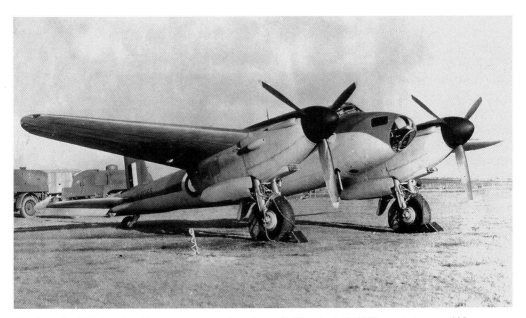

Newly arrived PR/Bomber Conversion type Mosquito as B.IV series i: W4065 awaits its new 105 Squadron identification code GB:N. This aircraft first flew operationally on 31 May 1942 and failed to return from a high-level attack on the heavily defended German port of Bremen, on 19 August 1942. (Via Keith Rowland)

observer W/O Jobson took W4069:M for a low-level photographic reconnaissance only of the burning city, in the hope that at least some photographs of the destruction could be obtained. Their aircraft flew all the way over the North Sea, hugging the wave-tops at 60ft. Peter Channer remembers: 'The weather was right down on the deck. We flew out over the coast and navigated our way to Cologne on DR. We flew into a weather front, and an area of low pressure, and as we neared the target we flew into cloud. As the pressure drop causes the altimeter to read higher than we were, I went up to what I considered to be a safe height at 2/300ft to avoid hitting anything. We could smell smoke [from the burning city below] in the cockpit, and I circled the top of the cloud and searched for a break – there was no break!' Once again, this had made photography impossible and so S/L Channer left the target area and dropped back down on to the deck for the flight back across the sea to RAF Horsham St Faith, where he landed safely at 19.25 hours.

The next day, there was another unfortunate attempt to gain some reconnaissance information by attempting to photograph Köln from high level this time. That evening at 19.30 hours Sgt Monaghan and his observer Sgt A.W. Dean took off in W4065:N, accompanied by F/O L.L. Pearman and P/O R.L. Scott, who took to the air and set course for their target in W4068:B. Once again a valuable Mosquito, this time 'B' for Bertie, failed to return. However, there was a happier note to the circumstances, as both crew members survived to be taken as PoWs. They ended up in the infamous Stalag Luft 3 at Sagan [now Zagań] in Poland, where two years later in 1944 fifty escapees were murdered, shot in cold blood by the Gestapo under the direct orders of their Führer, Adolf Hitler. Mercifully, Pearman and Scott were not included in the roll of fifty. Returning to the operation, all was not lost, as 'N' for Nuts reached Köln, managed to drop the bombs and take the urgently required photographs before their flight home, where they landed safely at 21.55 hours.

This role of bombing and damage inspection, following Bomber Command's area bombing of targets, was to continue throughout June 1942. Major cities such as Essen, Emden and Bremen became the targets of mass destruction, with breaking the morale of their civilian populations at the forefront of Bomber Command's policy. As an example of this, on the night of 1/2 June, Essen was the target. This was to be the second 'Thousand Plan' following that on Köln, but in the event only 956 aircraft were despatched. Many flares were dropped, followed by high explosive. The nearby towns of Müllheim, Duisburg and Oberhausen received many of the bombs intended for Köln, despite the use of Gee. On the morning of 2 June, 105 Squadron despatched three Mosquitos at two-hourly intervals to view the damage. F/L Parry, Sgt Rowland and P/O Paget all managed to take photos from 19,000ft, as well as drop bombs to stoke the fires below.

Aerodromes were also targets. On 5 June, W4069: 'M' for Mother was purring its way at high level across the Netherlands over Schipol aerodrome with the camera clicking away, when the observer, F/O Thomas Gabe, had a problem with the oxygen supply. Hypoxia set in and he passed out. Happily, he recovered and the aircraft returned to RAF Horsham St Faith just in time for lunch. It was clear that the instruction on the effects of lack of oxygen at altitude had been justified, yet again.

On 8 June, an Air Ministry signal 0.1862 was sent out and No. 139 (Jamaica) Squadron re-formed at RAF Horsham St Faith. Their Hudson III aircraft had been left at Dum Dum, India, on 30 April 1942, where they had been renumbered as No. 62 Squadron. No. 139 Squadron was soon to re-equip with Mosquitos as and when they became available and in the short term were to borrow aircraft from 105 Squadron. In an effort to get the squadron operational, some aircrew from 105 were posted and although still located at RAF Horsham St Faith, several well-known faces became 139 Squadron aircrew. G/C J.C. MacDonald DFC, AFC, assumed command of RAF Horsham St Faith from G/C Cockie Spencer, and on 15 June received S/L Jesse Oakeshott, who was appointed to the new rank of acting Wing Commander, assuming command of 139 Squadron. F/O (Acting F/L) Jack Houlston became an acting S/L and F/O Robert Bagguley assumed the rank of Flight Lieutenant. In addition, 105 lost F/O C.K. Hayden, F/O Vernon 'Titch' Treherne and F/Sgt J.L. Armitage to 139 Squadron, which further augmented its ranks by an influx of crews from No. 17 OTU based at RAF Upwood.

Meanwhile, amid much low-level cross-country flying practice in Blenheims and Masters, 105 Squadron continued its photographic and bombing operations. On 18 June, Sgt Lawrence W. Deeth and his observer W/O Frank E.M. Hicks took W4071:L on a cloud-cover sortie to Bremen but returned owing to lack of cloud. That same morning, P/O Downe and F/O Skelton also tried in W4070:C and, ending up in the same predicament, bombed the East Frisian island of Langeoog instead. Wilhelmshaven was also given some attention by P/O 'Jock' Pringle and P/O Robin Thomas in W4072:D, who disgorged their bombs on it from 2,000ft. Robin Thomas takes up the story:

The idea was to fly over the North Sea, off shore from the Frisian Islands, just above the clouds forecast as being 10/10ths [complete cover] all the way, pop down through the clouds – with a bit of luck – over Wilhelmshaven, drop our bombs and nip back into the clouds to go back as we had come, just above the clouds, so that in the unlikely event of a fighter coming up with us, we would disappear into them. All went well until, still over the sea and north of where our target should have been, the cloud stopped in a neat line parallel to the coast and about 20 miles from it. Our orders were clear, 'if the cloud runs out the bombs are to be jettisoned in the sea and return to base'. We had done that once already and it seemed a great waste of time, effort and bombs to come all this way for nothing. After all, if we came home safely there was unlikely to be too much bother and if we did not get back there would be no bother at all, not with us anyway. So we turned in to the shore and there was Wilhelmshaven. We were not the only ones to be surprised at this masterly feat of navigation. The Germans were certainly not expecting us; not a shot was fired as we cruised across the town and harbour. I noticed a large merchant ship alongside the quay with the hold covers off and it seemed to me, if I could put our bomb-load in the open hold then it would be congratulations all round for us and great confusion for the enemy. We went round again, to come back to the ship from the east, somewhat conscious of only being at 2,000ft. This height, we had been assured, was ideal for light anti-aircraft fire to be positively lethal. I am sorry to say the ship survived my onslaught. They were beginning to shoot at us by now, thus inducing a modicum of panic and causing the bombs to overshoot and knock down some bungalows in the town. At the debriefing, when I sadly admitted missing the ship, a kindly intelligence officer told me it was a good thing I had, because the bombs were designed for blast effect and knocking down houses and would have been wasted on the ship. I still wished I had proved that for myself.

The next 105 Squadron operations were flown on 20 June to Emden on Ostfriesland, which had received the attention of 194 aircraft the night before. It had been the second major attack on the town since 6/7 June. On this occasion the town of Osnabrück some 85 miles south-south-east of Emden had taken most of the punishment, as a significant portion of the marker flares had landed there. Two new Mosquitos were detailed to photograph and bomb. P/O Paget and P/O Addinsell took DK292:B and completed their mission on Schütroff, and Sgts Rowland and Carreck flew DK294:F to Emden. Their bombs fell on the target and the camera took photos through a hole in the cloud at 24,000ft. Mike Carreck notes that: 'On solo high-level ops, you tracked over the briefed objective with camera switched on and automatically shooting a sequence of stills. On photo-recce ops we also bombed our objective. Since all 105 Squadron Mosquitos carried cameras and every bomb run was photographed, PR ops were little different from normal high-level daylight operations.'

The month continued with attacks on 25 June on enemy aerodromes at Schleswig (Jugal) by F/L Parry and P/O Costello-Bowen. Although Parry could not locate the target, W4070: 'C' for Charlie bombed a small town for good measure. Costello-Bowen was more successful and bombed the main runway before speeding back home to land safely in W4066: 'A' for Apple at 01.15 hours on the 26th. Meanwhile, 139 Squadron had been busy with borrowed 105 Squadron Mosquitos, and S/L Jack Houlston in DK296:G bombed the aerodrome at Stade, west of Hamburg, catching enemy aircraft taking off. Meanwhile, F/L Bagguley dropped to 50ft and bombed the town of Dorum north of Bremerhaven, instead of Stade. Unfortunately, having selected the flaps by mistake, instead of operating the bomb door closing lever, the flaps were ripped from the aircraft. On return to RAF Horsham St Faith, W4072:D made a low and necessarily flapless landing, which resulted in the aircraft careering down the aerodrome and beyond the flare path. Their troubles were not yet over, as before coming to a halt a wheel caught in a trench and the starboard undercarriage collapsed, damaging the Mosquito severely but not beyond repair.

Final operations for the month were carried out on 26 June, when the intention was to photograph Bremen from 24,000ft. Bremen had last been attacked by Bomber Command on the night of 25/26 June, when another 'Thousand Raid' had been ordered. In the event, 960 Bomber Command aircraft of all shapes and sizes had taken part, with a supplementary contribution coming from Coastal Command and Army Co-operation Command. The final tally was indeed over the thousand and resulted in a force of 1,067 aircraft taking to the skies. P/O Downe and his observer F/O Skelton took off in their Mosquito, W4069:M, at ten minutes after midday, but failed to locate Bremen. Instead, they bombed Hannover and two aerodromes on the way back. Sgts Rowland and Carreck were more accurate though, for having located Bremen satisfactorily, they proceeded to take photographs as planned before bringing DK292:B back safely to land at 16.55 hours.

So the first month of operations was over for 105 Squadron in their new wonder aircraft. The lives of one crew had been lost already, and sadly there would be more to come. But what was it like to fly ops in the Mosquito? Mike Carreck gives his viewpoint:

On ops it was fatal to brood. Fear was like a tiger in a cage. You couldn't help doing sums – 105 was soon to lose a crew a week. It was six weeks until your next leave – forget it, lock the tiger's door. Once an op was flown you put it out of your mind, never dwelt on the near miss or life-saving moment of luck. The secret was to treat each op as routine, from the briefing to the exhilaration as your wheels touched down, to the relief and achievement and the glorious knowledge that you were one op closer to the end of your tour – thank God for that!

The groundcrews were always busy on the aircraft trying to ensure that the aircrews would be as safe as possible, as Cliff Streeter describes:

A typical day would start with the DIs (daily inspections) on our allotted aircraft. This would normally entail two of us going to each aircraft. One would be in the cockpit operating the switches etc., while the other would check from the outside, the navigation lights, landing lights, pitot head heater, bomb door and landing gear micro-switches connected to warning lights in the cockpit. Also in the cockpit were such things as battery voltage indicator (24 volts), bomb release switch and selector, cockpit lighting and rheostats, and a few other things. If any faults turned up they had to be rectified. When all was satisfactory, one of us would sign the Form 700, signifying that everything electrical was serviceable. If a plane flew during the day after this, a similar between-flights check had to be made and again, any faults found rectified. There were also Ministry modifications to be made as they came up. Any fault that occurred on an operation also had to be traced and repaired, of course. When an operation was on, an electrician had to be on duty prior to take-off along with other trades. Then the often long wait for their return and hopefully, relief when you asked 'Any snags, sir?' and he replied, 'No problems'. Engine and airframe fitters always called electricians, wireless, instrument repairers and armourers etc., 'gash trades', although each flight was pretty close-knit. Your flight, whether A, B or (as later) C, was of course, the best!

Bob Woodhouse, who had been stationed at RAF Swanton Morley as a flight electrician on Blenheims, had returned from electrical courses at Plessey at Ilford and from Hatfield, the birthplace of the Mosquito. As a senior NCO in the Electrical Section, he recalled a specific event that indicates the shortage of labour at the time:

I well remember an incident that happened on B-Flight. On the occasion I recall, there was just one electrician doing the check. All checks could be done of course taking longer, except for the warning lights and audible warning of the position of the undercarriage in flight. The micro-switches which operated the warning circuits were in the wheel nacelles and had two switches operating to energize the horn. A coin was used while the throttles were operated in the cockpit. The idea being that when the pilot came in to land and his wheels were up, on

105 Squadron A-Flight groundcrews assembled in front of a Mosquito. (Via Cliff Streeter)

Electrical Section and B-Flight groundcrew proudly displayed at RAF Marham with Sgt L. Hogan (sixth from left) and F/O F.M. Fisher (third from right) in front of Mosquito 'Uncle Sam'. (Via Cliff Streeter)

throttling back, the horn warned him to check his undercarriage. This particular aircraft went on ops successfully and returned safely, but the aircrew were very, very annoyed, as each time they throttled back during the flight the warning horn operated. It was my duty to investigate, report on the fault, and correct it. When personnel had left the dispersal point, I removed the coin (a penny) from the micro-switch, where it had been accidentally left. I was able to report back to the aircrew with an apology and an explanation. Having already berated the 'spark', I would imagine that pilot has the old penny in his collection to this day!

CHAPTER 5

Submarines and Steel

July 1942 began with a successful attack on the 1st, by F/Sgt L.G. Collins and P/O Phadric W. Kerry in W4069:M, against Kiel. They dropped their bombs from high level at 26,000ft and were back just after 16.00 hours. Otherwise the day was spent on a Mosquito training programme. However, the peace was not to last, as the next morning an attack was to be made on the U-boat submarine slips and construction yards at Flensburg, situated at the top of the Flensburg Fjord near the border between Germany and Denmark. Three 105 Squadron aircraft undertook this low-level bombing operation, accompanied by two 139 Squadron crews flying borrowed 105 Squadron machines.

At two-minute intervals, starting at 11.45 hours, the 105 Squadron aircraft took off and formed up with the two 139 Squadron crews. The first up at 11.45 hours was F/L G.P. Hughes with F/O Gabe in DK299:S, followed by 139's W/C Alan Robertson Oakeshott DFC with F/O Treherne in a 105 Squadron Mosquito, DK298:H. They were accompanied by S/L Houlston with F/Sgt Armitage in another Mosquito on loan from 105 Squadron, DK296:G. 105's P/O Costello-Bowen with W/O Broom took off at 11.47 hours in DK295:P and finally, G/C MacDonald with F/L Skelton in DK294:F at 11.49 hours.

The Mosquitos formed up and headed for their target. On arrival, 'S' for Sugar and 'P' for Popsie successfully bombed the slipways. Oakeshott was intercepted by FW 190 'Butcher Birds' and both he and his observer, F/O Vernon Frank Evans 'Titch' Treherne DFM perished when they were shot down 9 miles north-north-east of Husum, at Sönnebüll, Germany. Tony Spong, a general staff officer who, as mentioned previously, was responsible to the CO of the station, remembered Jesse Oakeshott. 'W/C Oakeshott, a regular officer, had been transferred from a Wellington squadron to 105 Squadron, and I got to know him well. I strongly agreed with his idea that the bomber force should consist almost entirely of Mosquitos; the argument which I supported was that a high-speed wooden aircraft carrying a useful load of 4,000lb [latterly] was more effective than four-engined aircraft with a larger bomb-load but a considerably lower top speed. The other advantage of the wooden aircraft was that most moderate damage could be repaired on the station, while the same damage to the larger aircraft had to be dealt with at the manufacturer's base. Unfortunately, his arguments were cut short by his demise.' Both W/C Oakeshott and F/O Treherne are commemorated on the Runnymede Memorial.

MacDonald and Skelton were last seen flying slowly across the coast on the return leg, off Pellworm Island. They did not return to base but both survived to become PoWs. They too ended up at Stalag Luft 3. Messerschmitt Bf 109 and Focke-Wulf FW 190 fighters made concerted efforts to kill their prey. S/L Houlston was pursued but managed to evade three of the latter. F/L Hughes had two more to contend with, having already suffered damage from the anti-aircraft fire local to the target. Despite the efforts of the fighters, at 15.00 hours Hughes landed back at base, closely followed by Houlston three minutes later. P/O Costello-Bowen had touched down earlier at 14.46 hours. The FW 190s had tried hard to complete their work over the sea, but the superior speed of the unarmed Mosquitos at sea level had won the day.

Mike Carreck commented on the German fighters of the time: 'Nonsense has been written about the Mosquito showing a clean pair of heels to the Bf 109. Diving down, the Bf 109 had all the speed it wanted to engage a Mosquito. Two Bf 109s and you're a dead duck; as you turn from one's attack, you fly into the guns of the other. As for the FW 190, the Luftwaffe called it "Butcher Bird" with good reason.'

The Focke-Wulf FW 190A was a very functional and, to some, an aesthetically pleasing aircraft. Its air-cooled radial engine combined with its sleek slender lines made it a very dangerous foe indeed. Even the Spitfire MkV, one of our best fighters of the time, was outclassed by the 'Butcher Bird', which was some 20 mph faster and stable in the dive. It possessed superior manoeuvrability, and was initially armed with two MG17s in the cowling and two in the wing roots which were augmented by 20mm Oerlikon MG FF cannons outboard of the undercarriage attachment points. This was later modified in the FW 190A-3 version with two fast-operating synchronized 20mm Mauser MG151 cannons replacing the wing root mounted MG17s, thus presenting a very dangerous adversary for the unarmed Mosquito bomber. However, the saving grace of the Mosquito was that while in a straight chase it could outpace the Bf 109s, under certain conditions it was just faster than the FW 190. S/L Charles Patterson DSO, DFC, made the following comment regarding the FW 190's performance at high level: 'The correct deduction was that it depended on the rating of the Merlin engines. If the engines were rated to give maximum performance at high level, the Mosquito could just outdistance the FW 190. And if it was fitted with engines rated for low level, it could also just outdistance the FW 190. Until this time, the only engines fitted were, if I remember rightly, the Merlin 21s and they fell somewhere in the middle range. That meant that although they were just fast enough at low level, they certainly weren't at high level. Later on they fitted different engines so that the MkIX was able to do PRU and Met. reconnaissance at high level without a higher than acceptable risk. In fact, even fitted with the Merlin 21 engines, the Mosquito at high level was still very fast. It was as fast as a Spitfire with comparable engines, and therefore FW 190 interceptions were by no means inevitable, but if they did take place, you were pretty well for it!'

Fortunately, the high-level photographic operation to assess the damage at Flensburg, undertaken on the afternoon of the raid, was successful. P/O Jim Lang and W/O D. Robson in W4069:M returned at 16.10 hours without having met any enemy fighters or 'snappers' as they had become known to the RAF crews.

The same day, S/L Channer was up in W4066:A at 26,000ft with his observer, Sgt Frank Holland, to observe the weather in the Bremen area where there had been heavy rain. The crew were briefed by the 'Met. people' and they were given codes to be utilized to transmit their information from the aircraft. The information was duly obtained and transmitted. That night, a force of 325 aircraft left England to bomb the town, where much damage was done to ships, industrial companies and about a thousand houses.

Apart from a high-level attack on Wilhelmshaven on the 9th, the next major event was a repeat attack at Flensburg on the 11th, by six Mosquitos, providing a diversion for an attack by 44 Lancasters in semi-daylight on the northern Polish port of Danzig. Gdansk, as it is now named, lies on the south-eastern part of the Gulf of Danzig. The diversion was to back up this operation, and led the heavy bombers far beyond the range of any Bomber Command operations at the time.

At 17.14 hours, the first wave of three Mosquitos left RAF Horsham St Faith, followed at 17.21 hours by the remaining three. S/L Channer and Sgt Holland in W4070:C led the first vic of three. Their wingmen were P/O Joseph Roy George Ralston with P/O Syd Clayton in DK300:N occupying the no. 2 position on his right and the Australian F/O Downe with observer, P/O Alfred W. Groves in DK297:O occupying the no. 3 position on his left. Their formation flew initially through good weather, but it worsened as they continued. The cumulonimbus clouds they had been warned about at briefing appeared, followed by atrocious weather with heavy rainstorms, which became clearer only when south of the border on the German coast. The low pressure caused an over-reading of their altimeters, so the formation climbed up to about 500ft to avoid any obstacles. As the vic reached the target area, a tall radio mast came into view which was used as a reference point. When ready, Channer turned his vic on to a 180°, or reciprocal, course to the left and climbed slightly to be able to dive at the target. In discussion he recalled: 'We had a wonderful view of the slipways. Our bombs burst straight up the slipways where a submarine and more alongside and to the rear were all damaged. We then flew low over the town. There were Bofors guns on flak towers and one shell in front went into the roof of a house as we went over the town. We then turned north into Denmark where there was a nice lot of cloud. We turned west in the cloud and then flew down to sea level.'

While over the town, Channer had been flying about 10ft over the buildings when Holland observed Ralston and Downe coming along to formate on him. Slightly more than an hour later they arrived over the coast of Norfolk. The three arrived home safely, with S/L Channer touching down last at 21.07 hours after P/O Ralston at 20.50 hours. Ralston's logbook entry notes that his aircraft had been 'hit in the tail unit by flak', the result being a safely executed crash-landing back at base.

While Channer's vic had returned successfully, what became of the second vic? The three crews who took part were F/L Hughes, with his observer, P/O Gabe in Mosquito DK299:S, followed by their wingmen comprising P/O Lang with W/O Jobson in DK295:P and Sgt Rowland with Sgt Carreck in DK296:G. Mike Carreck remembered this attack:

> Three of us took off from RAF Horsham St Faith on that dull dirty afternoon of low cloud, Hughes leading. We crossed the Norfolk coast at a comfortable 500ft and then settled down to 50ft to hide from the German radar screens in the scribble of returns from the water just below. There were some 300 miles to fly over the empty sea before we made landfall at the island of Sylt. That is, we hoped the sea would be empty with not a sign of 'squealers', enemy lookout ships on patrol. Our luck was in, no 'squealers', and at long last we were passing over Sylt. Two minutes later we crossed the coast into Denmark, a couple of miles north of the German border. We turned with Hughes and Jim, as we altered course for Flensburg and then very quietly, and without any fuss, we hit a farmhouse. There was just a gentle tap on the fuselage. The Mosquito took no notice and flew serenely on, and there were lots of little pieces of chimney and a thick layer of dust all over the Mercator chart on my knees. I swallowed down my astonishment and then was amazed again: there was green grass passing just below me and a huge hole was gaping in the side of the Mosquito. I well remember that neither Pete nor I made any comment, it wasn't the time nor place for conversation and the port engine was making very peculiar noises. The fields of Denmark spread out flat before us and what I said was, 'Where shall we land, old boy?' Pete said, 'We're going home' and as we banked in the turn we saw Hughes and Jim Lang far ahead, disappearing eastward into the murk for Flensburg. Sadly, Hughes didn't get back.

Both F/L George Pryce Hughes who was an Argentinian and a member of the RCAF and his observer F/O Thomas Albert Gabe died when their Mosquito crashed, apparently avoiding light flak over Danish territory. Both were buried in Esbjerg (Fourfelt) cemetery. However, it has recently been alleged that an FW 190 fighter may have intercepted their aircraft. Mike Carreck continued:

27

Bound for Flensburg, Germany, on 11 July 1942,
Sgt Peter Rowland (pilot) with observer
Sgt Michael Carreck hit a farmhouse and removed a
chimneypot which entered their Mosquito DK296, GB:G,
leaving this hole in the fuselage. (Via Keith Rowland)

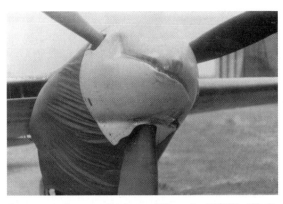

Damage to the propeller boss of Mosquito DK296, GB:G,
sustained during the same flight. (Via Keith Rowland)

We had a long way to go again over all that water but Pete did a superb job of nursing us along. We saw no fighters looking for us or the Lancasters; our marvellous Mosquito didn't let us down and after an eternity we landed, thankfully, at Horsham St Faith. I've thought since then that it would have been the safer option to head our damaged aircraft for Sweden, rather than risk that long haul over the sea, but Pete and I never even considered it, we had such faith in the Mosquito. We climbed down from good old DK296, gave her affectionate pats and stood about looking modestly heroic, as a dense crowd began to gather and make low whistles at the size of the hole in the starboard fuselage. Then, someone called out, 'Hey, look at this!' He was pointing up at the port engine. It looked as if a gigantic sword had smashed it; there were deep scars on the airscrew spinner, and the radiator. To all appearances we'd hit a cable of a balloon barrage at 280 knots – something unlikely to escape your attention. What a noise, like a thunderclap and the Mosquito going out of control, rather fatal at a height of 50ft. Yet we'd heard nothing, seen nothing, felt nothing. The mystery was never solved, nor was another – why didn't the starboard airscrew tear itself off on the roof of that unfortunate Danish house? Next day, Pete was awarded a Green Endorsement in his logbook for his skill in bringing DK296 safely back to base. All I got was a hell of a line to shoot!

The Green Endorsement stated that he was: 'Commended by AOC 2 Group for skill in handling his aircraft after colliding with an obstacle during an operational flight.' This presented an example of the 'ease of maintenance' theory as expounded by W/C Oakeshott as Tony Spong recalls: 'In the event two riggers/carpenters from de Havilland came over to Norwich, cut out the damage with a saw, plastered the hole over using a resin and the plane was back in service in two days!'

The other Mosquito flown by P/O Jim Lang became separated from the formation and returned early due to the bad weather, landing back at base at 19.55 hours.

Five days later on 16 July, two aircraft left RAF Horsham St Faith to attack a target well known to the squadron from its Blenheim days – the iron and steelworks at IJmuiden in the Netherlands. Ralston and his navigator Syd Clayton set off at 14.53 hours, followed by Monaghan with Dean in W4065:N. After a low-level flight over the North Sea, they made landfall and arrived over the target at 15.35 hours where they both successfully let their bombs go, not on the steelworks but on the gas plant. P/O Ralston scored a direct hit from Mosquito DK302:D, damaging the ammonia gas-holder. Fire also broke out in the gas plant as both aircraft sped back to base.

On the same day at 15:35 hours Mosquito W4069:M took off, with P/O J.W.G. Paget at the controls, accompanied by his observer F/O Paul Addinsell. They were briefed to operate a cloud-cover attack on the shipbuilding yards at Wilhelmshaven. Their machine, 'M' for Mother, did not return from the operation but the news was not as tragic as one might expect. The Grim Reaper had been denied his harvest that day, and both of the young airmen were reported as being safe, having been taken PoW.

The month continued with high-level bombing attempts at Essen, Bremen, Düsseldorf, Emden, Osnabrück, Münster and Köln with varying degrees of success. Several alternative targets received punishment due to cloud obscuring the target or, as was the case at IJmuiden and Köln, where there was insufficient cloud cover and the aircraft turned back.

There was some excitement on the 22nd, when the station received a visit from His Royal Highness the Duke of Kent, who inspected the squadron. However, not all of the aircrew were impressed, as one of the squadron considered that he had 'never seen a man so insultingly bored by the squadron flying an incredible new aircraft and suffering heavy casualties to keep his family on the throne'. Some three days later, the Right Honourable Sir Archibald Sinclair Bt, KT, CMG, MP, Secretary of State for Air, visited and repeated the inspection which went down in a similar vein and the comment was made that 'an absolute horde of highly senior RAF officers descended on us at Horsham St Faith. We noted how brown-nosing the visiting group captains were to the air commodores, and the air commodores to the air vice-marshals. There was a civilian too; I think he was Sir Archibald Sinclair, Secretary of State for Air – looked like a lightweight.'

Meanwhile, cloud-cover operations were attempted on Köln at the Knapsack and Quadrath power stations on the 23rd but lack of the vital element, cloud, prevented attacks, and a factory at Königshofen was attacked from 5,000ft instead. High-level bombing and PR continued at Mannheim, Frankfurt, Duisburg, Köln, Lübeck, Flensburg and Essen. It was on a sortie to Essen that the squadron lost yet another crew. On 28 July, F/O Frank Watson Weekes RAAF took Mosquito DK295:P aloft at 17:40 hours, accompanied by his observer P/O Frank Arthur Hurley. Sadly, both were killed and were laid to rest in the Reichwald Forest war cemetery.

August opened with high-level attacks at 21,000ft planned for Kiel, Frankfurt, Bremen, Hannover and Wilhelmshaven. P/O Pringle had engine trouble on his operation to Kiel and jettisoned his fused bombs in the North Sea some 92 miles east of Bridlington, before bringing W4066:A home safely, to land one hour and forty-two minutes from take-off at 13.25 hours. Mosquito DZ312:K also had a narrow escape, as having bombed a target at Frankfurt, its luck began to run out. The bombs were believed to have been fused 'safe', so no damage would have resulted from the raid, and to cap it all, on the way back one of the engines packed up. The pilot, Sgt Wilkinson, managed to land at base, but overshot and crashed. The observer, Sgt Bastow, was doubtless shaken; however Sgt Wilkinson was injured in the crash. While the Hannover and Wilhelmshaven attacks were completed without incident, the operation to Bremen claimed yet another crew. Nothing was heard of F/Sgt L.G. Collins RCAF and observer

P/O Phadric Woodrow Kerry after departing RAF Horsham St Faith at 11.39 hours in DK308:J. They did not return and the worst was feared. However, it transpired that their aircraft had come down, and F/O Collins survived to be a PoW. Unfortunately, P/O Kerry was killed and was subsequently buried in the Sage war cemetery, about 25 miles south-west of Bremen, near Huntlosen.

A happier and most significant event also took place on 1 August 1942. A posting was made and a familiar face appeared at RAF Horsham St Faith. W/C Hughie Idwal Edwards had returned to command 105 Squadron from his previous post of CFI at Wellesbourne Mountford. Edwards was a tough, strict disciplinarian and pugnacious leader who was born at Mosman Park, Perth, Western Australia on 1 August 1914. What better present for this young 28-year-old officer on his birthday than to be presented with the command once more of his beloved 105 Squadron, with whom he had previously won his VC. Those who did not know him from his Blenheim days would once again witness the quality of the man under whose command the squadron would climb to even further heights of acclaim.

It was about this time that the first Mosquito diplomatic flights to Stockholm began and it was the Australian station commander from Perth, G/C 'Digger' Kyle, who was to select a suitable crew for the first of these missions. He chose F/L George Parry and his observer P/O 'Robbie' Robson for the task. George Parry agreed and now describes what happened:

British Airways carried diplomatic mail and were suffering losses, particularly on the Stockholm run. As there had not been a flight to Stockholm for more than six weeks, the situation was becoming serious. It was decided that a Mosquito would have the best chance to get through German defences. My station commander asked Robbie, my navigator, and me if we would undertake courier runs as civilians. We jumped at the idea and went up to the Air Ministry [by train] and Foreign Office for briefing and passports. As we were leaving, we were presented with a van load of diplomatic bags for Stockholm.

DK301[:H] was stripped out and painted pale grey, with no markings or identification. The bags (approximately 1,000lb) were roped into the bomb bay and we took off for Leuchars with Sidcots over our civilian clothes, to await the go-ahead. Take-off time was fairly critical, as we had no communications and had to land before dark. As we heard nothing, I contacted the Foreign Office to find that they could not get through to Stockholm. As the matter was urgent, I said that I would go as arranged which would give them time to contact Stockholm before my arrival. The trip took three hours. We climbed to 20,000ft, and when in fighter range, I put the nose down and went over Denmark and into Sweden at 450 mph. On arrival at Bromma, we found a JU52 doing a wide circuit, so I cut in and landed, taxied to dispersal, shut down and awaited the arrival of the embassy [staff]. The JU52 landed and taxied up to the airport buildings and about 20 Germans got off the aircraft. We were later told it was Göbbels' deputy and various officials visiting Stockholm, before going on to Finland. [Paul Josef Göbbels was Hitler's 'Minister of Public Enlightenment and Propaganda'.] After the Germans had gone inside, there was no movement about the terminal, and after about ten minutes, I began to feel that something had gone wrong and we would have to destroy the aircraft. We kept a close watch and after half an hour, to our great relief, an envoy from the embassy came out to meet us. They did not know of our flight until we landed.

We unloaded our cargo and a guard was put on the aircraft. We were taken off to the embassy, and were later taken out to dinner and to a hotel for the night. We were collected very early the next morning and taken to the airport and we loaded up our return cargo and took off for Leuchars. We climbed up and cleared out over Denmark, but ran into a front off

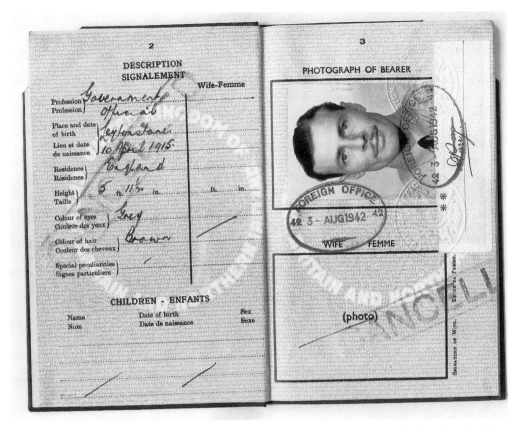

'Civilian' passport issued on 3 August 1942 to 'Mr D.A.G. Parry' for his Mosquito flight to Sweden. (Via George Parry)

Denmark and eventually broke cloud at 400ft. As we approached the Firth of Forth, two Hurricanes came out to intercept us. Not being sure of my reception, I made all speed to Leuchars and landed, handed over my cargo, refuelled and flew back to base.

I had some explaining to do that evening. A mess party had been arranged and I had invited my wife, telling her that I would make final arrangements later. When she did not hear from me, she rang up. The person who answered the call knew I was on a special assignment, and as a cover, said I had gone to London on a 48-hour pass but thought I would be back for the party. I had some difficulty convincing my wife that I had not been to London because I could not tell her where I had been.

W/C Peter Channer noted an interesting caveat to this story. He heard a mention on the radio in the 1990s, suggesting that whereas the British had received sneering German broadcasts in English, direct from Hamburg from the traitor William Joyce or 'Lord Haw-Haw' as he was known, the Germans were provided with radio broadcasts from England in German. This was to make them believe they were hearing the voices of unrest and dissatisfaction in the Nazi ranks. To reinforce the point, it was suggested that the Mosquito Stockholm run was the vehicle by which recordings of music (which had only just been released in Germany) were smuggled back to England in some of the diplomatic bags. Thus they could be broadcast to the German population as background music in an attempt to gain authenticity, under the premise that the 'Englanders' could not possibly have such up-to-date German music, and hence the radio station had to be authentic.

Back at RAF Horsham St Faith the war continued, with cloud-cover attacks on Hagen, Vagesack, IJmuiden and the Brauweiler electrical switching station at Köln. All were attempted between 6 and 9 July, but were again frustrated by lack of cloud. The only successes were during high-level operations that were not without their problems, such as the operations to Kiel and Essen on the 6th. P/O Lang and his observer in DK292:B carried out the Kiel operation. They took off at 10.52 hours on a sortie that would last just 1 hour and 40 minutes, for as they approached north-east Polden, the records show that three FW 190s appeared and intercepted the Mosquito. However, Jim Lang remembers the incident with some regret:

> We were on our way to Kiel, and we turned back at the coast. Official records show that three FW 190s intercepted us – I never saw them, although my observer gave me evasive actions for several minutes. He completed the interrogation and I believe I realised then that he was a very scared man, and had been, on our previous few trips together. I was called in by the Wing Commander [Hughie Edwards] who was suspicious about our flight ops report. I told him that I had no wish to fly with 'X' again, as he was not reliable, and very scared. I have been led to believe that S/L Channer took 'X' on a low-level to Holland and that 'X' could not complete the task. He was brought home and later demoted by the Wing Commander for what was known as LMF [lack of moral fibre]. I met 'X' later when he had been dealt with and he pleaded with me to take him on again as my navigator, but I declined. I do not know what happened to him, and I was fortunate to find P/O Thomas without a pilot; we established a wonderful communication in the air as well as on the ground.

The observer in question was posted from the squadron soon thereafter. The same day, however, F/O Downe and P/O Groves had a bit of a 'shaky do' themselves as a result of meeting the 'Butcher Birds'. They had taken off at 11.55 hours in Mosquito DK313: 'M' for Mother, and were attacked at 13.22 hours. Derek C. Ransom in *Battle-Axe* noted the following account of the operation as told by the crew themselves in a report which stated that:

> The journey was uneventful and the aircraft was over the Ruhr when numerous bursts of heavy flak were seen bursting behind and on both sides (mainly starboard), being accurate as regards height. The nearest bursts were in the region of 100yds away. On ETA the target was obscured by cloud but we anticipated that another minute's flying would take us to the edge of this cloud where we thought we could see some large town. I was about to select bomb doors open and my observer was about to go forward to bomb when he saw a condensation trail which appeared to be overtaking us from the rear at a fast rate. This trail was caused by a FW 190, which we first saw clearly at approx. 3,000ft above us and diving steeply. We immediately decided not to bomb, as the time to open and close the bomb doors would have put us at too great a disadvantage. I decided our best height to escape would be at 21,000ft (rated altitude) and accordingly commenced to dive. Our IAS at this stage was 180 mph and our height 28,000ft. Before we had reached 27,000ft, one of the enemy aircraft (another had appeared behind the first) attacked, and on instructions from my observer I turned to port, the attack being made from almost astern and above. The FW 190 fired at approximately 500yds and continued firing until about 200yds when he broke away to starboard, whereupon the other FW attacked from the starboard quarter from about the same distance away.

We then turned sharply to starboard and the attacking aircraft turned with us, continuing to fire. We could feel some bullets entering the aircraft, but at the time could not see the damage. After continuing the turn for about 50° this FW broke off his attack, and the other one came in once more from above and astern. By this time our aircraft had reached 21,000ft and an IAS of 390 (550 TAS). As this one overtook us we levelled out and turned sharply to starboard. As we did this, our aircraft was hit in both engine nacelles and a portion of the starboard aileron shot away. At the same time the hydraulics failed and the port wheel fell down, the combined effect being to cause the aircraft to roll over on to its back, and control was temporarily lost. At one stage whilst the aircraft was out of control we experienced some negative G and one motor cut out temporarily. (*Note*: the Merlin at this time was fitted with a carburettor that drained under conditions of negative G. German engines had direct fuel injection that was not affected by aerobatics.) Aileron control had become exceedingly heavy and difficulty was experienced in lifting the port wing. All this time the aircraft was spiralling around to the left and rapidly losing height. By turning on full starboard aileron trim and throttling back the starboard engine, control was regained at approx. 16,000ft.

On getting back into an ordinary dive again both motors were opened up again and we continued our evasive action although the ailerons felt pretty stiff and heavy. During this time one FW had remained on our tail and again attacked from the rear. We decided to make for the protection of layer-type clouds that were at 7,000ft and accordingly continued to dive and turn about 15° either way. At this time our intercom failed and I turned around but could not see the enemy aircraft as his attack was made from the rear. However, I could see tracers flying about 10ft from the aircraft and appearing to come from the port quarter. A turn was made to port but the FW turned with us. We endeavoured to shake him off, by turning first one way and then the other, but failed to do so and he continued to fire at us at intervals until we reached cloud and he was lost to sight.

We subsequently returned to base and landed with bombs owing to failure of hydraulic and electrical systems. From our experience it appears that the FW 190 is somewhat faster and just as manoeuvrable as our own aircraft. It also appears that the German pilots are aware of our lack of guns as all the attacks were made from astern and they made no attempt to break off the engagement after having made a burst or two. It is of interest to note that at no time during the engagement did I (the pilot) see the enemy owing to the pilot's restricted rear vision.

This last comment is most interesting considering the problems associated with the operation to Kiel that day. P/O Lang and his new observer P/O Robin Thomas returned to Kiel the next day, but were unable to identify the town due to poor visibility.

Met. reconnaissance and high-level attacks continued and on the night of 11/12 August Bomber Command attacked Mainz with 154 aircraft, comprising Wellingtons, Stirlings, Halifaxes and Lancasters. They lost six aircraft in the process but caused much damage to the centre of Mainz, so much so that when P/O Ralston and P/O Clayton took DK317:K over the next day to bomb and photograph the results, they noted a large amount of smoke still hanging over the town. On the afternoon of the 15th, Mainz was again the target, this time for P/O Geoffrey William Downe RAAF and P/O Alfred William Groves DFM in Mosquito DK309:S. Unfortunately, unlike their operation on the 6th, their luck ran out as they again encountered enemy fighters. It is thought that Unteroffizier [Corporal] Kolschek of 4./JG1 [4th Flight of the 1st Day Fighter Wing] met the Mosquito and succeeded in shooting it down near Gent-Mariakerke, north-west Gent in the area of Vlaanderen, Belgium. The crew were both laid to rest in the Gent City cemetery.

Only four days later, on the 19th and yet again during a high-level daylight attack, ordered this time for Germany's most heavily defended town of Bremen, another Mosquito was lost. This time F/Sgt Charles Dermot Kelly RAAF and his observer, P/O F.J. Harniman, were posted missing. Mosquito W4065:N failed to return and it transpired that the pilot had been killed but the observer was a PoW. F/Sgt Kelly was buried in Becklingen war cemetery in Soltau, which lies about 40 miles east of Bremen.

On the 23rd, a photographic sortie was proposed to Choques, Pont-à-Vendin, Sequedin and Sluiskil as undertaken by F/L Parry but the Lille area could only be photographed, due to cloud obscuring the target. Ironically, this was followed on the 24th by a cloud-cover operation to Flensburg which proved impossible, due this time to lack of cloud and an alternative target at Westerland on the island of Sylt, the most northerly part of Germany's coast, was attacked from 6,500ft instead.

There was a change of emphasis for the remainder of August with the high-level raids being temporarily replaced by low-level operations against the enemy's power plants. The air was electric on the 25th, when Köln was again the target, as F/L Costello-Bowen and W/O Broom took off at 19.08 hours in DK297:O, accompanied by P/O Ralston in DK303:V and F/L Parry in DK292:B. The three Mosquitos purred their way over the North Sea, as far as the mouth of the Schelde, where they went their separate ways. Ralston bombed the power station at Stolberg from 300ft, and Parry did the same from 500ft on the power station at Knapsack. Meanwhile, Costello-Bowen was heading for the electricity switching station at Brauweiler. He made his landfall, and as he raced over the ground, hugging the tree-tops, there suddenly loomed up before him a very dangerous obstacle: an electricity tower, carrying its lethal high-voltage wires. The Mosquito was hauled up in the hope of missing the tower, but the starboard engine struck the top of the obstacle and then, out of control, they plummeted down to earth, 'O' for Orange scything its way through pine trees. Unbelievably, both airmen escaped death. Costello-Bowen was badly injured, and Broom was uninjured but was knocked out cold for a while. The Belgian Resistance subsequently rescued both airmen. After a long trip via France and Spain, they were returned to their unit, having sailed from a port well known to those of the squadron who, during the Blenheim era, had gone out to attack shipping from Malta: Gibraltar.

There were more electrical targets on the 27th, when two Mosquitos left RAF Horsham St Faith. The first away was F/C S/L Raymond Noel Collins DFC at 18.17 hours in W4070:C, followed by F/Sgt Monaghan one minute later in DK303:V. Both aircraft set course for the power station at Vagesack. 'V' for Victor attacked at 150ft, dropping its bombs in the target area before returning to base at 21.40 hours. Unfortunately, the same cannot be said for 'C' for Charlie – it flew too low and hit the sea on the outward journey. The crew ditched in the North Sea, north of the Frisian Islands, and about 105 miles west of the island of Pellworm. Sadly, both crew members perished. S/L Collins is commemorated on the Runnymede Memorial and the observer, P/O William May, who was found off Medemblik in the Zuider Zee on 14 September, was subsequently buried at sea.

The new CO took off for his first operation, again on 27 August, accompanied by his new observer, P/O H.H.E.P. 'Bladder' or 'Tubby' Cairns DFC. Edwards recalled: 'Whilst awaiting Quinn's transformation from WOp/AG to Navigator [P/O Gerry Quinn DFM and bar who was Edwards' WOp/AG on the Bremen raid on 4 July 1941, for which Edwards won the VC and Quinn the bar to his DFM], I commenced an association with P/O Tubby Cairns. He had joined the squadron as a navigator from No. 5 Group and had the advantage of being a wireless tradesman before opting for aircrew duties. Navigators who accepted the pattern of navigation as a science were never in great demand by pilots in the 2 Group day force, especially on low-level operations. The requisites were navigation rudiments, native cunning, intuition, quick thinking and, most important of all, the ability to read a map as well. Anybody lacking these assets would be struggling.'

On this operation, W/C Edwards took Mosquito DK292:B to, and quite successfully plastered, a power station at Langerbrugge, near Gent in Belgium, which they attacked from 100ft. They met light flak, but survived to return home to base at 21.40 hours. Meanwhile, S/L Channer was about to attack yet another power station at a factory at Sluiskil in the Netherlands. He took DK325:S in at 50ft and dropped his bombs along the target. Three bombs hit the power station and sulphuric acid sheds before the aircraft sped back home.

The last operation of the month was on the 29th and proved very dramatic. As P/O Cairns was away on leave, W/C Edwards was accompanied by observer P/O Robin Thomas, the Squadron Navigation Officer, in Mosquito DK323:N to lead a raid on the power station at Pont-à-Vendin. Sgt Charles Atkinson and his observer Sgt Pomeroy flew the other aircraft, DK303:V. Robin Thomas takes up the story:

> I had never flown with him [Edwards] before and therefore knew nothing beyond his reputation which made him, to me, a rather daunting prospect, held much in awe and to be avoided as far as possible. After a little while, as we headed towards the coast, I was surprised to hear the Wing Commander say he thought we were off course. I was perfectly happy with the way we were going, and said so. 'No' he insisted, we were off track and getting further off by the moment. I believe he thought he had recognized some feature on the ground, over which he knew we should not be passing. Here was the situation, he thought he was right, and I knew I was, but he was rather important and I was not. So I did the bravest thing in my life, and with polite deference, oozing humility, I placed the map on his lap and said, 'Then you'd better get on with it, hadn't you?' I have no idea what I expected or recollection of his reaction beyond realising the map was not accepted, the course was not altered, the departure point on the coast near Adderburgh came up precisely as planned and there was no more bother then, later, or ever.
>
> There was some 80 miles of sea to cross at low level before reaching our landfall east of Dunkirk. The sea was calm, the sun shone and at about half-way, we overtook two Bostons going in the same direction but not nearly so quickly. Then suddenly, the war took on a very personal guise, and time went into slow motion as the beach in front revealed a Bofors gun pointing at us, with its crew staring from under their coal-scuttle helmets as they aimed and fired their gun and I realized those faces had, at that moment, only one ambition – to bring down our plane and kill us. It is not agreeable to be shot at, at the best of times, but to look into the face of the unknown person bent on your destruction adds another dimension altogether. Slow motion stopped, the gun and its crew were behind us having failed to hit us, I am happy to say, and we were streaking some 30ft above the French countryside towards the next landmark, Armentières, where the Mademoiselle came from, and where we made the course alteration to bring us to the target about 18 miles away.
>
> Bomb doors were opened, the bombs fused, and the camera made ready. The Wing Commander made a shallow dive on to the target and as he pulled up, dropped the bombs. We stayed on course for the 11 seconds of time it took for the delayed action fuses to detonate the bombs and for the camera to take photographs (via a mirror looking backwards underneath the aircraft), before turning away, closing the bomb doors and at the same time, looking back over his shoulder to see the bombs burst. It will be remembered there was another Mosquito with us, and as I looked behind I saw to my horror it was flying over the target and looked as if it might be blown up in the explosion of our bombs. Fortunately, our bombs went off about 5 seconds after they were past; it appeared the Wing Commander had made a direct hit.

While all this excitement was happening, the Wing Commander was shouting at me to give him a new course. I could not hear him and, so it seemed, he could not hear me. A quick look established that the intercom plug had pulled from its socket during the agitations of trying to do so many things at the same time. I wriggled across him, found the plug dangling from his helmet (somewhat to his surprise as he had not yet realised why I could not hear him), pushed it into the socket, and once again we could hear each other. I gave him the course and was surprised to hear him say, 'If we get back from this, I'll buy you the biggest pint you've ever seen!' I applauded the sentiment but unless he was clairvoyant and had just received a presentiment, then I could not see what there was to worry about. The job seemed well done, the nasty men on the beach were long past and we were on our way home to tea.

Up to now, I had doubted his map reading, wondered at his unwitting ability to detach his intercom plug from its socket and admired his skill in putting the bombs in the right place. Very shortly I was to be astonished at his powers of clairvoyance. The way home was planned to cross the sea near Le Touquet, then over some 40 miles of the Channel to the neighbourhood of Folkestone and thence to Norwich. The French coast faded behind us, the other Mossie was on our starboard side, the sea 30ft below was calm and in about 5 minutes the sea would become England, and then I saw the splashes in the sea below. 'Oh, look,' I said, 'Bullets in the water'. 'School of porpoises? Where?' 'No, not porpoises, bullets, and there are fighters behind us! Turn left, left.' It is very good advice when there is a fighter on your tail, to turn towards him, thereby increasing the rate of his turn to an extent where he is unable to aim in front of you, which he would like to do, so that you may hopefully fly into his bullets. This you do not want, so by turning steeply his bullets will go harmlessly behind you. The Wing Commander knew this as well as I did, and since I was the only one who could see behind, he would now do as I told him.

We were at full throttle. 'Right, right', I cried, almost in the same breath as saying 'Left, left'. 'He can't have got across as quickly as that', said the Wing Commander, suddenly losing his faith in his navigator. 'It's not a "him" sir, there are six of them, FW 190s.' [There may have been more than this, as W/C Edwards recorded this as 12 FW 190s in his log entry for that day.] No more arguments, he pulled the 'panic tit', and we wove appropriately, lots more bullets in the water but none in us until – BANG, and the port engine exuded a white stream of vapour. The inflictor of this wound flashed by from in front! He had come at us head-on at a [combined] approach speed in the region of 600 mph and put a bullet through the glycol tank. About 20 seconds later, the engine, kept at full throttle and boost, having lost the coolant from the radiator, seized up and was feathered. All the fighters had gone home, I dare say they thought the plume of white 'smoke' meant we were done for. We flew on with the one good engine and looked around to see how the other Mossie had fared, but it was nowhere to be seen, either then, or ever after.

The Wing Commander decided we should land at the earliest opportunity – Lympne aerodrome was nearest, so that is where we went. The control tower was informed of our plight and of our intention to land, a tricky business on one engine, but I had no doubt well within the capability of my pilot. Then there was a snag. The undercarriage would not go down, owing to the hydraulic power for this operation being generated from the port engine, which we no longer had. 'You will have to pump it down', he said, and I agreed. This was totally a new experience, only vaguely remembered as a thing that could be done in such a predicament. Undoing my belt, I searched for and found the pump handle, put it into its socket and started to pump. This had to be done by kneeling on the floor, and was going to take some time. So there I was on the floor, unable to see anything, pumping like mad, the wheels half down when the plane lurched into a shallow dive. 'What's happening, sir?' I said, getting up from the floor and seeing the aerodrome right ahead. 'The wheels are causing too much drag and it is becoming difficult to hold flying speed, so I'm going in to make a belly landing'. 'Well, you might have told me', was my retort, forgetting the 'sir', as I quickly regained my seat and fastened my seat belt. Lympne was a small, grass aerodrome and we made its acquaintance in surprisingly gentle fashion. The wheels being half down absorbed any initial shock as they were pushed back up into their housings. The good engine stopped very suddenly. The momentary silence was followed by a sustained crumpling/scraping noise from underneath, as the poor Mossie skidded and slithered over the grass, leaving a forlorn trail of bits and pieces, bomb doors, engine nacelle covers, undercarriage doors, etc. Silence, very nearly complete except for the dying-down whine of various gyros, returned when the depleted aeroplane came to rest not more than 20ft from the boundary hedge.

The Wing Commander and I came through the top hatch to see an apprehensive crowd of assorted airmen standing well back, who it turned out, had never before seen a Mosquito and had no intention of finding out the hard way; was it carrying bombs, were there loaded machine-guns, or was it prone to catching fire when belly landing on strange airfields? It was a little early for tea so they opened the bar and he [W/C Edwards] bought me my large pint, or two, while we waited for, I think it was the Anson, to come and fetch us.

In fact, P/O Walker of 139 Squadron provided the transport back to RAF Horsham St Faith in a Blenheim MkV or 'Bisley' as it was known.

As for the other crew, sadly they had not made the coast before they fell prey to the 'Butcher Birds'. They had been shot down 9 miles off Dungeness. Unfortunately, Sgt Atkinson had been killed; Sgt Pomeroy was alive but injured and was picked up by an Air Sea Rescue launch. He survived, but lost a leg in the process. Yet another highly trained young airman had been killed. His body was subsequently laid to rest in Folkestone new cemetery. The losses were beginning to mount and with them concern about the future of the Mosquito.

CHAPTER 6

Exploring Tactics

The beginning of September 1942 saw the return of high-level operations, punctuated by cloud-cover operations within Germany and the Netherlands. Many of the targets were not attacked successfully, due to either too much or not enough of that vital ingredient, cloud. Where there was too much cloud, bombs were merely dropped on ETA with the hope of hitting the target.

There was yet another tragedy on the 6th, when Frankfurt was the target for a high-level attack by Sgt K.C. Pickett and his observer, Sgt Herbert Edmund Evans in Mosquito DK322:P. Having departed at 15.02 hours, it is believed that their machine was intercepted by Feldwebel [Sergeant] Roden of 12./JG1 [12th Flight of the 1st Day Fighter Wing]. The Mosquito fell to the ground at 18.30 hours, 11km south-south-east of Leuven in Belgium, near the town of Tourinnes-la-Grosse in the area of Brabant. The pilot was taken PoW, but sadly the observer was killed and is buried in the Haverlee war cemetery.

Sgt Smith and Sgt Bastow also had a close call on the 6th during a high-level attack on Frankfurt. They had left base at 15.06 hours in Mosquito DK330:N, and finding 10/10ths cloud over the target, located a small town in the Karlsruhe area, where they dropped their bombs from 21,000ft. They were soon flying home at 26,000ft, with clear skies above and only 2/10ths cloud at 1,500ft below them. The view ahead stretched for 30km and all seemed well. However, at 16.00 hours, some 250 miles from Karlsruhe at a position around 10 miles east of Cambrai, France, there appeared two enemy aircraft (snappers) on the starboard quarter, about 2,000ft below. The enemy were flying on a course south-east of the Mosquito, but when they saw it they immediately broke away to starboard and took up positions, one on the Mosquito's port beam, 1,000ft above, and the other on its starboard beam, 100ft below. Both fighters were now ready to pounce.

The first to attack was the 'Butcher Bird' on the starboard beam. It opened fire, damaging the fuselage and petrol tanks of the Mosquito. As had become standard practice, Sgt Smith hauled the Mosquito round to head into the enemy, whereupon the FW 190 on the port side saw its chance, and leapt down from above to attack its quarry below. The desperate fight continued with the enemy twice more zigzagging across the Mosquito, firing many rounds at it each time. In what had become a frantic battle for life or death, both fighters converged on the Mosquito simultaneously. One chose to attack from the port again, 200ft above this time, followed by his wingman, who closed in from starboard, 200ft below. The first to open fire was the FW 190 on the port side. The Mosquito again replied by turning steeply in towards its attacker, whereupon it received a crippling blow from the fighter's cannon shells. They ripped into one of the Mosquito's ailerons, and instantly Sgt Smith lost control. The aircraft span helplessly, spiralling downwards for thousands of feet until control was regained only 4,000ft above the earth's surface. The enemy must have considered the aircraft to be doomed, as they were nowhere to be seen as Sgts Smith and Bastow fled towards the English Channel, flying right down on the deck for safety. Due to damage sustained to their aircraft, they decided to land at RAF Oakington, 5 miles north-north-west of Cambridge, where they crash-landed safely at 18.40 hours, alive but severely shaken.

High-level attacks were therefore still proving extremely dangerous, a fact of which W/C Edwards was all too aware:

It was to be a battle to kill off this policy of high-flying intruder raids by day. The Station Commander saw the problems quickly, but it had to be played carefully because of the Mosquito's unpopularity as part of the strategic offensive. We had to do something with it that would pay dividends and make it seem a worthwhile venture and an adjunct to the command.

The results were not immediate though, as Edwards explains:

From the end of August we, the antagonists, began to win the battle against high flying by day. We were fortunate in having 'Digger' Kyle as CO who was prepared to argue his case against operations from all levels, and he had plenty. So gradually, the pattern of our future operations took place. A straightforward low-level operation in daylight was considered to be a fair bet. To ring the changes took the odds our way. We could go to the target at low level in daylight, bomb at least light, and withdraw under the cover of darkness [dusk attacks].

Such a change of tactics was therefore tried out on the 9th, when dusk attacks were launched at Osnabrück and Münster, from varying heights between 3,000 and 19,000ft. P/O Lang and observer F/O Thomas made one such attack in Mosquito DK316:J. Robin Thomas wrote in *Student to Stalag*:

Münster is a German city some 40 miles east of the Dutch border. One day it was decided that it should be irritated by Jim and I at dusk. The main object of the exercise was, although we were not told this, to assess the merits of a dusk raid when related to a Mosquito. The plan was to fly at our best height, 27,000ft, arrive with enough light to see the target, descend to 2,000ft, aim, drop the bombs and return in the dark. The outward journey, very high and fast, made us almost immune to fighter interception and flak would have to be extremely lucky, even if it could reach that height, to score a hit. It had to be sheer misfortune if a night-fighter found or could match, let alone exceed, the speed of a Mosquito as we fled home in the dark. Light flak at the lower height was a hazard if you flew over defended areas. This we tried not to do, but not always with success as we found on another occasion.

One or two things did not go according to plan. No trouble in arriving at dusk, but the predicted break in the clouds did not materialize at the ETA, and there was of course no sign of Münster. So we descended in a large spiral to where it ought to be, still above 10/10ths cloud, and then someone started to shoot at us. Not only could we see the shell bursts following us round in our descent, but also the muzzle flashes of guns on the ground seen through the cloud which may have been a thick ground mist. There was no future, it seemed, in going through the cloud only to find Münster very adjacent to the underside, so I aimed the bombs for the middle of the greatest cluster of muzzle flashes and we set out for home, hoping it had indeed been Münster and we had made a worthwhile contribution to the war effort.

As we climbed away towards home it became quite dark and the port engine was seen to be giving out a continuous stream of sparks. Had we, without being aware, been hit by flak? Was the engine about to burst into flames? Would a night-fighter see our trail of sparks and sneak up behind while we were climbing and vulnerable? All things considered, it was decided to stop the engine and see if this stopped the sparks – it did. Fire now seemed unlikely, and invisibility desirable, so we stayed on one engine. The Mosquito did not mind a bit and even maintained a good rate of climb at over 180 mph. This was considerably below our planned speed and taking into account we did not know for certain our point of departure from what might have been Münster, the navigation was becoming more and more tenuous.

We flew on, using the flight plan, modified to acknowledge the lower speed, until we would seem to be over the sea. Jim then started the faulty engine from which the streams of sparks had diminished owing to the gasket, the cause of the bother, having burnt itself out. I then tried to get a QDM on the wireless, which, had I been successful, would have given us a course to steer to arrive back at base. I do not remember if success attended my effort; knowing my luck with the radio, probably not. I do remember we both became aware of a moaning noise in the earphones, and there was no doubt it was getting louder by the second. One of us suddenly recalled an instructor mentioning balloon squeakers. These were radio devices transmitting a continuous undulating signal from the centre of a balloon barrage. They had a limited range to warn anyone hearing the signal that they were near a barrage. If the signal became stronger, you were getting nearer and vice versa. The sound had never been demonstrated but had been described as being 'the final agonies of a dying cow', and that seemed a fair description of the noise in the earphones. Assuming London was in front, we turned smartly towards the west and the dying cow faded from the earphones.

Now was the time to try for another QDM, but before this could be done the cow came back again, faintly at first, but getting louder. The immediate and sensible reaction when finding danger lurks ahead, is to go in the opposite direction. We were sensible, the cow became fainter, great relief and then it came back again! The dying cow was determined to have us as its audience. After the same thing happened three or four more times, our twisting and turning seemed to shake it off, but by now, from being unsure of our position, we were completely lost. There was however, always 'Darkie', another radio aid never before used by us. The pilot had a radio with which to speak to the control tower, nearby aircraft, etc. Indeed the same radio recently dominated by the dying cow, had, like the balloon squeaker transmitter, a range of about 10 miles. So, if anyone heard its transmission, then it followed they were within 10 miles of you. 'Hello Darkie, Hello Darkie, this is "J" for Jig calling', said Jim into the microphone. 'Please, where are we?' Almost at once came back the reply: 'Hello "J" Jig, you are off the coast of Bradwell Bay, we will light up the aerodrome for you.' Suddenly, about 5 miles away an enormous cone of searchlights went up. There must have been at least 50 of them, all meeting at a point over the aerodrome. We flew towards it and coming in to land was like flying through the side of the biggest tent you are ever likely to see. We made a somewhat bumpy landing and stopped as soon as possible, because Mosquitos needed quite a lot of room and we didn't know how long a strange runway might be. Jim facetiously remarked into the radio, 'I have just made an attempt at landing', at which he was told to go around and try again, but on explaining he was actually on the ground was told to taxi to the end of the runway. This took 5 or 10 minutes, it being the longest runway we could ever have imagined. It transpired the aerodrome had been constructed exclusively for the reception of 'lame ducks', four-engined bombers coming back from Germany, after having been badly shot up and unable to make it back to their own bases. We stayed the night and flew back to our own aerodrome the next morning, and were able to see from the air, the extent of the airfield. There were three runways of incredible length, forming a triangle with, in the centre, a cluster of the original farm buildings.

The squadron thereafter reverted to high-level attacks on Wilhelmshaven, Kiel, Cuxhaven, Lübeck and Emden, until on the 16th the chemical works at Wiesbaden were to receive dusk attacks by six crews between 2,500 and 4,000ft which were largely successful. Yet another tactic was tried out on the 18th when roving commissions were given to three crews, assigned areas in Wilhelmshaven, Bremerhaven and Emden in which to choose a target and bomb, all of which were unsuccessful owing to lack of cloud cover.

Then came the chance everybody was waiting for, a chance to drop bombs on the 'big city' – Berlin. Six Mosquitos took off around 12.30 hours on 19 September and formed up to set course for the target. In the event Berlin escaped unscathed, mostly due to cloud obscuring the target and the protection of the Luftwaffe. F/L George Parry was first away in Mosquito DK339:C and remembers the sortie as follows:

It was the first daylight raid on Berlin, and was unsuccessful due to weather. We were intercepted twice by Bf 109s on the way to Berlin, which we evaded by going into cloud and changing height and course. There was heavy cloud over the target so we made for Hamburg where we were intercepted again by Bf 109s. We evaded them [at 16,000ft] by going into cloud, which we had all the way back. Robbie [P/O Robson] asked me to go under the cloud as we were near the Dutch coast. We broke cloud at 1,000ft inside the Dutch coast and were immediately attacked by two FW 190s. We evaded the first attack by going into a steep turn and found myself head-on to a second FW 190 which fired a burst as we closed. There were several hits, but no serious damage. We climbed into cloud [at 1,500ft] and headed for home. The cloud gave out just beyond the Dutch coast, so we dived down to sea level and outran our pursuers.

The remaining Mosquitos all landed back at base late in the afternoon. All, that is, except DK326, 'M' for Mother. S/L Norman Henry Edward Messervy DFC was an Australian from Point Cook, who had completed a previous tour on Blenheims, then on PR Spitfires, earning him a DFC after 68 operations. He and his observer, P/O Frank Holland, had taken off at 12.34 hours but failed to return. They had been flying in company with two other Mosquitos. The formation had just climbed up through cloud and had emerged at 21,000ft heading for 26,000ft, when they were attacked from astern, 500ft below, by a FW 190. The enemy aircraft fired bursts into the climbing Mosquito, from which black smoke began to pour from the port engine. The result was a stall turn to port and the Mosquito then spiralled vertically downwards, pursued by the FW 190. 'M' for Mother crashed 30km north-north-west of Osnabrück, just south of Ankum, killing both of the occupants. Although initially interred at the Evangelical Friedhof cemetery at Quakenbrück, 16km north-north-east of Ankum, the bodies of the crew were transferred to the Rheinberg war cemetery where they now rest.

The next operation the squadron was to embark upon was on the 22nd. It was to be a low-level attack intended for the Koninklijke Nederlandsche Hoogovens & Staalfabrieken NV (Royal Dutch Blast-Furnace and Steel-Mill Limited) at IJmuiden in the Netherlands. The attacks were in two waves, one in the morning with a follow-up in the afternoon. F/L Roy Ralston in DZ313:E with F/Sgt Armitige led the morning's attack. W/O Ray Noseda in DK336:P and P/O Jim Lang in DK296:G, the repaired aircraft in which Sgt Pete Rowland had previously collected a chimney pot, accompanied him. The weather was fine as the vic crossed the coast and headed at sea-level until landfall. When they arrived at the Dutch coast, the bomb doors were already open and the cameras were ready. They expected to be south of IJmuiden and north of Haarlem, but when they swung north IJmuiden seemed a little closer than expected – it was in fact Haarlem, and the target was now erroneously to be the gas works. A gas-holder was the target for P/O Lang's machine and he dropped his bombs alongside it, causing a fire at the gas-holder and the adjacent oil tanks. W/O Noseda also dropped his 500lb bombs on the factory before making for the coast. The largest gas-holder, although not destroyed, did suffer splinter damage. Consequently, gas to Haarlem and the surrounding areas had to be delivered directly, without the storage facility. By 5 October it was back in service again. Meanwhile, F/L Ralston had obviously realized the navigational error and made for the steelworks further north at IJmuiden, where he dropped his bomb-load from 100ft on the coke ovens. He met some light flak before beating a retreat safely back to base.

The afternoon attack was again in vic formation, this time led by F/L Charles Patterson with Sgt Joseph Egan in DK338:O. Patterson, who eventually became S/L Patterson DSO, DFC, was on his second tour and on his first operation with 105 Squadron, having secured a posting to the squadron after a chance discussion with Hughie Edwards while in the Officers' Mess at RAF Swanton Morley late in 1941. S/L Patterson describes what happened next: 'Well, it was a very quick and fairly easy operation. We crossed the coast, turned just north of IJmuiden and then turned south, and there straight ahead of us was the steelworks. We just went straight at it, and a lot of light flak came up. I threw the Mosquito all over the sky, over the roof with evasive action against all the light flak and then down the other side. I do remember coming out of the coast on this first Mosquito operation for me and the flak started opening up as it used to do. They depressed the heavy guns and fired shells out to sea which were pretty inaccurate, but there was a certain danger from them. You would see a huge column of water go up from the shell bursting on the water.'

With F/L Patterson that day was Mosquito DK328:V, flown by P/O Jimmy Bruce DFM, who hailed from Dundee in Scotland and was also on his first Mosquito operation. His observer on this operation was P/O Mike Carreck, who remembers him as: 'Five foot ten, of medium build, and approximately 26 years old. An unmarried chap with craggy features and a serious

S/L Charles Patterson. (Via Charles Patterson)

expression, very Scottish looks but no Scots accent; spoke BBC. He was very mature for his age, and flying with him I felt he was my elder brother, not only in years but also in ops experience. He was on his second tour after 30/35 Blenheim ops on his first tour on which he won the DFM, which took some winning in those earlier days. [He was a veteran of the anti-shipping campaign when the Blenheims of 105 Squadron went to Malta.] He was a 'press-on' type, with a very strong sense of duty. We were friends of course, but he saw our pilot/navigator relationship not in social terms, but as two workmates with an important job to do.' Regarding the IJmuiden operation, Mike Carreck remembers:

Everything was reassuringly ordinary as we settled in our Mosquito and strapped ourselves in. We waited a moment or two, and then the leader's airscrew started to spin. Almost immediately, the no. 2 of our formation of three opened up [F/O Bristow in DK337:N], and Jimmy stabbed the starter button – nothing happened. He jabbed again and again, but 'no dice' and by now the other two Mosquitos were taxiing away. 'Standby Mossie!' said Jimmy, a man of few words. We scrambled out and set off for the reserve aircraft 50yds away, not an easy run with a hanging dinghy or dinghy plus parachute banging the back of one's legs. We climbed into reserve Mosquito DZ314 [:F], the starter trolley was plugged in, engines roared and we taxied off like a bat out of hell and leapt into the air.

It felt as if we'd carried out that change-over in about 30 seconds, but several minutes had gone by with Jimmy running through his pre-flight checks and giving the engines time to warm up. Each minute at 240 knots meant another 4 nautical miles ahead for the other two Mosquitos. We stormed across the Norfolk coast, came down over the sea to a beneath-the-radar 50ft and, taps wide open, started using up the North Sea. On and on we raced, with not a sign of Mosquitos; it seemed less and less likely we would ever catch them. Until, at the very last minute, we saw two tiny specks far ahead hugging the wave-tops. We joined them just as they were crossing the Dutch coast, and if they were surprised to see us, IJmuiden wasn't. All the flak in creation started coming up: red, yellow and white tracer over, under, ahead and all round us bursting cannon shells and climbing up, what looked like strings of coloured Chinese lanterns. Bomb doors open – inside this cage of flak we were among the dockside cranes, warehouses and machines sheds. A building loomed up and Jimmy pressed the button on the control column. The 11-second delay bombs fell away, and he lifted us up over the roof. There was the sea ahead of us, and when we were out of range, they were still firing at us. I unclenched my teeth and, one by one, my muscles and my breathing slowly came back to normal. Jimmy was gazing idly at the sea and humming quietly to himself; if you'd survived a tour on Blenheims, any Mosquito op was a piece of cake.

Returning home, Charles Patterson described a diversion to the plan: 'I saw a large shipping fleet about 2 miles off-shore, a bit to the south. So I promptly left. Of course on Mosquitos there was no defensive armament. You didn't come out in formation, it was every man for himself, but we were roughly in sight of each other coming out of the coast. When these guns opened up I thought well, they're not going to fire at their fishing fleet if they've got two Mosquitos that are quite free and open. So I promptly turned south and flew straight at the fishing fleet, and sure enough, the guns stopped firing in my direction, and carried on firing very firmly at the other two. When we got back, my young navigator – I think it was only his first trip, and had been given to me as a second-tour man – had boasted to the other crews what a great pilot he had got. I can't say it made me feel very pleased with myself, just rather amused me. He was an awfully nice little chap, Sgt Egan – very nervous but determined to go and do it, but conquered his fear marvellously.' The other two Mosquitos each arrived back safely at RAF Horsham St Faith.

CHAPTER 7

Oslo

The next target for the squadron was to remain prominent in the annals of RAF history. As far back as 11 December 1939, Adolf Hitler had met the Norwegian politician Vidkun Quisling, who was born in 1887 and founded the pro-Nazi National Union movement. Subsequently, on 2 April 1940, Hitler gave orders for the start of Operation Weserübung against Norway and Denmark. By 9 April, Germany had begun its invasion of Norway and a Nazi occupation began which heralded a reign of terror and despotism which lasted until 1945. The Norwegian King Håkon and his government left for London in summer 1940, and were declared as deposed. Quisling remained, pandering to Nazi doctrines such as obliging all boys over the age of nine to join the Nationalist Socialist Youth Organization, having banned other youth organizations, including the Boy Scouts. In place of the Håkon régime, a puppet government was formed on 1 February 1942, and the traitor, Quisling, became its 'Ministerpresident'. Quisling's association with the reign of terror lasted until the Nazis in Norway capitulated on 7 May 1945. A month later, on 7 June, the legal Norwegian government and King Håkon returned and subsequently, on 24 October of that year, Vidkun Quisling paid the price of his treachery. He was found to be a war criminal and was shot.

George Parry provided the following insight: 'After the Nazi occupation of Norway, life for the Norwegians was pretty grim, as it was for the other occupied countries. By 1942, with no Allied action taking place over Norway, and with the constant struggle by the Resistance against the Gestapo, people were feeling isolated and maybe forgotten. Tor Skjønsberg, head of the Norwegian Resistance, contacted London to explain the situation and to ask if some action could be sanctioned to show that his people were not forgotten and to raise morale. It was decided to lay on a low-level daylight raid on the Gestapo HQ [Victoria Terrasse] in Oslo. The raid was to coincide with the Quisling rally [Quisling was to give a speech to the Nasjonal Samling] and parade, to be held on 25 September 1942. The Gestapo headquarters was an imposing building surmounted by three domes, located near the university and the royal palace in the centre of Oslo. Four aircraft led by myself, each carrying four 500lb bombs with eleven second delay fuses, would make the attack. A few days before the attack, the route was finalized and tactics discussed. We were able to study photographs that had been taken by the Norwegian Resistance from the roofs of nearby buildings and we were told the time that they wished us to attack.' Above the central Norwegian torture chamber was a building where the rally was to take place. The attack was not only to interrupt Quisling's rally, but also to try and destroy Gestapo records that were kept there, and indeed to end the lives of as many Gestapo officers as possible.

The operation commenced on the afternoon of 24 September 1942, when W/C Hughie Edwards led a formation of Mosquitos to RAF Leuchars, in what is known to the locals as the 'Kingdom of Fife', in the east of Scotland. This was to be the starting point for this precision Mosquito attack. Six aircraft had left RAF Horsham St Faith, to arrive after a 1 hour 35 minute flight. Edwards and his observer P/O H.H.E.P. Cairns in DK328:V led the crew who were to lead the actual raid: S/L Parry in DK296:G, with P/O Victor George Robson. Accompanying them were P/O Peter Wilton Townsend Rowland with P/O Richard 'Dick' L. Reily in DZ313:E;

44

Leaders of the raid on Gestapo HQ in Oslo: P/O Victor Robson (observer, left) and S/L George Parry. (Via George Parry)

F/O Alec Norman Bristow with P/O Bernard Willis Marshall in DK338:O; F/Sgt Gordon Kenneth Carter with Sgt William Shirley Young in DK325:S, as well as P/O James 'Jimmy' George Bruce with P/O Mike Carreck.

Mike Carreck remembers the trip: 'We flew up in DZ312:U from Horsham St Faith with the other Mosquitos to Leuchars on the 24th. That evening, a bunch of us went out for a noggin or two in nearby St Andrews. In the garden of an excellent pub, Carter told us about his parachute jump from a doomed aircraft. His harness unbuckled, he made a frantic grab and floated down hanging by his hands.' On the morning of the 25th, P/O Pete Rowland went to the briefing and recalled:

As the fixed bayonets of the sentries lifted to let me into the briefing room, I saluted the Wing Commander who was standing on a raised platform. My eyes lifted immediately to the big map on the wall behind him. I was wondering where we were going, how far we had to go and whether any of us would have to die. A black ribbon on the map stretched eastwards from Leuchars, on, on, endlessly on across the North Sea to the Norwegian coast, then on across Norway until it turned sharply up the fjord that led to Oslo. Oslo? Why were we going to Oslo? The ribbon pointed back across the sea to Sumburgh airfield, on a tiny speck of an island remote from the Scottish coast [Shetland]. We had far to go. Dick Reily, my navigator, was busy at one of the trestle tables ranged before the platform. He looked very elegant, as always, even in the severely cut battledress. His table was neatly arranged, maps in tidy piles, ruler, dividers, Dalton computer, freshly sharpened pencils, all precisely set out. 'Hello Peter,' said Dick. 'Long one this.' He was fixing three charts together with transparent tape. 'Four Mosquitos going.' There were five tables, and at each sat a Mosquito pilot and navigator. 'What about Jimmy Bruce and Mike?' I asked. 'Standby crew. Wonder why we're off to Oslo.'

Mike Carreck recalls: 'Jimmy Bruce and I were touchline spectators, very much to our disappointment, on this famous operation. When we were issued with 1:250,000 maps of Norway, I was puzzled to see the great areas in white. "What are these?" I asked the station Navigation Officer. "Glaciers", he said. No ordinary op, this, I thought.' Pete Rowland continues: 'W/C Edwards surveyed us from the edge of the platform. He was massively built, an Australian famous throughout the RAF, and a man of few words. "Probably you'd like to know why you're going to Oslo", he said. "I'll tell you. You're going after a man called Quisling." "Quisling?" somebody said in surprise. Quisling – he was the traitor who had sold Norway to the Germans. "Quisling", said somebody else with relish. "Some gallant Norwegians", the W/C was speaking again, "have risked their lives to tell us where Quisling will be, on what day, at what time. S/L Parry, let's have that model." From a corner of the room George Parry pushed forward a trolley, covered with green cloth. W/C Edwards pulled the cloth away, and there before us were streets, churches, houses with brightly coloured roofs – a city, built in miniature, in careful detail. "Oslo", he said. "Quisling will be here today, at four o'clock Oslo time." He pointed to a building, surmounted by a dome. "Here, at Gestapo headquarters, and four Mosquitos will be there to greet him with high explosive."'

Regarding the briefing for the operation George Parry notes: 'At our final briefing, we were told that we could expect cloud cover if required, and that there were no enemy fighters close enough to our route to cause trouble.' This remained to be seen, as Pete Rowland concluded: 'After briefing was over, with all its details of call-signs, bomb fuses and formation orders, I found myself walking back to the mess with Jimmy Bruce. "Standby crew, eh?" I said. "Got a trip to Scotland, anyhow", answered Jimmy. He took a deep breath of the icy air, inhaling the fragrance of long-forgotten fish from the quay a mile away. "God's own country", he said in a rich Scottish burr.'

Pete Rowland and Dick Reily were soon sitting in Mosquito DZ313:E, and were getting ready to go, as Pete explains: 'I finished the cockpit check and once again ran over the string of letters TTMFCOBRF – Trim; Throttles; Magnetos; Fuel; Coolant; Oil; Brakes; Rudder; Flaps. Drills were done, prayers said, superstitions observed. Dick and I were strapped in our cramped cockpit, with its sports car smell of warm leather with a whiff of petrol, overlaid by the sickly-sweet pear-drop scent of aircraft dope. "Okay, Dick?" Dick took a rapier-sharp pencil from between his teeth and clicked on his microphone. "'Kay", he replied. Ahead of us, George's Mosquito [DK296:G] began to roll down the runway, gathered speed, and took off, banking away in a graceful climbing turn. I pushed the throttles forward, and the two big Rolls-Royce Merlin engines began to roar. We sped down the runway, lifted into the air and began climbing to take our position on George's left. Two more Mosquitos came sliding up into place [F/O Bristow in DK328:V and F/Sgt Carter in DK325:S], and our loose diamond formation swept in a gentle turn over Leuchars airfield. Below us, a toy Mosquito was taxiing back to its dispersal point. Jimmy and Mike had the day off.' Mike Carreck explained: 'On the 25th, Jimmy and I took off and waited above while the first XI got airborne. We hoped somebody would stay on the deck so we could join them. Nobody did. Since then I hold my manhood cheap while any speaks of the op they flew that day. After a discussion about marmalade, Jimmy went off to visit his family in Dundee. I spent the afternoon sightseeing in Edinburgh.'

At this point George Parry recalls that: 'Having taken off from Leuchars, the Mosquitos headed out over the North Sea, in echelon-starboard formation at 50ft above the sea.' Pete Rowland continues: 'The numbers on my gyro settled down to zero-eight-four, the course for Norway. At 1,000ft we skimmed across the Scottish coast, and Dick checked our position on one of his maps, and now we were out over the North Sea. No more map checks until we reached Norway; no radar to guide us; precious little radio. We had a long way to go and a long way to come back, [approximately 1,068 miles in total] beneath a sunny sky with clouds building up. "Drift 4° starboard", said Dick. "We're right on track." '

The plan was to fly 227 miles from Leuchars to position 'A' at 57°08'N; 03°00'E, where they arrived at 14.12 hours. Then it was on to a position 'B' some 215 miles further on at 57°50'N; 08°40'E in the Skagerrak, where they arrived dead on ETA, at 15.08 hours and 30 seconds. This splitting up of the course was done for accuracy, in order to take account of a large change in magnetic variation along the track. The aircraft flew on in open formation, two to a section. Pete Rowland takes up the story:

What a beautiful little aircraft this is, I thought, looking to my right at the trim silhouette of the leading Mosquito, its carpentered lines, slender, its tail cockily high, the big Rolls-Royce engines gulping down the miles. It was camouflaged earth-brown and tree-green above, sky-blue below; on the fuselage stood out the letters GB, for 105 Squadron. The Mosquito, tough, belligerent, swashbuckling – fastest two-seater in the world. Now George was leading us right down to the sea, just above the white caps of the waves. Down so low that a moment's lapse of concentration could mean splintering destruction; staying down meant hours of grim, sweating work, but to fly a few feet higher would expose us to the gaze of German radar, and would show us up as four glinting specks on a green-lit dial. German voices would report our minute-by-minute position and other German voices would order up fighters to meet us. Although we were flying Mosquitos, one German fighter was at least as fast – the Focke-Wulf 190; squat and ugly, with its huge, blunt, round-fronted engine and its four murderous heavy-calibre cannons. So we stayed low on the waves, hidden among the dense scribbling which the sea itself wrote on the screens. Out of radar sight, as long as we kept the hurtling Mosquitos below roof-top height, on our way over the sea to Norway. On and on we went, hugging the waves. Time and time again, Dick took further drift readings, checked track and speed, calculated changing winds, as we moved across his charts in a line of neatly pencilled dots. Always we scanned the sky for fighters that would appear out of nowhere, to swoop instantly down – beware the Hun in the sun! The scratch of the horizon thickened, and grew in size all too slowly. 'Thirty-three minutes to the Norwegian coast', said Dick. Now we could see the mountains, snow on their peaks, looming higher and higher. Suddenly, fishing boats were flashing by beneath us.

Two large merchant ships near Kristiansand were ignored as the Mosquitos pressed on. George Parry recalls the scene: 'On entering the Skagerrak we could see the northern tip of Denmark on the horizon away to our right, but there was blue sky with no cloud. Unknown to us, FW 190s had been flown to Oslo from Stavanger that morning to take part in a fly-past during the Quisling rally. We made landfall at the south-east corner of Oslo Fjord [at 15.40 hours, just west of Fredrikstad, aiming for position 'C': 59°10'N; 10°50'E, about 5 miles east of Fredrikstad] and flew just inland from the fjord.' Pete Rowland further recalls: 'We crossed a small stretch of sand. "Wizard landfall", said Dick, as our low-flying Mosquitos were speeding across a landscape of dark green firs and grey barren rock.'

The Mosquitos then flew at low level over the houses in Fredrikstad, and onwards just east of the Fredrikstad–Råde railway line, until they met the Vam Lake north of Råde, from where they crossed the Moss–Oslo railway line. At the southern tip of the Bunde Fjord, the formation wheeled around to starboard in a wide circuit before approaching Oslo from the east. Pete Rowland noted: 'Abruptly, a city came into view; bright coloured houses, pinks and blues and greens, just like the model we'd seen that morning – Oslo. Up ahead was a big building with a domed roof, a Nazi swastika flag floating above it. George Parry's bomb doors gaped open. I disengaged the safety lever and yanked down the red bomb door handle. The Mosquito shuddered as the slipstream snatched at the opening doors. A green light winks on and Dick said "Bomb doors open. Bombs fused, eleven seconds delay." He turned around in his seat, "Formation closed up." We came over the edge of Oslo, storming just above the roof-tops, the building with the domes leaping towards us. A church steeple shot by on the left; a golden weathervane above our heads. I saw the clock – just on four. Black blobs hung for a moment below George's Mosquito and plummeted into the domed building.' George Parry recalls: 'I released my bombs and my no. 2 aircraft saw debris rising as they struck the building, but it would be another eleven seconds before the bombs burst. As we passed over the target my navigator told me that the fourth aircraft had been hit and was turning south with his port engine on fire.'

Meanwhile Pete Rowland was about to drop his own bombs: 'I touched the rudder, here came the domes. My thumb whitened on the release button and the Mosquito lurched upwards as the bombs fell and I said "bombs gone". Dick was staring behind us, his eyes fixed on the target. I began counting off the seconds; one, two, three . . . nine, ten, eleven. "There it goes!" yelled Dick, "direct hit! direct hit! Right on the . . . Jesus Christ Almighty, fighters!" and immediately, calmly, he said, "two Focke-Wulf 190s, seven o'clock high, range 200yds." I snatched the toggle that gave our Mosquito maximum emergency speed, to be used for a few minutes only, otherwise the engines would shake themselves to pieces. A few feet below us water glistened as we flashed across a lake. Dick's voice again – "Two One-Nineties attacking rear Mosquito. They're firing now, the Mosquito's hit; smoke is coming from his starboard engine – he's going in, he's going in – he's crashed into the lake!" Tail-end Charlie I thought, they always get tail-end Charlie. Who's next?'

The aircraft, DK325, GB:S, had been intercepted by a FW190, flown by Unteroffizier Rudolf Fenten who was training on the FW 190. He had picked up the machine from Stavanger and had landed at Fornebu. Following a report of the Mosquitos' arrival at the fjord, he and another fighter pilot, Feldwebel Erich Klein who, like Fenten, was of 3./JG5 [3rd Flight of the 5th Day Fighter Wing], took to the air to intercept them. Fenten had tried to warn F/Sgt Carter and Sgt Young to land and had shot up their wing but the crew refused to set down. Seconds later, with fire streaming from their starboard engine, their fate was sealed. George Parry explained: 'He [Carter] attempted to make a crash landing on a lake in a valley a few miles south-west of Oslo, but unfortunately hit a tree on the edge of the lake and crashed. Both the pilot and navigator were killed.' The crew are buried in Oslo Western civil cemetery. Parry continues: 'I carried on my course after bombing, as I had a backward-facing camera, taking shots of the target. I noticed more tracer as the other two aircraft went ahead of me accelerating rapidly. I looked back to see a FW 190 behind me, so I too accelerated rapidly and made for the rising ground, where I flew up and down valleys as low as I could and finally lost my pursuer.' Pete Rowland, meanwhile, was to have difficulties of his own:

'Fighter, fighter, 190 at five o'clock level turning towards us, range one-fifty. Ready to turn starboard, turn NOW!' Right full rudder, control wheel hard down. The crushing force of the turn was thrusting us into our seats, and the lurid, yellow lines of tracer hose-piping by on our left; brilliant red balls, floating lazily in the air as the cannon shells exploded. We shaved the tops of pine trees, came down over open playing fields, pulled up to clear the coloured roofs of a village then on over a bridge. 'Here he comes again, eight o'clock high, ready to turn port . . . turn port NOW!' Again and again, the One-Ninety came in to the attack, with Dick telling me, moment by moment, the fighter's position, judging the instant for the crazy-angled turn that wrenched the Mosquito across the fighter's gunsight to offer the worst possible deflection shot; to make the curve of his pursuit diverge away from us; to force him to make a time-wasting S-turn to get in line for the next burst. On the fifth or perhaps the sixth attack, I saw the One-Ninety as we turned starboard, our wing almost touching the ground. For a brief moment I caught sight of the stubby scarlet-painted engine, and for a fraction of a second I saw the pilot's head in the cockpit. Then the fighter's wing splashed red with the fire of the cannons. Tracer arched towards us – CLACK! . . . Something slammed noisily into our starboard airscrew and steel splinters stabbed along the wooden fuselage.

I brought the Mosquito out of the heeling turn, held her straight and level, low over the tree-tops racing below, ready for the next crushing, horizontal-spinning turn. 'He's gone', said Dick flatly. Startled, I glanced behind us. I could see the One-Ninety turning away, already almost out of sight. 'He must have hit a tree, had a hole in his wing.' Dick rubbed his face with his fingertips. After a moment he said briskly, 'Course two-eight-seven compass.' So we came out over the sea on course for home, flying just above the waves, below the searching enemy radar, on and on for an eternity, my wrists like lead, straps biting into my shoulders. An airscrew was damaged, and our engines had to be nursed along after that over-long period of grinding emergency. Our fuel was low, squandered to strain out extra speed throughout the chase, and Dick had a tiny island to find with almost no navigational aids. More than once, we thought we saw land far ahead. Each time, the blur on the horizon was cloud, but at long last it wasn't cloud. Dick's superlative navigation had sought out the island; there below us, in the dusk, was Sumburgh airfield. We came in and landed, the damaged airscrew functioning perfectly, the fuel gauge needles rigid at zero.

George Parry also made it back, and noted after the attack: 'The three aircraft had now become separated, so I made my way over the mountains and down to and accessed the North Sea to Sumburgh at the southern end of the Shetlands.' Robson reported on his navigation for the return journey with George Parry as: 'Going up the valley we started climbing, steering a course of 281° (magnetic) and I passed an ETA of 16.40 [hours] for the coast. Very little map reading of DR was done at this point, as I was watching for any signs of fighters. At 16,000ft I levelled out above a 1,000ft cloud layer, flying over the tops. The cloud gradually dispersed and we descended to 6,000ft, flying over mountain-tops and glaciers. My next accurate pinpoint was the southern tip of the Folgefonna Glacier. We maintained course, leaving the coastline at 16.38 [hours] at Selbjörn Fjord. Here we altered course to 289° (magnetic) and I gave an ETA of 17.29 [hours] for Sumburgh. We were now flying at zero feet over the sea, and using the CSBS. I checked my drift and altered course to 285° (magnetic). The pilot altered his aircraft and my ETA became 17.32 [hours]. I was aiming to hit off the middle of the Shetlands, and my track was confirmed when I obtained a QDM of 278° (magnetic) at 17.15 [hours]. As this was a first class bearing, I altered course and reached Sumburgh at 17.35 [hours]. The flight had taken 4 hours and 45 minutes and the other two aircraft landed separately, 10 and 15 minutes later.'

F/O Bristow and his navigator, P/O Marshall, had also had a rough time of it as they too had been attacked by the FW 190s. Having managed to evade them, they too returned safely to Sumburgh. Their aircraft was the one George Parry mentioned, touching down 10 minutes after him. Pete Rowland's flight lasted 5 hours exactly and they landed last. George Parry was greeted on arrival by W/C Hughie Edwards, who had flown a 1 hour, 15 minute hop up to

Sumburgh and remembers the first characteristic words to greet him: 'Did you arrive on time as you were a minute late taking off?' Parry assured him that he had indeed arrived on time at the target.

On arrival at Sumburgh, Pete Rowland and Dick Reilly were taken by RAF van to be debriefed. Pete Rowland described the scene: 'The other two Mosquito crews were there and so was W/C Edwards. "Thought you'd had it", he said, seemingly casual. The Intelligence Officer questioned us, gave us coffee and showed us to our rooms in a Nissen hut. I fell into bed. When I awoke, it was bright morning, and Dick was handing me a cup of steaming tea. I took a sip, "Did we get Quisling?" I asked. Dick was spick and span in a well-pressed uniform and sparkling shoes. "No", he said. "Quisling bravely ran downstairs as soon as the sirens went and hid in the cellar, but the radio did say we got the Gestapo in heaps. All last night Oslo was crammed with Norwegians singing in the streets, and. . . ." He went over to the window. "That lake – you know, where Carter and Young went in – men, women and kids are coming in their hundreds to chuck flowers on the water, it's all covered." Then Dick looked back at me. "That chap in the One-Ninety, I'd like to know how he's feeling today." I said, "I wonder if we will ever see him again?" '

That morning W/C Edwards, reunited with his Mosquito GB:V and the remaining four Mosquitos, flew the 2 hours and 15 minute sortie back south to RAF Horsham St Faith. Some time later, George Parry had some interesting news: 'We heard afterwards that the Oslo police were annoyed, as I took away the radio antennae on the roof of their HQ, so that they had no radio communications to marshal their own, and other, emergency services after the raid. The Germans also accused us of machine-gunning the palace, but as we had no guns, it was the fire from the pursuing fighters that hit the palace.'

The press had a field day, and the public was, for the first time, made aware of the existence of the Mosquito and all its high adventures of the Oslo raid. Sadly, some civilian damage had also occurred, and a few houses had been hit during the raid. Four bombs had hit the target, however three had scythed their way through to the other side without exploding. Another also failed to explode but had entered the building. However, the point had been brought home and Norwegian morale was successfully lifted from the doldrums.

As a postscript to the raid, George Parry wrote: 'Fifty years later, I had a telephone call from Rudolf Fenten, the pilot of the FW 190 that attacked me over Oslo. He had heard of my whereabouts and wished to meet me. He had his own aircraft so I arranged for him to land at Norwich Airport (once RAF Horsham St Faith) and we spent a pleasant weekend together at my home. Norwich impressed him, and we spent a lot of time exchanging experiences of both during and after the war. We even went flying together before he returned home. He was not as fortunate as myself, as he was taken prisoner by the Russians in 1945 after a forced landing following an engine failure, and spent seven years in a labour camp.'

Pete Rowland also had an answer to his question, 'I wonder if we will ever see him again?' as he explained: 'Well, I was going to see that chap in the One-Ninety again, this very afternoon, twenty-one years later. His name was Erich Klein; he lived in Hamburg. A friend of mine had seen the story of the Oslo raid in a German magazine for ex-fighter pilots, and arranged for us to meet.' Erich Klein came limping into the room they had put aside, surrounded by reporters. The two shook hands formally for the photographers and then were left alone to talk. Rowland continued: 'We shook hands, properly this time. He was tall, dark-haired, grey at the temples, well built. I liked him at sight. I said "You're limping." Klein's hands became two fighter planes. He imitated a cannon burst – "Frrrrrrrrrp". "An American fighter shot me down – a Mustang. I lost a leg." "Oh, I'm sorry", I said. I was, deeply sorry.' Klein explained that he had landed after the fight at Oslo with a branch of a tree sticking through his wing. The two airmen chatted further before they parted. Rowland concluded: 'He then turned round and punched me lightly on the shoulder – "Auf Weidersehen, mein Freund". "Goodbye my friend", I said, "See you soon".'

The raid was noticed by the AOC RAF Bomber Command, who sent a despatch to the AOC 2 Group stating: 'Please convey my congratulations to all concerned for a first class show today.' Doubtless the operation had done much in the Air Ministry to improve the reputation of the much-maligned Mosquito.

One final point of interest concerns the security surrounding the operation to Oslo. W/C Peter Channer recalled that a Norwegian pilot who was under training at 1655 MTU, and was later to join 139 Squadron, had found out about the forthcoming raid on Oslo. His name was 2nd Lieutenant Haakon Wenger of the Royal Norwegian Air Force. He was insistent that if the raid was coming off, he should be included as he was a Norwegian who lived there. Channer brought this to the Station Commander's attention, and it was decided that if he were to be allowed to go, as he was not nearly as experienced as the crews who were to be on the operation, bombs would be put on his aircraft; however they would be 'rigged' so that they would 'hang up', i.e. could not be dropped, thereby saving the Oslo people from inaccurate bombing. Although allegedly this was discussed, Wenger was persuaded not to go after all. The question still remains as to how he knew in advance of this top-secret operation. We may never know the answer.

Following the heroic exploits of the 105 Squadron crews to Oslo, tucked in at the end of September's operational flying, on the 26th, was a lone Met. Reconnaissance of the Hamburg–Kiel area. Mosquito DK336:P was prepared, and S/L Charles Patterson DSO, DFC, takes up the story:

About lunch time, I was sent for, to go to the ops room. My route was up on the map. Even by Mosquito standards I was pretty appalled at what I saw. High-level daylight Mosquitos were being shot down in very high numbers by Focke-Wulf 190s. I saw the route on the map and what was involved. Bomber Harris had decided that he wanted to know what the weather was – quite definitely was – over Germany, because the Met. people were apparently rather vague about it. It was for a night bombing attack that night, with a deep penetration to Magdeburg or somewhere like that. If there was some cloud they could do it, and if there wasn't they'd have to call it off.

It was a glorious, clear September day without a cloud in the sky over England. The route I was told to fly was: at 25,000ft I was to cross the Dutch coast and fly straight down to Magdeburg. Then I was not to turn for home, but was to turn north, and slightly north-east, and fly past Berlin and up to Rostock. From Rostock, I still had to carry on and fly up to north-west Denmark, to Esbjerg and then back, which apart from anything else, was at the very limit of Mosquito range. I was told that I was the only Allied aircraft that would be operating over Germany at all that day, so the chances of my getting back, and not being intercepted by fighters, seemed impossible. There was no chance of diving down to ground level unless intercepted. That wasn't part of the flight plan, but I was to bring back this weather report. To show how bad it was, even Eddie [W/C Edwards], the squadron commander, said he was sorry he'd had to send me on this, but it had to be done. Someone had to do it, and he looked at me and said with a twinkle in his eye, 'You're not married, you see, which is a factor we have to take into account.' And so I went off, the challenge being so great, I didn't really have much time to worry. I had to get off the ground virtually right away and go.

I set off and climbed to 25,000ft, which in the flight plan I would reach about 50 or 60 miles off the Suffolk coast, but as I climbed I began to feel not myself and then the feeling got worse. I thought 'this is awful'. It had crossed my mind that what was wrong with me was panic which I couldn't control and was taking me over, and that this physical feeling of malady was nothing physical, it was mental, and turning fear into a physical panic. Of course, immediately, the thing which came to mind was that if I went back, I would have to say to Eddie when he said 'Why have you come back?', because I don't feel well. I thought of that and then suddenly saw in my mind, clear as day, him standing in front of me as I said it. The thought of that was so appalling that I just kept on going, climbing. Then, when I was really very woozy, and was having to concentrate on the instruments like anything, quite suddenly it became very clear. I looked out of the window, and there underneath me in full view was the Dutch coast and Holland spread out like a great map in front of me. I felt absolutely normal. What had happened was that my oxygen tube had been disconnected, and Sgt J.W. Egan had noticed it when I was already up to 25,000ft. This feeling had been lack of oxygen, not fear at all. The interesting thing was that such was the force of Eddie's influence over his pilots and his crews, that it was purely the thought of him that made me keep going even when I was running out of oxygen at 25,000ft. I was so relieved at feeling so well, that it lessened the concern that lay ahead.

Anyway, we flew on, the aeroplane at that height seeming to stand absolutely still. Every minute or two we'd dip the wings and look round to see if there was a fighter. Somewhere, about half-way to Magdeburg, quite suddenly Egan screamed 'Snappers, snappers', which meant a fighter of course. Immediately, I flew the thing into a vertical turning dive, and thought, 'Oh, my God, we've had it now!' Then he [Sgt Egan] sort of tried to keep level in his seat and suddenly told me as we were in this dive, 'Oh, I'm very sorry, it's only a fly!' I was so relieved that that again took away the worry of what lay ahead, and I resumed the flight. Again, at that height you have to watch back all the time that you're not letting out vapour trails, and if you do, you have to drop height immediately. Well, we carried on right down to Magdeburg, in this glorious blue sky. You could see for a hundred miles round the aeroplane, and no interception. Then, when we got to Magdeburg and turned north-east, we mercifully ran into a bank of cloud. It was below me a bit but I dived down a few thousand feet and got into it. That carried on until we were just short of Rostock, which I suppose was the most dangerous part of the trip. We then emerged out of the cloud at Rostock, still with no interception and still no cloud. All the Baltic spread out underneath us, and of course I had this awful grind of getting across the Baltic, across Denmark and up the north-west. We just seemed to go on and on and were never intercepted. We got as far as Esbjerg and with a great sigh of relief, I was able to dive down to sea-level and safety.

I got back to Horsham [at 19.09 hours]. It had been a very long trip, and stretched the Mosquito near the limits of its endurance. There was to be one of our wartime officers' parties that evening, and I realized that I would get back in time for it, and that was the big thing. Sgt Egan and I were thrilled to bits to have survived and got away with it; couldn't believe how we'd done it . . . still don't know. I whizzed over Horsham and came in and landed. It was nearly dusk as I switched off the engines. Just as I did, and got out, a little van came racing up towards me. Out jumped Wing Commander Hughie Edwards, looking slightly flustered. He said, 'Oh, incredible, you've made it. Well done. Come in the van and I'll take you back to the ops room.' So Egan and I got in, and as we were driving back he said, 'Well, you've made it in time for the party, but the reason the van was not there when you switched off was that, quite frankly, Digger Kyle and I had written you off. We heard nothing but wire reports all afternoon of these German fighters trying to intercept you, and we took it for granted you couldn't possibly survive. We were each having a bath, when we got the news you were coming in. We were getting ready to change for the party.'

On 13 September 1942, a signal had heralded major changes at RAF Horsham St Faith. The USAAF was to arrive and was to inhabit this station as well as RAF Attlebridge. RAF Attlebridge and RAF Horsham St Faith both became home to the Martin B-26 Marauders of the 319th Bomb Group. The resident squadrons were therefore to move out, and those at RAF Horsham St Faith were earmarked to move to RAF Marham, 9 miles south-east of Kings Lynn, which was to be available to receive its new incumbents by 28 September. During the change-over period, life became a little fraught as groundcrew member Stan Twigg recalls: 'During the last week or so of 105 Squadron's stay at Horsham St Faith, some Yanks appeared on the airfield and for a few of the "erks", it was a trying time.' In conclusion, a note was made in the station ORB recording that at 08:00 hours on 30 September 1942 '2nd Bombardment Group moved in'.

CHAPTER 8

New Beginnings

R AF Marham had been under the control of No. 3 Group, which was, from 28 September 1942, to relinquish command in favour of No. 2 Group and consequently 115 and 218 Squadrons moved out. Subsequently, 105 and 139 squadrons, followed by 1509 BATF and some time later, 109 Squadron (another Mosquito squadron) were posted there. The aerodrome was protected by the RAF Regiment and the 11th AA Battery, with illumination provided by the 446/65 Searchlight Battery. The first to move was 105 Squadron which was ready for operations by the 29th. No. 139 Squadron sent an advance party on the 28th, followed the next day by the main party, with Bristol Blenheim MkV (Bisleys) and any Mosquitos they had. They were finally ready when a rear party arrived on the 30th, as did 1655 MTU. No. 109 Squadron was to arrive some time later, on 5 July 1943. The station also received a new Commander in the Australian, G/C Wallace H. 'Digger' Kyle DFC, later to become ACM Sir Wallace Kyle.

Arrival at RAF Marham was remembered by W/C Edwards: 'The change-over was to take place without affecting operations. I led the squadron across in a very disciplined manner. There

Australian flying crews at RAF Marham in 1943 (left to right): P/O B.W. Coyle; F/O R.B. Smith; C/O, G/C W.H. 'Digger' Kyle DFC; F/O W.A. Christensen; F/O D.C. Dixon and W/O H.C. 'Gary' Herbert. (Via E.B. Sismore)

was to be no showing off to the existing tenants, less fortunately equipped. After landing, the crews taxied to dispersals previously arranged and I taxied to the tarmac, where there was a large American automobile with a group captain [McNee] at the wheel. He was a little shaken when out of my Mosquito emerged Sallie, our bulldog, followed by F/O Shirley Peake, Intelligence Officer and Tubby Cairns.'

Mike Carreck also remembers the new station: 'W/C Edwards led us in formation from Horsham St Faith on 29 September 1942. Praise be, it was another permanent station, so life went on as before. The airfield itself was like a bird sanctuary: curlews, lapwings, etc. It was a bird-watcher's dream. What a pleasure to see them on the airfield, but they were a worry because there was always a chance on take-off or landing that one might burst through the windscreen and explode in the pilot's face. However, no bird caused a crash at Marham while I was there. [There were incidents due to bird strike though, as we shall see.] Marham village was tiny. I do recall an excellent supper – unrationed pigeon pie, in a delightful restaurant in Kings Lynn. If you cycled into Marham to catch the train, you could leave your bike at a house just by the train station and for a few pennies, they'd look after it for you until you collected it for the ride back to the airfield.' Bill Rilley, who was a F/O navigator at RAF Marham and destined to become a F/L with a DFC and bar, also commented on life there: 'Marham was a very comfortable place – a peacetime station. Nice mess, nice rooms, and I had a staid old civilian batman. Distinguished people visited there and generally stayed to lunch. I remember the then Duke of Gloucester and other notables [reference to a visit of 11 February 1944 by HRH the Duke of Kent, in the uniform of an air marshal, accompanied by AVM D.C.T. Bennett CBE, DSO, AOC No. 8 Group, and presented to the squadron by the squadron commander, W/C (later G/C) H.J. 'Butch' Cundall DFC, AFC]. An event I sometimes chuckle about even now [in 1997] – when I first walked into the mess for a meal, I think it was lunch, we had pheasant for the main course. I said to the chap next to me, "This is all right, pheasant for lunch!" He replied, "F—— pheasant again!"' Indeed, the perpetrator of such culinary replenishment may have been the CO himself, as W/C Edwards recalled: 'The area around the mess teemed with game. In the early winter evenings, we used to set off on a squadron drive, which produced profitable bags to supplement the mess kitchen.'

October started with further low-level attacks at dusk on the 1st, by three Mosquitos on oil and chemical works. On the 2nd, shallow-dive attacks were made by six aircraft on a steel works at Liège, Belgium, from between 1,700 and 3,000ft. A couple of high-level attacks were made from 15,000 and 26,000ft on Essen and Bremen respectively on the 6th and on the same day, a low-level dusk attack was made on the Dutch town of Hengelo. This was to be the first of several attacks on Hengelo and was led by Edwards in his favourite Mosquito, DK328: 'V' for Victory. Three aircraft were to attack the Stork diesel engine works and the fourth, DK317:K flown by Parry, was to attack the Twente central power station.

The aircraft departed at 17.04 hours and formed up for the flight over the North Sea to the Netherlands. Edwards was in the lead, followed by F/O Alec Bristow with P/O B.W. Marshall in DK316:J and F/Sgt K. Monaghan with observer F/Sgt A.W. Dean in DK339:C. To the rear of the formation were S/L George Parry and his observer P/O Robbie Robson, who were in a separate position as a solo aircraft, as they had been allocated a different target from the others. Henk F. van Baaren, a Dutchman from Hengelo, provided the author with information on the Hengelo raid from his book *Bommen Vielen Op Hengelo*. He advised that Parry noted on the way over to the target, at a position about 14 miles from their landfall near the town of Sneek: 'One aircraft in the leading formation was struck by birds, breaking the windscreen and [temporarily] blinding the pilot. The plane pulled up steeply, almost stalled and then dived towards my formation. Luckily, it pulled out of its dive and missed us then disappeared in the opposite direction. As we were flying at 50ft above the ground there was very little we could do to avoid collision.' The aircraft was DK316:J, and P/O Marshall the pilot. Jim Lang, although not directly involved in the incident, had been particularly fond of Mosquito DK316:J, as it was in his opinion a particularly good aeroplane to fly. He warned Bristow before he went 'to take care of it and to make sure it comes back in one piece'. He recalls the crew's return to base where they landed at 19.10 hours: 'He [Bristow] arrived in my room in the early hours with his head covered in bandages, feeling all in. He had run into a flock of birds at low level. Gulls had broken the windscreen and hit him on the head, knocking him unconscious. The observer, P/O Marshall, having seen the danger, immediately pulled the stick back and of course went into a steep climb. The motion apparently brought Alec around again.' Mike Carreck recalled: 'Then he [Marshall] handed control back to Bristow, and went up front to lie down in the "office". By kicking Bristow's legs, he guided him back to Marham for a safe landing.' Jim Lang concluded: 'We saw the plane the next morning and I have never seen such a mess; broken Perspex, and the leading edge radiators completely full of feathers, guts and gulls. He deserved a medal that night.'

Meanwhile, the remainder of the formation headed south-east towards Hengelo, with Edwards still in the lead. On they flew until about 9 miles north-east of Hengelo, when Edwards with Cairns attacked the target they thought was the diesel engine works. The bombs exploded, sending debris high into the air, from the eight storeys of the building that suffered below. They had in fact dropped their bombs on the town of Almelo. The bombs had 11-second delay fuses, however, the rear aircraft flown by Parry, flew over them as they detonated, nearly knocking DK317:K out of the sky. By skilful handling, S/L Parry was able to regain control and continued on to the target. In the event, F/Sgt Monaghan did manage to reach the Stork works, and dropped three 500lb bombs from 250ft into the target. In their enthusiasm to shut the bomb doors, the forth bomb hung up and it was not until over the North Sea about 28 miles west of the coastal town of Bergen aan Zee, that they managed to jettison it safely.

As for Parry, he carried on to the TCS power station, situated on the edge of Hengelo, close to the road to the neighbouring town of Borne. Henk van Baaren described the attack: 'Just after this raid, I was hanging out of the window of my attic and I could just see the swiftly disappearing Mossie, DK317. The power station had been hit. It was a pin-point job; on the dot. There were flames, smoke, debris, damaged walls, and machinery, but no casualties at all.' He continued to evaluate the worth of the attack thus: 'It was a pity that the part of the power station which was damaged had just been taken out of service, so electricity kept being delivered to the factories where work should have been interrupted for some time.'

Once back at base, there had been some heated discussions, and W/C Edwards recalled: 'Back at base, George Parry claimed that I had bombed Almelo, a few miles from Hengelo. "Tubby" was adamant on the justness of his cause but I was not certain. Intelligence reports some two weeks later described a highly successful attack by Mosquitos on a factory in Almelo, which turned out clothing for the German Army – George Parry and Robson, his navigator, had been right!' Regarding the bombs which did fall on Hengelo, Henk van Baaren concluded: 'There was however something else, more important to the people of Hengelo; a British plane had successfully bombed the target and the Germans had been unable to intervene. It meant to us, in fact more or less sitting in the waiting room of war, that we knew there were people working for us. They had showed it now, and that gave us a kick. It was good for our morale. Had we known the Mosquito flights were still in a developmental phase and that these airmen, only less than a fortnight before, had successfully attacked the Gestapo headquarters in Oslo, we would have been even more excited. We would have understood that there were still people risking their lives for us, hitting the Hun that we despised so much. It was the talk of the town on the night of 6 October 1942.'

Thereafter, Edwards noted a change in operational emphasis: 'As an alternative, popular with some, not all, we started what we called dawn raids. This involved using the last hour of darkness and flying to the bigger cities at altitude, bombing at high level or in a dive at first light, then returning low or at altitude. I found this exhilarating and favoured an approach to the target about 25,000ft, then gradually using the remaining height to come home at reducing altitude and great speed.'

The town of Hengelo was not to be left in peace. In the intervening period, such high-level dawn attacks were mounted on various targets in Germany. On the 9th Limburg, Siegburg and Koblenz were all attacked, as the primary targets were obscured by cloud. W/C Edwards also flew that day, leaving RAF Marham at 05.25 hours in DK328:V. Edwards remembered the raid:

This morning winds were forecast above 20,000ft. I, with another crew, W/O Bools and navigator Jackson, were allotted Duisburg. We took off approximately one hour before dawn [at 05.24 hours] and climbed in the direction of the target, gaining height. I intended to bomb at 25,000ft, or diving down as necessary. The problem with this sort of raid was that the Mosquito had no sort of navigational aid other than DR, therefore there was no check until it was sufficiently light enough to match up DR with ground detail. As ever then, my navigator was confident. When ground details started to emerge in the early morning light, I could see nothing tangible to recognize apart from rivers, but none so big as the Rhein. I knew that if we did not pin-point ourselves in the vicinity of Duisburg, the last thing I wanted to do was to spend much time over the highly flak-defended Ruhr in daylight, with the menace of fighters.

However, on ETA, we were not where we should have been and after a few minutes flying I said, 'There is a bloody great lake down there, where is it?' The reply I got was that there was no such lake near our target. I decided to fly east, and after a minute or so we came across what was unmistakably the Rhein. This was better – we had always decided to strike the Rhein and follow it north to Duisburg. We turned left and then flew to a built-up area. 'There's Duisburg', said my navigator triumphantly. 'Lucky for you' was my reply. We were at 25,000ft, perfectly positioned to bomb it, so down we went. All was quiet below; too quiet, I thought. We were congratulating ourselves on this effort when all hell broke loose. We were now over a tremendously built-up area and black, angry flak was bursting all around us in great quantities – they had our height. In my predominantly low-level role, I had never seen flak bursting since my Blenheim 'circus' days. That was a flea-bite compared with this – this was frightening. 'Thank God the night pilots don't see their flak' I thought, they only feel and smell it.

I commenced to climb and reached 29,000ft but the flak was tremendous in quantity. I could not go on forever, and thought 'Where the hell are we?' I could not be bothered asking questions. This was never-ending; they had my changes in height perfectly, and we were being used as target practice. In desperation, I changed altitude and stuffed the nose down. The speed fairly built up and the altimeter unwound. After a minute or so we were out of it but I kept the nose pointing towards the ground. After recovering my breath I shouted, 'Where the hell was that place? Flying north-west from Duisburg we should have been in clear country in no time.' For once my navigator was stuck for an answer. We reached ground level, travelling fast. Then a very large town or city loomed ahead of us, with more shooting of light flak from the opposition. 'Where the hell is this?' 'Rotterdam', my companion in trouble said quickly. 'Turn south, fly west and we will be over the Hook of Holland in no time.' I was obedient. No sea came into view, but a similar, large town with more shooting of light flak. This was beginning to test the nerves – we did not know where

A turbine in the central power station at Hengelo lies amid the wreckage, following S/L George Parry's low-level dusk attack of 6 October 1942, in Mosquito B.IV, DK317, GB:K (Via Henk van Baaren)

No. 105 Squadron in front of Mosquito 'V' at Marham with W/C Henry John Cundall with his dog. (Via W.E.G. Humphrey/Bill Riley)

we were and I began to get angry. 'Keep flying west', said my adviser. This we did until it became absurd. Another 15 minutes of travelling at nearly 5 miles per minute ensued, and we were just eating up flat country. 'We must have been miles south of Duisburg', I ventured, 'I am going to fly north.' After two or three minutes of this we sighted sea. Neither of us knew where we were, but we soon did. We flashed over the coast with guns from Gravelines blazing at us.

   When out of range, I turned to Tubby Cairns. 'You clown, what a performance!' All he offered was 'The winds must have been out'. How right he was. All returning crews reported great difficulties in locating targets as forecast winds were about 50 mph less than actual. The lake I had seen had been near Bonn and we had bombed Siegburg, and then received our great hammering from Köln which is roughly 40 miles from Duisburg. Tubby's Rotterdam proved to be Antwerp, and then we fell foul of Gravelines and finally Dunkirk. The only joy of the flight had been streaking across Belgium and France at 300 knots, on an early autumn morning, but this was counterbalanced by wondering what was to come next.

Edwards landed at RAF Marham at 07.54 hours, approximately two and a half hours from departure, but there was no sign yet of W/O Bools. W/C Edwards noted the following about his No 2: 'Bools was an experienced pilot, but not operationally. Although we took off within one minute of each other, I saw nothing of him.' Unfortunately, W/O Charles Ronald Kernick Bools MiD and his observer Sgt George William Jackson in DK339:C failed to return. It transpired that they had fallen foul of a fighter of 12./JG1 [12th Flight of the 1st Day Fighter Wing], flown by Feldwebel Fritz Timm. The two young airmen were subsequently laid to rest at Heverlee war cemetery, south-east Louvain, Belgium.

CHAPTER 9

'Chutes and Ships

Dusk attacks returned on Sunday 11 October, which left one crew dead, and proved particularly traumatic for another. Around 13.00 hours, a message came over the tannoy; six crews were summoned immediately to the ops room. The target was to be Hannover at dusk, at high level. S/L Jimmy Knowles DFC, having completed a tour on Blenheims doing suicidal low-level anti-shipping strikes, had just returned from a 'rest' at 13 OTU at Bicester with his observer, F/Sgt G. Gartside. On 3 August 1942 they had been posted to 139 Squadron. This was to be their first Mosquito operation, for which they borrowed a 105 Squadron aircraft.

There were to be three directions of attack, one of which was allotted to each of three pairs of Mosquitos. The first wave to leave was P/O Pete Rowland with P/O Dick Reily in DZ340:X at 16.35 hours, accompanied by F/Sgt Monaghan with F/Sgt A.W. Dean in DK336:P. Next away were 139 Squadron's S/L Knowles with P/O C.D. Gartside in 105 Squadron's DK317:K with P/O Lang and his observer, F/O Robin P. 'Tommy' Thomas, at 16.41 hours. Thomas considered that having been late for briefing, they had been left with the route entering enemy territory at the Zuider Zee; the worst of the three possible routes. P/O Lang was to be S/L Knowles' wingman in DZ341:A at his no. 2 position on his leader's port side. Lastly, at 16.49 hours, F/L Charles Patterson with his observer Sgt J.W. Egan in DK338:O led P/O Jimmy Bruce with P/O Mike Carreck in DZ320:Y.

The first wave attempted to make their way to the target, but Rowland's trimming tabs froze up and so he could not get to Hannover. Not to be beaten, however, he managed to drop his bombs from 18,000ft on Emden instead. His wingman carried on to the target and bursts were seen to the north of the built-up area, having received his bombs from 15,000ft. The third wave managed to reach the target and from 18,000ft each aircraft let go their load. Unfortunately, due to cloud the results remained unobserved. However, the second wave had not been so fortunate, as Jim Lang recalls having climbed somewhat erratically, trying to keep station with Knowles. They should have been at 29,000ft five minutes before but were still in the climb as they crossed the coast and approached their first course change point, later than anticipated. As Lang pointed out in *In the Clutch of Circumstance*: 'In the past, crews had not been intercepted on the way in to the target, as a general rule, because of our height, speed and surprise. The fighter squadrons did not get high enough early enough before we crossed the Dutch coast, but today was to be an exception (and we were to be the victims).' Unteroffizier [Corporal] Gunter Kirchner of 5 Staffel [Flight] of II./JG1 [2 Squadron of the 1st Day Fighter Wing], based in Holland, took off from Katwijk and intercepted Lang's Mosquito, 2 kilometres from Utrecht at 18.20 hours local time. Kirchner was the holder of the Iron Cross Second Class, which he won shortly after having shot down a Wellington MkIII, Z1577 of 9 Squadron on an operation to Duisburg on 23 July 1942.

Jim Lang explains what happened next, in his account from the Vancouver Aircrew Association's *Listen to Us*:

> Suddenly, there was an enormous explosion, the aircraft shuddered, the ailerons refused to respond and I lost control of the aircraft. Having wondered for months how it would feel to be

Unteroffizier [Corporal] Gunter Kirchner of 5 Staffel [Flight] of II./JG1 [2 Squadron of the 1st Day Fighter Wing] who shot down P/O Jim Lang and F/O Robin Thomas in Mosquito DZ341:A over Utrecht on 11 October 1942, has a bite to eat at readiness in the sidecar of Unteroffizier Schmid's BMW motorcycle at Schipol. Note the 5 Staffel emblem, a 'tatzelwurm' (tapeworm), on the front of the sidecar, inverted coal-scuttle helmet on the back, and an FW 190 at readiness in the background. Kirchner was killed on 19 April 1945 when his Heinkel He 162 jet fighter crashed for unknown reasons after having shot down a Spitfire. (Via Robin Thomas/Aad Neeven/Eric Mombeek)

hit by enemy fire, there was no doubt in our minds that this was it! I shouted to Tommy to get out. He clipped his parachute to the hooks on his harness [unlike the pilot who had his clipped permanently and sat on it, the observer's chest parachute was not clipped to allow mobility] and lifted the floor hatch. He performed a somersault as he had been trained to do, but the parachute snagged on the hatch and tore away from the harness, and he could not find it nor its rip-cord, where it should have been on his chest. As he fell, he saw from the corner of his eye a bulky object floating next to him. He grabbed it, recognized it as his parachute and pulled the rip-cord. After a severe jerk that pulled his flying boot off, he found himself descending from a great height with pieces of aircraft all around him. In the meantime we were hit a second time. This made the aircraft want to turn over on its back, while I tried not too effectively to prevent it. I jettisoned the narrow hood above me, released my seat straps, and took off my helmet and oxygen mask. I really had nowhere to go, since I could not get across the floor hatch because the stick [control column] was in the way. The hood above was too narrow for me to get through under normal circumstances, and I was trapped in a plane that was spinning out of control.

The third attack was a near miss, although I have never seen so many cannon shells exploding about me. I must have blacked out, since my next recollection, the most memorable of my life, was of being suspended in mid-air under my parachute, with my watch still going. 'Thank God I'm alive!' was my first thought. I was unhurt, although I have no recollection of what happened in those lost five minutes; perhaps my brain suffered from lack of oxygen when I took off my mask. What I did I do not know, but I have had nightmares for years, where I have been trapped with my legs and arms pinned. I do not remember pulling the rip-cord, and the handle was not in my hand when I regained consciousness. I am still happy to believe it was a miracle.

I saw my Mosquito blazing as it swirled towards the ground, but I did not see Tommy, my observer. It was very cold at 29,000ft; my gloves had vanished and the 'chute harness prevented me from putting my hands in my pockets. It was very quiet. Some 15 minutes later I hit clouds at about 4,000ft, and then I made a hard landing near Utrecht. After hiding my 'chute and dinghy in a ditch, I walked to a nearby farm where an old Dutchman was leaning on a fence smoking a pipe as though nothing unusual had happened. I told him, in English, that I would hide in a nearby farm but the farmer looked at me in complete non-comprehension. I hid in the barn until I heard voices below. Someone called to me in German, which I did not understand, but when I had established the fact that I was an RAF flier, the Dutch people were ready to help me. They gave me a raincoat and a bicycle and told me to follow them at a distance. I pedalled by a group of German soldiers returning to barracks singing 'Roll Out the Barrel', and almost ran down a German patrol in Utrecht. Without thinking I said 'Whoops, sorry!' and got away with it.

I was given refuge with a Dutch family in Utrecht living next to a German officers' mess. Next, I was smuggled into a little cottage outside the city. The Utrecht Underground tried to contact the British, to arrange for a rescue plane to pick me up somewhere in the Frisian Islands, but the agent was caught. To hold me longer was dangerous, so I had to move on. I was soon picked up by the Dutch police during the curfew in De Bilt. They had to turn me over to the Germans when a German patrol burst into the police station, Schmeissers pointed. I was escorted to a waiting patrol-car and seated between armed German guards. At Soesterberg airfield I was interrogated by a major to establish that I was in fact a pilot, not an agent, since it was ten days since I had been shot down. I was told that my observer had been captured also.

P/O Jim Lang, who was shot down over Utrecht on 11 October 1942. (Jim Lang)

F/O Thomas had landed in Oudenrijn, 2km south-west of Utrecht, and was concerned on his descent to see the spires of Utrecht below him getting closer as he drifted in the westerly wind. Having cleared the city, it looked for a time as though he would land in a lake. Fortunately the wind took him clear of the lake but he ended up hanging from the branches of a tree which projected out over a water-filled moat of a circular ancient earth-work, which had proved useful on other occasions for navigation over the area. Thomas continues:

I grabbed one of the springy overhanging branches and came to a stop with no more shock than as if landing on a spring mattress, still suspended by the harness, now caught in the higher branches, with one stockinged foot and one booted foot, a few inches below the surface of the water. Releasing the harness, I dropped into less than 2 feet of water, and at the same time, became aware I had an audience. Standing awkwardly on the steep bank was an extremely nervous German soldier, it takes a nervous person to recognize one! He was looking from beneath his coal scuttle [helmet] and pointing a gun in my direction at a range of about 10 feet. 'Good evening', I said, hoping to put him at ease, at the same time raising my hands within the limitations of the inflated [Mae West] jacket and the branches. 'I do not have a pistol or any other weapon.' 'Kommen Sie mit' [come with me] said he, gesturing with the rifle, so I did.

It soon became apparent that this ancient fortification was now occupied by a large number of soldiers, some sort of camp or even a barracks. So much for the instruction and all the equipment designed to enable the newly shot down to evade and escape! Landing in a barracks has to be the quickest way ever of getting to a prisoner of war camp, short of landing in the camp. I was taken to a sort of Nissen hut and allowed to sit down while a small crowd of soldiers gathered around to admire their catch. I took out my cigarette case and, as one would in company, offered it around. Only one accepted, fortunately, as it was going to be some time before a refill would be available.

An officer turned up and the cigarette was very nervously stamped out before, under the warning that if he attempted to escape he would be shot, F/O Thomas was taken to a military HQ in Utrecht, where he was fed and allowed to dry out. Here, 'Tommy' was to see German training at its best: 'Some discussion was conducted over a wall-type telephone by an NCO who stood in front of the instrument talking to an officer on the other end, and as far as he was concerned, the telephone was the officer. He came smartly to attention, with a thunderous clicking of heels, and throughout his conversation, every time it became necessary, which was every ten seconds or so, to shout "Jawohl Herr Hauptmann". He re-snapped uprightly and savagely clicked his heels. The performance ended with a shout "Heil Hitler", another click of the heel, this time accompanied by an immaculate Nazi salute. Up to then, in my experience, such goings-on had been confined to cartoon caricatures and burlesque on film and stage, and here it was, quite real, happening within a few feet of me. I quite forgot my cold, damp, and soggy nether regions.' From here, Thomas was taken to a city jail, where he was made to turn out his pockets before being shown to a small cell. Before entering it, a German officer decided it would be more fitting for an officer to have a larger, more comfortable cell and the prisoner was immediately transferred to one with three beds in it, where he was tucked up for the night in a bed.

Both Lang and Thomas were transferred to Dulag Luft on the outskirts of Wiesbaden, a holding unit and transit camp for the interrogation of newly captured prisoners. Jim Lang further recalls from his interview in *In the Clutch of Circumstance*:

Our treatment was not at all pleasant. The guards made our life as difficult as they could. Our clothes were taken away from us for twelve hours and the heating system was turned on and off with great frequency. I awoke in the middle of the night, lying on the floor alongside the door, almost unconscious, struggling for breath. The cell was quite airless and hot. Eventually, it was my turn to be sent to the main assembly camp, where I would finally meet the other aircrew, before being sent further into Germany to Stalag Luft 3. Here I finally caught up with my observer, Tommy.

As this camp [Dulag Luft] was a transit camp, it was another week before there were enough of us to make up a train-load for the long trip to Sagan. It was good to feel relatively settled among other aircrew at last after being alone for so long, not knowing what the

In the bag: the exercise compound in the infamous German PoW camp Stalag Luft 3 at Sagan. Three 'Kriegies' keeping themselves fit are (left to right) John Madge; F/O Robin Thomas DFC; P/O Jim Lang. (Via Robin Thomas)

In a hut in Stalag Luft 3: 105 Squadron's F/O Robin Thomas DFC relaxes smoking a pipe and reading a book (left) while pilot B. Bowler plays the saxophone. Others read to pass the time and Jack Steel (centre) makes his move on the draughts board. (Via Robin Thomas)

business of being a PoW was leading to. If my 20-minute ride from the ground from 29,000ft was the most memorable one of my life, I believe that the next two days and nights, sitting upright in a third-class railway carriage with fifty or sixty others, was a close second. Closely guarded, with little or no food, we became a very demoralized group – but together, we survived the journey and arrived at Sagan in the early morning. We got our first view of the famous Stalag Luft 3, the large barbed wire enclosure, with raised sentry boxes and searchlights. At approximately 07.30 that morning a large, cheerful, red-faced squadron leader, Jennings, the Camp Adjutant, greeted us and led us through the various protective wire enclosures into the main camp. We struggled through the main gate and were greeted by a crowd of prisoners; some who had been there since September 1939, some perhaps only a few weeks, but all anxious to look over and see whether they would know anyone and to get the latest news from England. Each of us was intercepted and escorted to a room, in one of the blocks in the camp, by another prisoner, and given a 'brew', and asked questions that would enable them to identify us as genuine aircrew.

Here, the 'Great Escape' was masterminded and Jim Lang was one of those who assisted and carried dirt in bags hidden under their clothing for dispersal in the compound. As was mentioned earlier, following the escape the Gestapo shot fifty escapees, and Jim's room-mate F/L James L.R. 'Cookie' Long and another from the room opposite, F/L Alastair D.M. 'Sandy' Gunn, were but two of them. Fortunately, Jim Lang and Robin Thomas survived the war. Sadly,

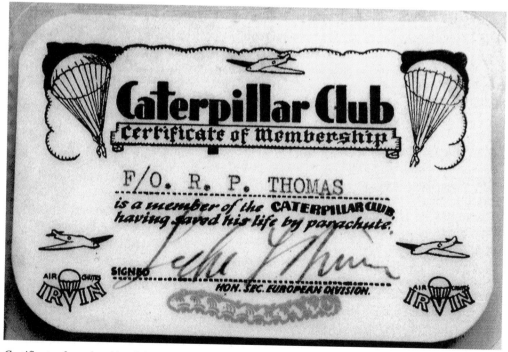

Certificate of membership of the Caterpillar Club for observer F/O Robin P. Thomas, awarded in recognition of his safe descent by parachute when shot down with P/O Jim Lang over Utrecht in the Netherlands, on 11 October 1942. (Via Robin Thomas)

however, the crew with whom they had been flying in no. 2 position, S/L James Gerald Leslie Knowles and observer P/O Charles Douglas Alan Gartside did not survive the operation and were lost without trace. Both airmen are commemorated on the Runnymede Memorial. As for the German who had shot them down, Unteroffizier Gunther Kirchner was killed on 19 April 1945, when his Heinkel He162 jet crashed for unknown reasons while returning to base, having just shot down a Spitfire.

Returning our thoughts to operations once more, Hengelo's Stork diesel works was visited yet again on the 15th in a successful dusk shallow-dive attack. Four Mosquitos of 105 Squadron were to attack, led by Ralston with his navigator Syd Clayton in DK338:O. F/L Ralston noted in his log book that the dive was from 4,000ft. The other crews were Pete Rowland and Dick Reily in DZ314:F, Jimmy Bruce with Mike Carreck in DZ320:Y and F/Sgt Norman Booth with observer Sgt Fred A. Turner in DZ341:A. They left at 16.55 hours; none had been to the target before, but all returned safely. Henk van Baaren commented: 'The second raid on Hengelo was much more impressive, as it was heavier. A total of 2,000lb HE bombs came down – more than the raid on the power station. Besides three civilians that were killed when a couple of houses near the factory were hit, this raid caused enough commotion to make the Germans take measures to protect the labourers of the factories and neighbouring civilians. At this time I went to a secondary school which was housed in a building in the centre of the Stork diesel works, who owned the building. We were lucky that at the time of the bombing there were no pupils in the building. However, soon after this raid, our school was evacuated and we were sent to other schools, further from the centre of town.'

The next day, the attack was repeated. By now 139 Squadron were becoming operational, and 105 were joined by one of their number, S/L Jack E. Houlston AFC and his observer W/O J.L. Armitage DFC in a 139 Squadron Mosquito DZ346, XD:J. The 105 Squadron crews were: George Parry with Vic Robson in DK296:G; Roy Ralston and Syd Clayton in DK336:P; Pete Rowland and Dick Reily in DZ314:F; Norman Booth with observer Fred Turner in DZ341:A and Jimmy Bruce with Mike Carreck in DZ320:Y. This time, the attack was made at low level from 100ft and all claimed to have hit the target. Henk van Baaren noted that: 'Only Hengelo is mentioned in the debriefing reports for this raid, but again some bombs fell on Almelo! Nothing explains the bombs dropped in Almelo, where three Mosquitos were observed. I myself saw three planes in Hengelo, where two factories were hit: Stork and the neighbouring Dikkers works. The bombs on Dikkers territory did not explode. It is likely that one flight of three aircraft mistook Almelo again for Hengelo.'

On the 20th there were cloud-cover attacks on Bremen, as well as an unknown village on the coast of the Jade Basin, Minden and an abortive attempt on Osnabrück. One aircraft was detailed to attack Hannover. F/Sgt Laurence Walter Deeth and observer W/O Frank Edward Malcolm Hicks in DZ313:E failed to return. They are buried in Sage war cemetery, 24km south of Oldenburg.

The following day, roving commissions were given to three crews but, due to cloud cover over the primary targets, alternative targets were found at 800ft and bombs were dropped in the Netherlands at Leeuwarden aerodrome, Dokkum and Hengelo as well as on German targets at Nordhorn and Lingen. Ralston and Clayton delivered the attacks on Hengelo, Nordhorn and Lingen again, in a new Mosquito, DZ343:Z. Again Henk van Baaren noted the results: 'They dropped a 500lb HE bomb on the Stork diesel works. A German report states: "At 15.30 hours, three HE [bombs] dropped on Stork. Little damage. Two people were killed plus some persons wounded."' Roy told me that only one HE [bomb] was dropped. The other three bombs were thrown on to towns in nearby Germany [Nordhorn and Lingen]. At Stork, three diesel engines and an office were damaged. Roy's comments: 'On this trip we spent rather too long in the target area, so we were spotted by two FW 190s. Luckily I saw them as they saw us, and so after about 15 minutes' chase, we pulled away and they gave up.'

The attack had been a fairly good example of the Mosquito's ability to outpace the FW 190 at low level. Returning at 3,000ft over the East Frisian island of Ameland, at 15.15 hours two FW 190s were noticed creeping up behind at 500 yards range. F/L Ralston dived the aircraft to sea-level and then embarked on a series of skidding manoeuvres to try to escape the enemy fire, which came on five separate occasions from 400 yards. Fortunately, the FW 190s were astern due to the evasive actions, and consequently not able to deliver quarter attacks successfully. Their cannon fire splashed viciously into the sea about 50/100 yards behind the Mosquito. DZ343:Z was then hauled up into a steep climb and at 1,500ft disappeared from the enemy's gun sights into a layer of 8/10 stratus cloud, about 54 miles north of the island of Norderney. The Mosquito subsequently flew home undamaged to land at 16.44 hours.

On the 23rd, it was yet again the turn of Hengelo to receive punishment, this time by four crews, again at low level. There were to have been five, but one crew failed to get airborne due to technical difficulties. The four who did manage to get away were Ralston and Clayton in DZ351B; Booth and Turner in DZ353:E; Monaghan and Dean in DZ340:X and New Zealander S/L Joseph Cunningham Simpson MiD with observer F/L Claud Bransby Walter in DZ343:Z. They took off at one-minute intervals between 12.52 and 12.55 hours and were over the target by 15.00 hours Dutch time. The works was hit from 100ft and bombs were seen to explode, among other places on the machine turning shops. There were no civilian casualties, but the raid did cost the lives of yet another crew. S/L Simpson's Mosquito fell victim to light flak and was seen to crash in flames and explode at Raard in the Friesland area of the Netherlands, 3km west-south-west of Dokkum. Both airmen were laid to rest in Westdongeradeel (Raard) Protestant cemetery.

October continued with an assortment of low-level, high-level, cloud-cover and photographic sorties on a variety of targets in Germany and the Netherlands. All manner of attack scenarios were being evaluated. On the 29th, W/O T.R. Williams with Sgt J.W. Egan took off in DK302:D for a cloud-cover attack on the island of Langeoog. An enemy aerodrome was hit from 100ft and a large column of brown smoke was seen billowing up from the target area as the Mosquito sped for home low across the North Sea. The last operations of the month were on the 30th. Two aircraft set out on a low-level attack on Leeuwarden aerodrome, set to take place at 13.40 hours. An Australian from New South Wales, F/O 'Bill' Blessing, and Sgt J. Lawson took off in DZ348:K accompanied by Sgt Reginald Levey with his observer Sgt Les Hogan in Mosquito DZ340:X. In Ken Delve's *RAF Marham* Reginald Levey explained that he was hit having bombed the aerodrome, but had been hit by the ground defences as he crossed the boundary. He gave this account of the operation:

The port engine was set on fire, the instrument panel and windscreen disappeared with the nose of the aircraft. I was hit in the leg [left thigh] – although I didn't feel it at the time – and my observer, Les Hogan, in the [right fore-] arm. At 40ft or so, control was tricky, so I called Les to press the extinguisher button on the port engine, which I had feathered. He promptly pushed the starboard one! The good engine was filled with foam, coughed once or twice and then miraculously, the good old Merlin caught again and we snaked along almost sideways at about 160 mph. I had to jam my foot under the rudder bar to keep it straight as the rudder trim handle had been shot away. We went out over the aptly named Dutch island of Overflakkee straight between two German ships, which opened up on us. Luckily we were so low that they could not get their guns to bear down on us. The ship on the port side hit the ship on the starboard side, starting a fire in the bows. During the return flight over the sea, we wound down the trailing aerial to try and signal base. The aerial hit the sea and Les yelled that he had been hit again, but it was the handle whizzing round which had banged him in his seat. We managed to get back to Marham, but couldn't go into cloud as I had no instruments, and we were actually in the circuit when our long-suffering Merlin packed up. We went down into a nearby wood, skating along the tops of the trees, demolishing about 30 (according to the farmer who claimed compensation) before we came to a standstill [at Cockley Clay] and promptly blew up. My feet had gone through the side of the fuselage and I was helpless, but Les Hogan stepped out of the front (there was no nose, it was in Leeuwarden), took my boot off, and we ran like mad despite the wound in my leg, which was now making itself felt. We didn't have a scratch on us from the crash, which had completely demolished the Mosquito. Had the Mosquito been a metal aircraft I'm sure my foot would have been severed, and I am sure that we were saved by the complete break-up of the aeroplane. After three weeks in Ely hospital [following immediate treatment at Swaffham cottage hospital] we were back at Marham and operating again.

F/O Blessing had attacked the aerodrome at 50ft, but did not note the results as he was too busy observing a Messerschmitt Bf 110 circling the aerodrome. He had also met some flak over the target, and as the hydraulics on his machine were rendered u/s, he returned to RAF Marham to a safely executed belly landing. Not so fortunate however was another crew, who also left that morning at 11.48 hours on a cloud-cover attack on Lingen. The operation for Sgt Edward Leon Simon with Sgt Thomas Whiteley Balmforth in DK316:J ended tragically when they were shot down by flak at 14.20 hours and crashed into Californiaweg in Den Helder. The crew were laid to rest in Bergen op Zoom war cemetery, on the Ooster Schelde coast, 53 miles west of Eindhoven.

November started with an anti-shipping attack on the 7th. This type of operation was well known to 105, but this was the first time it had been attempted by a formation of Mosquitos. There had been no operations planned for that day, but at 11.00 hours W/C Edwards walked into the crew room and 'volunteered' six crews on the spot for an operation, announcing that they were to be available for briefing in thirty minutes. The crews gathered. Mike Carreck was to fly in DZ320:Y with his pilot Jimmy Bruce DFM, and recalls the event: 'Six crews on this op. It was unusual because we almost always flew alone or in formation of three, and what made it odder still was the speed they rushed us through briefing. The ribbon on the wall map of Europe that showed our route stretched across England, round and well clear of Brest and Lorient and on down the Bay of Biscay to the estuary of the Gironde, north of Bordeaux. It seemed a devil of a long way to go, hour after hour at wave-top height – six hours flying in all. There they told us we were to attack two "blockade runners", there was not a moment to lose.'

The ships were carrying a cargo of rubber from the Far East. They were a *Sperrbracher* and the 5,000-tonner *Elsa Essberger*, and were anchored 10 miles down the River Gironde, pending a passage to be cleared for them by minesweepers, before proceeding to dock, presumably at Bordeaux. Carreck continues: 'Coming back we were to land at St Mawgan in Cornwall. Next thing we knew, we were being hustled out to our Mosquitos. Roy Ralston led us [in DZ353:E], late that beautiful sunny afternoon [in a box of six Mosquitos] with Syd Clayton as navigator, perhaps the finest crew in Bomber Command. Jimmy and I didn't talk much during that never-ending flight over the sea. It took great concentration for him to hold our Mosquito right down on the waves and I was kept busy enough scanning the sky for little black specks that would instantly become Bf 109s and FW 190s.'

In W/C John de Lacy Wooldridge's *Low Attack*, S/L W.W. Blessing DSO, DFC, RAAF, who flew on the operation when a flying officer, relates:

About five minutes before our ETA the French coast was sighted, slightly to port. Immediately afterwards four ships were sighted on the horizon. The leader took these to be our targets, together with a couple of escorts, and altered course for them, opening his bomb doors. As he approached, however, Ralston decided that these were the wrong ships, and swerved away to starboard. It was at this moment that his bombs, for no reason at all, were seen to fall off into the sea. Something must have gone wrong with the electric circuit, but the crew knew nothing about it and carried on. We reached the French coast and pin-pointed ourselves accurately, but there was no sign anywhere of our two cargoes of rubber. In the event of our drawing a blank we had been ordered to bomb any shipping in the estuary itself, and now the leader did a grand piece of work. He turned south and then back on to north-east, leading us straight across the southern headland of the estuary at zero feet, taking the defences completely by surprise. No sooner were we across than we found ourselves right on top of two largish destroyers tied up in dock. Then straight ahead we saw two big ships steaming slowly up the middle of the river towards their berths.

Mike Carreck continued:

Three hours and 750 miles from Marham, Syd had brought us out nowhere precisely, over the mouth of the estuary catching those ships utterly by surprise; sailors in sweaters and sea-boots walking the decks. Roy too, did a magnificent job, as he led us below mast height between the two ships. Neither could fire without hitting the other. Jimmy pressed the [bomb release] button, and we were a mile away before our delayed-action bombs exploded. Not a shot was fired at us, and in moments we were come and gone, and back over the sea. The formation had scattered after the bombing, and we each had to find our way to St Mawgan. Jimmy still had to skim the waves, but in about an hour it was growing dark, and with no more danger from fighters, he was able to climb to a comfortable height.

Now he was able to relax a little, but as the night wore on, I was becoming more and more anxious. All I could use for navigation was the radio and, strangely, nobody was answering my signals. There was a strong chance that an unknown wind would take us west of Cornwall and we'd fly on over water until our fuel ran out. There was even the possibility of landing in France instead of England – it had happened before. We had a darkened world all to ourselves, two very lonely people, Jimmy and me. My finger ached as I tapped the key; never a reply. On we flew, then we saw gratefully that we weren't alone in the universe as the dim shape of a Coastal Command Hudson passed overhead. On and on we flew. Jimmy said, quite casually, 'Petrol gauge on zero; have to jump.' He pressed transmit, 'Mayday, Mayday, Mayday', but nobody answered; nobody ever did. On, endlessly on, my finger, sore at the Morse [code] key, until everything happened at once. Emerging from the black of the sea was an even blacker coastline and there was piercing Morse in my ears. It was St Mawgan at long last, giving me a bearing which I ignored, as the lights of an airfield switched on just ahead; if we were flying on a sniff and a whiff, sooner down the better. Jimmy lowered the undercarriage and flaps, and we touched down, taxied and rolled to a stop. Somebody was opening the hatch. 'Where are we?', I asked. The reply, thank God, was in English, 'St Eval'. Cornwall – at least I'd navigated to the right country.

In addition to Bruce and Carreck, the three other crews, Rowland with Reily in DK296:G, Monaghan with Dean in DK338:O, and Blessing with Lawson in DZ314:F, all landed safely at St Eval. The leader, however, landed at Predannack on the southern tip of Cornwall, after a flight of 5 hours, 30 minutes. He flew the one and a half hour flight back to RAF Marham the next day, as did the others, on a 1 hour, 20 minute hop from St Eval. The Gironde operation was recorded by P/O Rowland in his log book as 'Approx. distance 1,350 miles.' Prior to their return to RAF Marham, Mike Carreck recalls: 'Next morning after breakfast I met Jimmy, who had been to the hangar to check our Mosquito – "Had twenty minutes petrol left!" he said.'

One crew was not flying back to RAF Marham. F/L Alec Bristow, with P/O Bernard Marshall in Mosquito DK328:V, had presumably fallen foul of the flak, which was thrown up after the leading aircraft were departing. They were at least safe, having been taken prisoner, and were destined to survive the war, having been 'guests' of Hitler, as others of the squadron before them, at the infamous Stalag Luft 3 prison camp.

On 8 November another Mosquito was lost, fortunately without loss of life this time, when F/Sgt N. Booth crash-landed at Abbey Farm near Marham on a training flight. The undercarriage had jammed and DK301:H now ended its days, having been first flown operationally on 21 July 1942 with Sgts K.S. Wilkinson and J. Bastow on a high-level sortie to Bremen.

For the next five days there were to be no further operations, but the groundcrews were still busy. AC2 Stan Twigg was an 'erk' wireless operator, who joined 105 Squadron at RAF Horsham St Faith in July 1942. His duties were to see that all wireless equipment was serviceable, in good working order and the Form 700s signed by the pilot before take-off. After transferring to RAF Marham, he worked in the accumulator room recharging the batteries for the radios. He later also worked for a while as part of the crash tender crew, and was responsible for laying out the lighted 'goose-neck' lamps on the edges of the runway during foggy conditions, to assist the pilots coming in to land. Thereafter he was back at the signal section, and during an operational lull in November, recalled that: 'I went down to the dispersal area, all wrapped up with my headphones over my ears to help keep me warm. I got into the cockpit of aircraft "V" for Victor [DZ365], plugged my headphones into the intercom socket, and switched on the R/T set. I said, "Hello, Wagon Control [Marham's flying control call sign]; this is Reveille [105 Squadron's ground call sign]. 'V' for Victor calling, are you receiving me? Over." I received the message, "Hello, Reveille 'V' for Victor, this is Wagon Control calling; receiving you loud and clear, but a little weak in places." I concluded that it must be an intermittent fault on the transmitter, and so I made my way down from the cockpit, into the fuselage where the transmitter was located and started to slacken its fixing screws. My intention was to take it outside and give it the "drop test". However, I suddenly felt a prodding in the small of my back, which turned out to be the walking stick of the CO, W/C Hughie Edwards. He asked me what I was doing, and I explained that I was taking the transmitter back to the Signals Section for repairs. I wasn't sorry that he had not turned up a little later, or I may have been caught doing the drop test on the grass; I wonder what he would have said?'

Returning to operations, the 13th was an unlucky day when disaster struck. Two Mosquitos had been detailed for a low-level attack on the *Neumark* at Vlissingen (Flushing). The ship was bomb-damaged and had been transferred from Le Havre for repairs. At 12.08 hours, F/Sgt Norman Booth with Sgt Fred Arnold Turner in DZ361:C, accompanied by P/O Charles Andre Graham RAAF with P/O Robert Fred Lindsay Anderson RCAF in DZ320:Y, took off from RAF Marham to try and sink the ship, but nothing further was heard of them after take-off. That afternoon, when both Mosquitos were overdue at Marham, four other Mosquitos led by S/L George Parry took off at 15.39 hours to search for the missing crews to a point at 51°37'N; 03°06'E. The weather for the search was cloudy but light and fair, with 3 to 4 miles of visibility, but they found nothing. It later transpired that at 12.40 hours, having bombed and damaged the ship, P/O Graham's aircraft had been hit by flak and crashed about 10km north of Vlissingen near Oostkapelle, in Walcheren (Zeeland), Netherlands. He and his observer were laid to rest in Vlissingen northern cemetery. Five minutes later, F/Sgt Booth's Mosquito was also hit by flak, near Rittem in Zeeland, 3km east of Vlissingen. They were buried in the same cemetery as the other crew.

The remainder of November was taken up in pursuit of yet another role; that of low-level attacks on railway repair shops and railway marshalling yards. Lingen, Emmerich and Zulich in Germany were attacked on the 16th. For the next couple of weeks there was a lull in operational activity, but flying practice was kept up, as on the 28th when a low-level cross-country exercise for ten 105 and two 139 Squadron Mosquitos took place. It was during this sortie that the ever-present hazard of bird-strike nearly claimed a crew. P/O Pete Rowland with Richard L. Reily were flying DZ360:A at 280 mph, when a wood pigeon suddenly smashed violently through their windscreen, shattering the Perspex and striking Rowland in the face. Fortunately he was not blinded, but nevertheless suffered severe bruising to his forehead. In view of the circumstances, Rowland terminated the exercise and a successful forced landing followed at RAF Bottesford, 7 miles north-west of Grantham in Lincolnshire. Both occupants were safe but with feathers rather ruffled!

Not so fortunate however were W/O Tommy R. Williams with his observer Sgt Joseph William Egan, who were also on the training flight in Mosquito DZ369:B. An engine failure necessitated another emergency landing, this time at RAF Molesworth aerodrome, situated 11 miles west-north-west of Huntingdon in Northamptonshire. When the Mosquito was on final approach to land, the driver of a truck crossed the end of the runway, directly in the pilot's line of sight. He must have suddenly realized there was a Mosquito coming in and panicked. As a result he stalled the truck, then jumped out and ran. Unfortunately, there was no time to avoid the obstruction and the aircraft ploughed into the vehicle. Sadly, Sgt Egan died of a fractured skull ten minutes after admission to station sick quarters and his pilot, Tommy Williams, who had survived the slaughter of the 105 Squadron Blenheim operations when flying from Malta, was severely injured. He sustained a broken fibula and tibia in his left leg, and his right leg was so severely damaged that it had to be amputated. In addition, he sustained a crack in his left shoulder blade, as well as head and facial injuries. The flight surgeon made a very good job of his emergency treatment and when Williams was subsequently rushed to Ely hospital his correct initial diagnoses allowed direct admission to theatre. He remained in hospital for the next 9 months. Sgt Egan was laid to rest in St Joseph's Roman Catholic cemetery in Moston.

The next squadron operations followed on the 29th on Belgian targets at Mons-St Ghislain, Montzen, Liège and the Haine St Pierre/Monceau area, all with varying but generally good results. The raid on St Ghislain was remembered by W/C Edwards:

In November, we carried out our first complete night sortie. [In fact, the first Mosquito night raid by the RAF so far.] Hitherto I had taken off or landed in daylight. This was a crazy sortie, but I suppose it had a purpose. We had information that there was to be a big uprising of patriots in Belgium on the night of 29/30 November and they required some bombing to act as a diversion to keep the authorities occupied. One of the night bombing groups was involved and 2 Group were asked to assist. From the available crews, I decided that Ralston, Noseda, young Monaghan and I should go. The weather was foul and the night bomber group cancelled, as did the majority of 2 Group. The CO and I discussed the value of the exercise; he felt we should go if at all possible in order to help the Belgians. It was a filthy night. We took off at about midnight in pouring rain with a cloud base of 300ft. My target was to be the locomotive sheds in the area Mons-St Ghislain. I flew at 100ft in cloud and rain and then on DR we estimated we were in the target area. There was nothing to indicate where we were, so we flew around and up came a lot of light flak. In the circumstances this seemed as good a place as any to bomb, so we let them go and were pleased to return to England. We landed back at Marham two hours after take-off, having achieved what? As forecast, the conditions were clear on return, but what would have happened in the event of an early emergency return I am not clear. RAF Scampton in Lincolnshire was the only clear nearby airfield at take off; there were others in faraway Yorkshire. In later years, when instrument ratings became a necessary fetish in the RAF, I realised how lamentable my night flying ability was. My life could well have ended, not due to enemy action, on that night; when I think that 105 Squadron provided the only four RAF aeroplanes to operate over occupied Europe, and we were a day bomber force, I only hope the Belgians benefited.

CHAPTER 10

Eindhoven

As already mentioned, throughout November when not flying operationally, low-level practice had been stepped up with 'bulls'-eyes' (combined exercises with British ground defences simulating conditions over enemy targets) taking place over the flat East Anglian countryside. Cross-country flights were frequent, as were visits by crews to the bombing range at Grimstone Warren. Something big was in the air and W/C Edwards was determined his crews would be ready. He recalled: 'The entire Group [2 Group] became involved in training and it became obvious that this was to require split-second timing and much accuracy. We took part in three large-scale "bulls'-eyes" in which all three types simulated the envisaged raid. The problem was to get a large number of aircraft across the target in the shortest possible time in an effective raid, at the same time providing a measure of safety.'

After the sad demise of his aircraft DK328:V on 7 November, when on the Gironde operation, W/C Edwards had received a replacement. The Mosquito was DZ365, again 'V' for Victory, in which he did an acceptance flight test with Corporal Smith on the 10th. It passed the test and Edwards adopted the Mosquito, which was to be the machine he used throughout the month to practise what he logged as 'squadron bombing', 'formation bombing', 'dive bombing', 'pair bombing' and 'operational exercises'. During all the intensive training, on the morning of 20 November, W/C Edwards summoned F/L Charles Patterson to his office with an unusual operational requirement. Patterson explains: 'I was introduced to a flying officer navigator, whom I'd never before seen in my life – nothing to do with 105 Squadron. It was explained to me that he was from a thing called the RAF film unit, and he had a ciné-camera, which was to be fitted into my Mosquito. I was to take him on a low-level reconnaissance of the Schelde estuary. We would take a film of the route down the estuary, which the raid – the big operation – would follow when it took place.'

The briefing was to fly down the Ooster Schelde estuary from Noord Beveland, as far as Woensdrecht on the Dutch mainland, where a German fighter airfield was located, and then return to base. The filming part of the flight was to take place at 300ft to allow the ciné-camera to take pictures at the best angle for maximum information, which in itself presented a hazard, as the Mosquito would be in plain view in the enemy radar. Accompanied by the navigator/cameraman, F/O Hill, Patterson took-off in DK338:O at 13.07 hours. The flight went well, and he noted; 'We whizzed down the Schelde estuary and crossed the mainland. When on the horizon, I could see the hangars of Woensdrecht airfield and I turned sharply about and came home again.' When he touched down again at 14.47 hours, Gaumont British News were there and both Patterson and his pet spaniel dog Jamie were filmed. The news reporters were there as a prelude to the main attack, and the film was taken away and developed. The results were less than overwhelming however, as the route was somewhat featureless. Nevertheless, it had been taken to be used appropriately, and the crew were safe.

Bombing practice continued relentlessly, and soon news broke that the target was to be the Philips valve and radio works at Eindhoven in the Netherlands, lying on a due easterly track from the end of the Ooster Schelde estuary. Operation Oyster was to take place on 6 December 1942, and would be the largest combined operation 2 Group had ever attempted in daylight. The operation was fraught with difficulties, with approach and withdrawal routes being over very densely populated enemy fighter regions. As the works was in a highly populated area, it would be necessary to attack with great precision if civilian casualties were to be minimized. However, the attack should cripple the Germans' electronic counter-measures research and also their manufacturing facility, which at the time accounted for approximately one-third of their supply of radio valves and radar equipment.

The plan was that 105 Squadron (call sign: 7PM) was to join several other squadrons in attacking the main Stryp Group plant. No. 107 Squadron (call sign: BC1) were to field 12 Boston MkIIIs, 139 Squadron (call sign: 7PM) – 2 Mosquito MkIVs, 464 Squadron (call sign: N7G) – 14 Venturas, and 487 Squadron (call sign: UD5) – 16 Ventura MkIIs. The Emmasingle valve factory was to be attacked by 21 Squadron (call sign: B18) – 17 Venturas, 88 Squadron (call sign: 1WT) – 12 Boston MkIIIs, and 226 Squadron (call sign: 8UT) – 12 Boston MkIIIs. Fighter cover was to be provided on the way home by 11 Spitfires from 167 Squadron, 12 Spitfires from 411 Squadron, 10 Spitfires from 485 Squadron, and 13 Typhoons from 56 Squadron. A diversionary raid around Alkmaar was laid on by 8 Mustangs from 268 Squadron and the USAAF fielded 84 of their B-17 bombers in another diversionary raid against Lille, under Circus 241.

The 2 Group bombers were to follow the route Patterson had flown with his 35mm ciné-camera, and proceed from Colijnsplaat on Noord-Beveland, south-east along the Ooster Schelde. Landfall was to be south of Bergen op Zoom, where they would pass Woensdrecht and continue as far as Oostmalle in Belgium, before turning to fly just south of Tournhout. There the formation was to dog-leg east-north-east back into the Netherlands towards the lakes at Valkenswaard, before converging with the railway line travelling north into Eindhoven. The main problem that had to be considered was the relative flying speeds of the three aircraft. The slowest was the Ventura, followed by the Boston. Naturally, the Mosquito was the fastest. It was decided that the 88 Squadron Bostons would start the attack, followed by the Mosquitos and finally the Venturas.

On 2 December all the hard training was over and the squadrons were set to go. However, the weather was not acceptable and despite further aborts on the 3rd, as fighters could not get off from their bases, and further weather problems thereafter, it was not until the 6th that the operation was definitely on. There was cloud and slight rain on this morning; however the forecast over the target area was favourable and so the show began. The briefing for the Mosquito crews was held by W/C Edwards at RAF Marham before they went out to their machines and prepared for departure. The Mosquitos departing around 11.22 hours were as follows:

105 Squadron (coded: GB)

DZ365:V	W/C H.I. Edwards / F/O H.H.E.P. Cairns
DZ372:C	F/O S.G. Kimmel / F/O H. Kirkland
DZ374:X	W/O A.R. Noseda / Sgt J.W. Urquhart
DZ370:Z	P/O J.G. Bruce / P/O M. Carreck
DK296:G	S/L D.A.G. Parry / F/O V.G. Robson
DK336:P	F/Sgt K.L. Monaghan / F/Sgt A.W. Dean
DK338:O	F/L C.E.S. Patterson / F/O J. Hill
DZ367: J	F/L W.W. Blessing / Sgt J. Lawson

139 Squadron (coded: XD)

DZ373:B	F/L M.M. Wayman / F/L.C.K. Hayden
DZ371:A	F/O J.E. O'Grady / Sgt G.W. Lewis

The Mosquitos took off and after a circuit of the aerodrome, set off across the hangars, bound for the coast where they formed two sections. W/C Edwards led the formation and S/L Parry the second section. The Bostons were ahead by this time and were to bomb at Zero Hour, chosen to be 12.30 hours, when the minimum number of workers would be in the factory. As fate would have it, it also turned out to be a Sunday. The Bostons were to be followed on to the target by the Mosquitos at Zero + 2 minutes and the Venturas at Zero + 6 minutes. All aircraft were to approach at deck level and the first two Bostons would drop their 250lb 11-second delay bombs at low level, while the others would climb to bomb from 900–1,200ft before departing, again at low level. The Mosquitos were to follow, dropping their 500lb medium casing, TD.025 seconds bombs at 1,000ft in a shallow dive from 1,500ft, commencing 4 miles from the target. Finally, the Venturas would drop their incendiaries and long time-delay bombs from a height of 200ft, while simultaneously attending to the well-alerted defences with their machine-guns.

The Mosquitos flashed across the sea at low level, in two echelon-starboard formations of six. They passed Colijnsplaat and flew down the estuary before making landfall and flying over Bergen op Zoom, having slowed down to catch up with the Bostons. Charles Patterson recalled: 'When we got across the Dutch coast, flying low level, we had to fly past Woensdrecht airfield. The thing I remember most clearly was my memory of looking across to my port wing tip and seeing those 109s taking off along the runway to come up and shoot us. We only looked about two or three hundred yards away from them. It was actually about half a mile, but it looked like that, which was rather a strange feeling. They looked so sort of normal – just like Spitfires taking off in England – that it was hard to realize they were coming up to kill you.' The first to be attacked was P/O Jimmy Bruce who was flying at 50ft at 12.23 hours. His observer, P/O Mike Carreck, recalls:

Well before we crossed the Dutch coast at Colijnsplaat, I was kneeling backwards on the wooden spar that was my seat and searching the sky for the first life-or-death glimpse of an expected fighter. Well, before we were ten minutes into Holland near Woensdrecht, a barrel-engined FW 190 appeared. [1,500 yards away on the starboard quarter at 50ft]. I mentioned the fact to Jimmy, who warned 'Snappers!' on the useless TR9, followed by a 'split-arsed' turn. Standard operating procedure was to lead him away from the other unarmed Mosquitos and the chase began, he the hunter, we the hunted. We weren't sitting targets but well within the range of his cannons. We must both have been flying at almost precisely the same speed [the Mosquito was doing about 230 mph IAS], as he was always the same size, never bigger as he gained, never smaller as he drew away. He'd tilt a wing banking to port, and I'd call 'Starboard!' Jimmy would wrench the Mosquito across the attack to offer the most difficult possible deflection shot. Starboard, port, port, starboard, over and over again, as we streaked across the flat billiards table of the Dutch countryside. Once out of the corner of my eye, I saw flashing by, a church clock with the spire soaring above. Three minutes later, at 51°21' N; 05°02'E, south of Poppel, the Mosquito was doing 300 IAS and was somewhat north of the formation when another FW 190 appeared from astern at 200 yards.

For a dozen lifetimes we turned and twisted all over Holland, flat out at nought feet. Then, suddenly, he had us in his sights and for an eternity of maybe four seconds, cannon shells were bursting all around us and just as suddenly they stopped. 'He's turning away, Jimmy', I said. 'Going home – ammunition pans empty.' The immediate action was to dump our bomb-load. It had slowed us up with that FW 190, and if we met another, as the skies were full of them, we'd need every last inch of speed. With acres of green, empty field 50 feet below us, Jimmy opened the bomb doors. I had my hand on the jettison lever, ready to drop the delayed-action bombs, when something, somebody, made me ask Jimmy to go up to a thousand feet where I yanked the lever. Those bombs weren't delayed-action, and their blasts flung our Mosquito about the sky – if we had dropped them at low level at Eindhoven, we'd have gone up with them! There was not the time to congratulate each other, as it was vital at this very moment to find out exactly where we were, as we hadn't recently had time for much navigation. I picked maps up from the floor, gazed anxiously around at an utterly featureless Holland – nothing to give us the slightest clue of our position. Then, like the climax of a bad movie, here comes John Wayne with the seventh cavalry – a formation of Bostons appeared in front of us flying west, neat, tidy and dignified, like a ceremonial air display. Jimmy and I came up to them, flew alongside at a safe, respectful distance. We stood on one wing – look, we're a Mosquito, then stood on the other – see our RAF roundels. Then we tucked in among the formation. 'Guns' I thought happily, counting the turrets. Uneventful minutes later, we were crossing the Dutch coast, homeward bound and then over the sea when naval guns opened up. Huge spouts of water erupted optimistically around us until we passed out of range. Then, I'm afraid, Jimmy was just a trifle tactless. He waggled our wings – thank you – and throttles wide open, we rocketed away, leaving the Bostons standing. Showing off, yes; but we'd had a hard day.

During this encounter, the FW 190s had a swipe at more of the formation, which was disadvantaged, being not far above stalling speed to accommodate the Bostons. Charles Patterson recalls when the fighters attacked again: 'George Parry, taking with him one other pilot, Bill Blessing, with great coolness and decisiveness, in a split-second decision, told me over the VHF to carry on leading the formation, and told Bill Blessing to follow him. He broke away with Blessing and turned right to go home, and deliberately drew these 190s on to himself and Blessing.' Parry managed to evade the 190s before returning to join the formation. Blessing was attacked by a FW 190, which engaged him from the starboard quarter, firing at 300–400 yards. He turned into the attack and circled for ten minutes at 50ft in a desperate struggle for survival in his unarmed machine. He suffered three attacks to port, starboard and port quarters before he decided to abandon the fight at 12.40 hours, about 24 miles to the east of Woensdrecht. Blessing made for home on a 270° course, chased by the fighter that only abandoned the hunt about 8 miles east of Vlissingen, near Borssele on Zuid-Beveland. Miraculously, the Mosquito had not been hit after a chase of around 55 miles in total.

During the excitement, the formation had pressed on, as Patterson continues: 'I was now leading the formation, and ahead of me I saw the front formation of Mosquitos in the distance, already climbing up to 1,500ft. So I immediately took my formation, which was two short, climbed up myself and got out of the Bostons and climbed to 1,500ft. I went as fast as I could, without losing contact with my formation, to catch Edwards up and join on to his formation. When we actually arrived at 1,500ft, about two or three miles south of Eindhoven, I'd practically caught Edwards up. He banked over to port and started to dive down on to the Philips works in the centre of the town'. W/C Edwards recalled: 'With throttles fully open I climbed to 2,000ft, suddenly feeling naked and a sitting target. Below me, George Parry, with two others, was streaking towards what was already a well bombed target. I put the nose down and levelled at 1,000ft. The flak was spasmodic; wrong time of day perhaps!'

Patterson continued: 'The moment I turned to port, I could see this factory standing out unmistakably, very prominently, right in the centre of Eindhoven town. So there was little problem with identifying the target. Then we all went down in this shallow dive, full throttle down towards the target, and at the appropriate moment, dropped the bombs; pilot-dropped.' Edwards further recalled: 'We were heading for the main plant, and bombed at 1,000ft. I then pushed the stick forward to get as low as possible. A large clock face loomed up over Eindhoven; it showed 12.32 hours.'

Charles Patterson went on: 'Then of course, as I went across the Philips works the whole factory seemed to erupt in a cloud of smoke and flashes. Looking down on it at height, it looked as though the whole thing was completely eliminated. In the distance, I could see masses of Bostons whizzing about across the trees at low level, away to port.' Following this and having taken the required ciné-film of the raid, Patterson headed home at ground level. The Mosquitos split up and it was every man for himself. W/C Edwards did likewise: 'We cleared the target town and I remarked on the precision and success of the attack we had seen. I wondered about the Venturas [for whom Edwards had said a prayer when passing them on the way out, due to their comparative slowness and vulnerability]. After about five minutes at 300 knots, I questioned the course. "Keep on as we are" [came the reply]. I looked at the compass and realized we had not changed heading since the attack; we were travelling into Germany, the excitement had been too much. I cursed our ineptitude and implicated my navigator by pointing at the direction indicator with a despairing gesture. I yanked the aeroplane around and headed due west. Within minutes, we flashed over the coast between The Hague and Haarlem. My fears were that we would encounter fighters returning from chasing the Venturas, but we saw nothing but a Ventura or two heading towards sanctuary.'

Meanwhile, Patterson had an interesting trip home, and on leaving the target area noted: 'It was midday – lovely sunny day, no cloud, well virtually none. So I just set off across the Dutch countryside at high speed. I decided not to follow the given route, which was towards the coast of Holland and out into the North Sea. I decided that that was where the fighters would be, and therefore I turned north to the Zuider Zee. I reckoned that if I was over the Zuider Zee very low, I'd be under the radar, and be difficult to intercept. The fighters would be directed to the main formation. So I took my own route up and came all the way up the Zuider Zee. Another Mosquito, which it turned out was flown by F/L O'Grady on his very first trip, decided, not having been on a Mosquito operation of any kind before, that he'd be wise to latch on to another Mosquito to see him home.' F/L John Earl O'Grady and Sgt George William Lewis in DZ371:A had been hit by flak over the target and smoke was streaming from the aircraft on leaving the target area. Patterson was flying on an outbound track, via Utrecht and Amsterdam. The two aircraft continued north-east until they turned to port between Den Helder and Texel Island, where they were in range of light flak. They flew among the flak and weaving tracer until out over the North Sea to set a course for home. Charles Patterson continued: 'I was untouched and the Mosquito behind me appeared to be perfectly all right and carried on flying behind me. When we were about five or six minutes out into the North Sea, which I suppose would be about 30 miles or whatever it was, I'd already come up to 200–300ft, when suddenly my camera-navigator chap said "He's gone into the sea, he's gone into the sea." At first, I couldn't believe what he was saying, and then he said "The Mosquito behind has gone into the sea." I thought he must have made a mistake, because we were 30 miles out to sea by now, but I turned round to go back and I'm afraid it was only too true. [The Mosquito was believed to have climbed, then stalled before entering the water.] There was a big cauldron of water, a boiling circle of water, and it was obvious he had gone in. He wasn't there. He was a very nice, cheerful young Canadian, O'Grady. I'd known him as a pupil at Upwood when I was an instructor. He only looked about sixteen – I suppose he was about twenty. [He was actually twenty-one.]' Both airmen are commemorated on the Runnymede Memorial.

There was one other incident on the way home. Having bombed the target, W/O Ray Noseda was flying at 50ft on a course of 280°, when at Overflakkee his Mosquito was attacked. Just as Patterson had surmised, the fighters were waiting to pick off those returning. Off the starboard quarter, two 'Butcher Birds' appeared, slightly above the Mossie. At 400–500 yards they opened fire, damaging the starboard aileron as the Mosquito turned into the attack. The fighters attacked the Mosquito three more times. The first attack was from the starboard quarter and was evaded by again turning into the attack. As if this wasn't enough to put up with, another two attacks from astern ensued, as Noseda turned to starboard to avoid the assault. However, machine-gun fire ripped into the aileron trimming control this time, and did a good job on the engine nacelle on the port side. Fortunately, speed won the day and the Mosquito eventually outran its pursuers, to land safely back at base. The remaining Mosquitos also landed safely. W/C Edwards noted finally: 'We landed at Norfolk at 18 minutes after 2, after a flight of 2 hours and 20 minutes. Then I reported "practically the most effective and well organized operation I have done".'

One more Mosquito was to venture to Eindhoven that day, as 139 Squadron's S/L Jack Houlston with W/O J.L. Armitage took 105 Squadron's DZ314, GB:F to view the damage the bombing had done. The operation was officially described thus: 'The crew were detailed to take photographs of the damage at Eindhoven. Route followed in cloud to the target. Two Me 109s were sighted at 800 yards en route to the target, but these were soon lost. Two runs were completed over the primary target at 800ft, taking pictures of the damage. A pall of smoke covered the secondary target, while the high buildings in the primary and all the eastern side were burning like a furnace. Light and heavy flak was encountered at the target but no damage was caused to the aircraft which returned safely to base.' They landed at 14.05 hours.

The operation had caused the loss four Bostons, three of which were shot down by fighters, nine Venturas and one 139 Squadron Mosquito. Many aircraft were damaged due to flak and 23 aircraft suffered bird-strike. As Mike Carreck recalls: 'Back at Marham, the airfield was swarming with newspapermen. They took photographs of faithful DZ370:Z, of the hole a cannon shell had made. It had hit us without exploding, missing the bombs by inches. Guardian Angel day. In the crew room, everybody was talking over the Eindhoven op, how the Philips plant had caught fire, trapping the flak gunners on the roof, when someone asked, "Did you see that c—— give the Hitler salute, as he fell into the flames?" Next day we went on leave. At home they phoned us to say that Eindhoven was my final op with 105 Squadron, my tour was over.' Both he and P/O Pete Rowland were posted to 17 OTU 'on rest' as instructors.

For leading the Mosquito operation, W/C Edwards was awarded the DSO to add to the VC and DFC he already held, and F/O Cairns received the DFC. Edwards commented: 'Actually, I was elated. The press next day hailed me as the first Dominion officer in the war to win the VC, DSO and DFC or their equivalent. I was also particularly pleased that the same signal notified the award of the DFC to Tubby Cairns. He was a deserving case. I would have been disappointed and embarrassed if he had got nothing.'

In response to the operation, on Christmas Day 1942, Archibald Sinclair wrote his Christmas message from the Air Ministry to the AOC-in-C Bomber Command at RAF High Wycombe, AM Sir Arthur Harris: 'The Dutch Minister came to see me yesterday in order to express on behalf of his Government the admiration which they felt for the skill with which the attack on the Philips Works at Eindhoven was planned and executed. The admiration of the gallantry of the attacking crews was only equalled by their gratitude for the accuracy of their aim and for the consequent avoidance of unnecessary injury and suffering to the civilian population.'

Following the Eindhoven raid on the 8th, F/O S.P.L. Johnson and his observer Sgt E.C. Draper were lost in their Mosquito DZ314:F. They had taken off at 11.58 hours with the intention of performing a low-level attack on Den Helder's docks. They did not reappear, and it was discovered that the crew were safe as PoWs. They too ended up in the infamous Stalag Luft 3.

For the rest of the month, railway targets along the railway line from Emden to Münster were attacked from low level. The stations at Leer and Papenburg, as well as track in the railway yards at Lingen all received attention on the 8th. The next day, the sky was clear with no cloud and five miles of visibility when S/L Roy Ralston and F/L Syd Clayton were attacking a tunnel on the Paris–Soissons railway line. The tunnel starts at Vierzy some 8km south-south-west of Soissons, and emerges about 2km to the north-east near Léchelle. At 17.10 hours Ralston took DZ353:E to the western entrance and planted one 500lb, 11-second time-delayed bomb in the tunnel mouth from a height of only 200ft. With smoke coming from the entrance, he had tried a second run again at 200ft, but this time the bomb bounced off the entrance. Undaunted by this and with great coolness, he flew round to the other end and attempted, five minutes from the start of the attack, to drop another two bombs into the tunnel, this time from 1,000ft. Unfortunately, the bombs overshot, but a train entering the tunnel at 17.20 hours was unable to emerge while the Mosquito watched overhead for 10 minutes. The same day, more trains were attacked, and F/L Bill Blessing attacked an engine shed in a railway yard in the Montdidier to Hove area. For good measure, he also 'had a go' at a mooring coal train. Meanwhile, W/O Ray Noseda was also harassing an engine pulling about 60 goods vehicles behind it on the line from Amiens to Tergnier, 5 miles east of Ham. He let loose four 500-pounders as the train sped along. They detonated and the train was left stationary and engulfed in smoke.

On the 14th, a new crew carried out their first attack with 105 Squadron, flying in DZ378:K. S/L Reggie Reynolds DFC was with his observer, P/O (later to become A/Cdr) E.B. 'Ted' Sismore. Sismore recalls the operation and how he arrived on 105:

In 1941, I went to Malta with the Blenheims of 110 Squadron and after a time in the Army hospital, was evacuated by Sunderland to Gibraltar. There I spent three weeks on a troop ship, waiting to sail, with Lord Haw-Haw telling us on the radio that we would be sunk as soon as we left. During that time I heard about the new wooden bomber, the Mosquito. I

Portrait of W/C Roy Ralston. (Mrs Betty Ralston and Mr David Ralston)

decided that if all the tales were true, then that was the aeroplane for my next tour. For my rest tour, I served at the Blenheim OTU at Bicester and the Whitley OTU at Honeybourne, where I flew two of the thousand bomber raids. There I met Reggie Reynolds who had already completed a tour on Hampdens and, remarkably, a tour on Manchesters. He had been promised a choice for his third tour. He chose a tour on the Mosquito, at the time equipping only No. 105 Squadron, with No. 139 still converting. I managed to persuade him that I should go with him to make up his crew, and so off we went to Marham, where our introduction was not as smooth as I had hoped. During our interview, the Group Captain [Digger Kyle] said, 'Reynolds, I chose my crews and I did not choose you, so you will get just one chance to make the grade here.' Perhaps luckily he did not remember me. At our last meeting at Bicester he had taken me to task for not completing a bombing instructor's course, which would have taken me away from Bomber Command. I have never forgotten him saying 'Don't you know there is a war on?' We almost ran into trouble on our 'one chance'. Our first target as a 'trainer' was the railway marshalling yards at Gent. We ran in for a shallow dive attack and I was in the nose to release the bombs. I pressed the release, looked down – nothing! I said 'down to the deck and turn left 180°' to give me time to check the circuits. I found a loose plug and so we made a second run. This time the guns were firing at us, but we bombed successfully. At the debriefing we were reminded forcibly that the rule was one run only – no repeats, all in the interests of safety. We escaped further censure, probably because we had at least shown some determination.

Two days later on the 20th, S/L Reynolds was up again in DZ378:K, this time to attack railway targets in north-west Germany, accompanied by five crews of 105 Squadron with five of 139, two of which were flying borrowed 105 Squadron aircraft. Ted Sismore recalls: 'Our next operation was to attack railway targets in the Oldenburg/Bremen area. Near Delmenhorst [where, at 10.28 hours, their four 500lb GP bombs left a gasometer on fire] we were hit by 40mm flak, holing the port radiator and leaving us on one engine. We came home by way of Wilhelmshaven Bay, where a cruiser tried to "splash" us into the sea with its main armament. Our no. 2, W/O Ray Noseda, bravely stayed with us until we were clear of the coast. We had lost the hydraulics so we had to land wheels up. The drama continued when the escape hatch failed to release and we had to resort to a fireman's axe.' The crew got out safely and the aircraft was salvaged, but it had reached the end of its flying days and was sent to Technical Training Command as an instrument for ground-based tuition. Sadly, for one of the 139 Squadron crews, the ending to the operation was not so fortunate. S/L Jack Edward Houlston DFC, AFC with W/O James Lloyd Armitage DFC in DZ387, XD:M failed to return and were laid to rest in the Reichswald Forest war cemetery.

On the 22nd, there was yet another tragic incident. Sgt Joseph Edward Cloutier RCAF and his observer Sgt Albert Cecil Foxley were on their first 105 Squadron operation, and had been briefed to attack the engine sheds at Termonde, east of Gent. They took off in DZ360:A at 15.52 hours. While crossing the French coast near Dunkirk, they were met by a hail of intense light flak. They carried on, but at 16.30 hours their Mosquito came to grief, at Axel. This small village lies between Sluiskil and Hulst, just north of the Belgium border in the Netherlands, and some 30km north-north-west of the intended target. The airmen were laid to rest in the Northern cemetery at Vlissingen. That same day railway targets were attacked at railway junctions east of Bremen and Alost, half-way between Gent and Brussels. Engine sheds at Grammont (Geraardsbergen), west-south-west of Brussels were attacked from 100ft by F/L Gordon and his observer P/O Ralph Gamble Hayes in DK302:D, while others attacked marshalling yards at Amiens.

Mosquito B.IV, DZ378, GB:K standing defiantly on its undercarriage once more, following the raid to the gasworks near Delmenhorst in Germany, on 20 December 1942. Note the flak damage to the port radiator which hit the Mosquito as the bombs released. The aircraft had also been hit by birds, one in the port side of the nose and one in the starboard leading edge. Returning on one engine with complete loss of hydraulics necessitated a belly-landing, the damage from which can be seen to the undercarriage doors and the propeller blades. (Via E.B. Sismore)

On 27 December, S/L George Parry was up testing a Mosquito and raised a few eyebrows in consequence. He recalls: 'We went up to 30,000ft for tests and cloud travelling south closed in beneath us. When the tests were completed, we decided to fly south to see how far the cloud had travelled. So we went into a dive down to the cloud level, and found that we had gone further than expected. Robbie [P/O Robson] said we should go down, as we were getting near London. So, down we went, and broke cloud over Folkestone. We turned north and joined up with two Hurricanes returning to Hornchurch, which saved me from having to fly about London's defended area. On arrival at Hornchurch, we waved goodbye to the Hurricanes and returned to base. My trip had caused come consternation, however, as I was being tracked on radar, and had been seen going south at a high speed. It was felt that I might end up over enemy territory, and the aircraft might be lost. I was told that I had gone from Cambridge to Folkestone in under 8 minutes, which was almost 600 mph ground speed!'

The last day of the month saw attacks led by S/L Roy Ralston on more marshalling yards at Mons, and Monseau sur Sambre in Belgium as well as Lille in France. Ralston completed the damage by dropping his complement of four 500lb bombs from his leading Mosquito, DZ353:E, smack into a locomotive assembly shed and boiler shop at the French town of Raismes.

So ended 1942, a year of heightened experiences of the Mosquito, which had emerged from the doldrums as an excellent fighting machine, but for which the cost in lives had been dear. Even the horrendous losses of the Blenheim era had been exceeded in percentage terms!

CHAPTER 11

Fame and Fortune

January 1943 started as December had left off, with attacks on railway targets. Marshalling yards at Amiens and engine sheds at Tergnier were visited amid intense flak on the 3rd, and on the 9th, S/L Ralston led another five Mosquitos in DZ353:E, to attack engine sheds at Rouen. During this operation, W/O Raymond Noseda, who had survived the murderous anti-shipping Blenheim operations from Malta, failed to return with his observer, Sgt John Watson Urquhart. They had been flying Mosquito DZ315:L, having taken off in the first wave at 16.15 hours. The Mosquito was hit by anti-aircraft fire while over the target at 17.31 hours, and was last seen by the leader to climb to 1,000ft with the starboard engine on fire. Then, having turned to port, it crashed into a hill in the target area and blew up. The two airmen's bodies were buried in St Sever cemetery extension at Rouen; a very sad start to the month.

On the 13th, engine sheds and yards at Laons, Aulnoye, and Tergnier were successfully attacked. On the 20th, the old favourite Stork works at Hengelo received yet another visit from eight crews, the leading wave of which was led by S/L Roy Ralston again in DZ353:E. The attack, which was to be a combined low-level and shallow-dive from 2,000ft, diving to 1,000ft, took place in the afternoon. The formation flew in over the Netherlands, south-east over Lemmer on the shores of the Zuider Zee. Here flak batteries opened up and at 15.04 hours, flak damaged the leader's Mosquito, putting both the pitot tube on the tail fin and the elevator rudder trim out of action, as well as damaging the hydraulics. F/L Blessing, with his observer, Sgt J. Lawson, was leading the second wave in DZ413:K. They too sustained damage. The elevator controls were hit and they received a hole in the fuselage as well as a burst tail wheel, before deciding discretion was the better part of valour and returning to base. The formation pressed on and found Hengelo, where the 'low-levellers', comprising F/O C.R. Henry in DZ416:Q, F/O K. Wolstenholme in DZ379:H and F/O Leonard J. Skinner in DZ408:F, dropped their 11-second time-delay bombs on the target at 15.15 hours from 50ft, followed one minute later by the leader's damaged aircraft.

The remaining two 'shallow-divers' bombed the boiler shops from 1,000ft. The first in to drop instantaneous bombs was P/O Monaghan in DK337:N at 15.15 hours. He did a second run at 1,200ft to photograph a 1,000ft-high column of brown smoke belching skywards from the works. The other 'shallow-dive' crew, on their first Mosquito operation, were the Australian from Perth, W/O H.C. 'Gary' Herbert with observer Sgt C. 'Jake' Jacques in Mosquito DK302:D. Gary Herbert noted:

We were tail-end Charlie. The leader of our four [Blessing] was hit and turned for home. We started to follow but realized he was going home and turned after the formation again. We couldn't find them in the thick haze, so I decided to go on alone. Jake, my observer, did some good map reading and we found the target OK, climbed up to 2,000ft, dived to 1,000ft and let our four 500-pounders go. We hit the boiler room with two, and the two overshoots hit the houses nearby. We came out very fast and had no trouble at all. We saw a lot of Holland – windmills, barges, dykes, canals and even boys with big yellow clogs. When we got back we found that five out of the eight machines had been hit at the coast. We were not hit by flak, but a bird holed our tailplane.

Unfortunately, F/L Gordon, who had also been formating on Bill Blessing when he had returned, had lost the rest of the formation. Uncertain of their position, he eventually found lock gates, 4 miles south of Lingen in Germany, where he dropped his bombs and beat a retreat out via the island of Terschelling. Here they the met flak, which damaged the starboard radiator and hydraulics of his Mosquito, DK296:G. Both he and S/L Ralston belly-landed safely back at RAF Marham.

The next operation was on Saturday the 23rd. The target was to be the marshalling yards at Quakenbrück on the River Hase, on the Osnabrück–Oldenburg line in Germany. Gary Herbert remembers the operation: 'We were tail-end Charlie again, but couldn't get our undercart [wheels] up [on DZ415:A] and had to land again. We got another kite [DZ407:R] and went out alone [at 12.40 hours]. There was very poor visibility as we sneaked in over the Zuider Zee at deck level without being seen. We went across Holland pretty fast and made for a railway junction at Quakenbrück in western Germany. We found it after a bit of trouble, and climbed up to bomb. Cloud base was only 700ft, so I let the bombs go and climbed into the cloud quickly as I could to avoid the blast. The bombs shook the kite plenty. I dived down to the deck and came back at nought feet, climbed to 500ft and photographed the damage. We had thrown the bombs over the railway yards into the town and smashed plenty of houses, before we went down to the deck again and came out north, pretty fast. Later, it was very disappointing to find out the weather was too dull and the photos didn't come out. One kite with F/O Skinner and Freddy Saunders, one of our pals, didn't come back.' The missing aircraft was DZ311:Y. F/O Leonard John Skinner and Sgt Frederick Henry Saunders were last heard of off Zurich at the Waddenzee in the Netherlands. Both are commemorated on the Runnymede Memorial.

Thereafter bombing practice continued. W/C Edwards went to Wainfleet Sands on the 23rd, accompanied by F/O Cairns as usual plus one other – his white bulldog, Sallie. Sallie was not unfamiliar with sitting in the Mosquito while her master honed his bombing skills. Indeed, Edwards' dog was remembered by S/L Patterson, himself the proud owner of a black spaniel, Jamie, also accustomed to flying in the nose of his Mosquito when at low level on non-operational flights: 'Sallie took precedence over everything. If she entered the ops room, briefing came to a halt. Sallie would walk in and Eddie would say "quiet!" and we all had to wait until Sallie laid down, and only then could we continue.'

The intense practice had been for the next operation, which was to be a very big one indeed – the Burmeister & Wain diesel works at Copenhagen, Denmark. W/C Edwards wrote: 'This was to be the first planned daylight raid on the Danish capital since that country was occupied. The Burmeister & Wain works, the biggest in Scandinavia, at times employed 10,000 workers, many of them highly skilled. The works were famous for producing the diesel engine ship *Fionia* in about 1910. In the two years of occupation preceding our raid, they had turned out supplies of engines and parts for Raeder's U-boat fleet [Erich Raeder (1876–1960) was Grand Admiral and Commander-in-Chief of the German Navy]. The U-boat menace was a strangling one, jeopardizing Britain's existence. Any means of counteracting submarine warfare was important. So far, the Burmeister works had enjoyed uninterrupted production. This raid was a great opportunity; our task was to bring these activities to an end.'

Charles Patterson recalls: 'We all settled down to prepare for a major low-level daylight attack which was to be led by Hughie Edwards, our W/C. This was clearly going to be a major operation and Edwards, as always, put himself down to lead it. We were not unduly alarmed because Copenhagen and Denmark were not considered particularly dangerous areas. If we had the right amount of surprise, it should be possible to get over the yard without too much loss from flak. Also, coming home at dusk, there shouldn't be any fighter interception.' Edwards explained: 'Copenhagen is in two parts, separated by a sound or waterway. The diesel works were on the eastern portion of the city in a built-up area and just behind the target was a sugar factory. Adjoining this was a church, which to the British mind must provide further food for thought, but such a problem might recede in the heat of battle. There were many other difficulties presented by residential suburbs in the Amager district, but our main task was to destroy the diesel works and confine our bombs to the target if possible. Causing avoidable loss of life to the indigenous population of occupied countries was frowned upon, since in most cases they were pro-Allied cause, and were harassing the Germans. It was important not to alienate this goodwill. To do all things properly and be effective was not going to be easy. The target was by no means large. I considered it could accommodate an attacking force of 9 Mosquitos.'

Charles Patterson concluded with some disappointment: 'I was to go on this trip, but just at this time there was a sudden sweep of rumours – some major change in the Mosquito squadrons was planned. We were all called together and G/C Kyle, the Station Commander, told us that any crew could volunteer to join a new formation in Bomber Command, that was to be known as "the Path Finders". He couldn't tell us what sort of work would be involved, but if we did volunteer, it would mean promotion and a very interesting new job. It sounded interesting and exciting, so I thought I'd have a go. I never went on the Copenhagen raid, but joined 8 Group, 109 Squadron, PFF.'

The crews who went were a mixture from both 105 and 139 squadrons as follows:

105 Squadron

DZ365:V	W/C H.I. Edwards VC, DSO, DFC / F/O H.H.E.P. Cairns DFC
DK302:D	W/O H.C. Herbert / Sgt C. Jacques
DZ415:A	F/O A.T. Wickham / P/O W.E.D. Makin
DZ407:R	Sgt J.G. Dawson / Sgt R.H. Cox
DZ413:K	F/L W.W. Blessing / Sgt J. Lawson
DK338:O	F/L J. Gordon / F/O R. G. Hayes

105 Squadron aircraft flown by 139 Squadron crews

DZ416:Q	Sgt C.K. Chrysler / Sgt J. Der-Stepanian
DZ379:H	Sgt R.E. Leigh / Sgt A.W. Munro
DK336:P	Sgt R. Clare / F/O E. Doyle

Because of inclement weather, the formation took off at 14.27 hours on 27 January, a day later than expected. W/C Edwards explained the tactics:

The intention was to time the attack to take place 10 minutes after sunset, in the early twilight period between the end of the day and darkness. This was always difficult to time. We wanted sufficient daylight to see the target clearly, but the approaching darkness to hide from fighter attack. I planned to be over the diesel works at 4.40 p.m. London time. In general terms, the plan was to make landfall on the west Danish coast near Blåvands Huk, then fly practically due east across Denmark, its islands and waterways, then turning north from Køge to attack from the south. As usual, the final pieces of attack looked like being the most dangerous. In this particular case it was accentuated by the necessity to fly up a narrow causeway into Copenhagen, where, if they were so positioned, guns could be brought to bear from two sides. This could be extremely dangerous and fatal to the operation. By this time

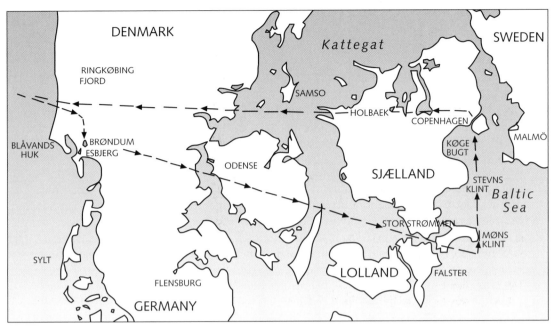

— ➤ — *Approximate Mosquito track en route to Copenhagen.*

there would be no doubt of aircraft crossing Denmark in an easterly direction, and if the gunners were standing at the approaches to the capital, the raiders would have a sticky time. However, this was an operation of which I was more than optimistic about success. It had to be, as it might be my last for some time [It was planned to be Edwards' last operation with 105]. It was to be a long journey of just over 500 miles each way; accurate navigation to the target would be vital.

The weather was very cold and wintry as the Mosquitos started their take-off rolls. Soon all were airborne, flying in echelon-starboard as usual, as the crews settled in for the long flight with Hughie Edwards in the lead. Edwards recalled the conditions:

The North Sea was at its most uninviting; cold, dull, grey with snow flurries. It was no day for ditching. We flew in loose formation for comfort. Our time to run to the Danish coast was approximately 1½ hours. We then had about a further 40 miles across Denmark to Copenhagen. Through the murk of a winter's day a coastline appeared, but not Blåvands Huk. It was a prerequisite in low-level flights over strange country, especially in war, to know the starting-off point. We could not scream across Denmark hoping to find our way as we progressed. However, fortune was with us and we saw the vast stretch of Ringkøbing Fjord. We were 20 miles too far north. This was excellent, having flown 400 miles with virtually no navigational aids. We altered course to the south and flew over the countryside. I commenced to get slightly apprehensive about keeping on track. Forty minutes in a Mosquito at nearly 300 knots at 50ft is not easy in good conditions. Today visibility was poor, the ground was covered in snow, and we would be flying in and out of flurries and light snowstorms. Apart from the snow on the ground, Denmark is a panorama of practically featureless, flat country, rivers and stretches of water. I also began to worry about the fineness of our timing, a problem accentuated by the short twilight period.

Soon the formation was over Brøndum (Bryndum) aerodrome, where it was a great concern that fighters would come up to intercept. Fortunately, luck was with the Mosquitos and none was scrambled. The course was then changed by steering a little north of east, until at a point north of Grimstrup near Arre, F/L Gordon decided to abandon the task. He saw what he thought was blue smoke around his starboard wing. It looked as though he had been hit by flak and so he took evasive action. Being at very low level, and in the heat of the moment, he clipped some telegraph wires with the port wing, damaging the aileron. Knowing he would now be unable to catch up with the others, he decided to abort the operation, jettisoning his bombs about 8 miles north-west of Esbjerg, before returning home. Meanwhile, the others pressed on but W/C Edwards was not at ease:

> As the miles sped by, sometimes over land, sometimes over water, I commenced to get querulous as the time factor was perturbing me. We were flying away from the setting sun, or what there was of it and the light was none too good, although it had not deteriorated much. I was trying to fly and look at Tubby Cairns' map, as though I disbelieved him. We could not pick up a positive landmark. The last quarter of an hour had been a succession of water and land, water and land – nothing else. It was not too easy for my navigator. What was going on in the minds of those behind I could not think – pilots engrossed in flying and navigators criticizing, presumably. At 4.25, we should have been over Sjaelland with 10 minutes to go. We ought soon to be ready to turn north, crossing Køge Bay [Køge Bugt] on the last rung to Copenhagen. Even with the most experienced crews, operations do not always go to plan; Sjaelland seemed to be a long time in appearing. Eventually, we crossed land. This must be it – or so I hoped; so did my navigator who remained supremely confident and unperturbed. The visibility had improved, and by chance and good fortune I espied on my left-hand side a rail and road bridge, quite 4–5 miles long, crossing a stretch of water. Then the heat was really on in the cockpit: 'What the hell was that? Where are we?'; maps went in all directions. The only bridge possible of a comparable size linked Falster with Sjaelland [across Stor Strømmen]. This was 30–40 miles south of our track. While this debate was taking place, we maintained our course, but ran out of land and we were over the Baltic. I commenced to turn north, slowly regaining my composure. At least we knew where we were and I turned to Tubby who offered no alibi.

Edwards then offered the get-out statement to Cairns: 'I see your point, you were deceiving the enemy into thinking we were going to a Baltic port. Good man!' This reasoning must have been promulgated, as when relating the events, S/L Charles Patterson later explained: 'W/C Edwards hit on the very clever idea that, instead of going across Denmark to Copenhagen, he would go across Denmark to the south, into the Baltic, before turning to port and coming straight into Copenhagen at low level, which would achieve complete surprise.' Edwards continued: 'I do not know what they were thinking behind me, it did not matter.' However, in no. 2 position was Gary Herbert, who had his own opinion and noted in his diary on return from the operation: 'The leader got lost on the way out and led us around Denmark for over half an hour before we found the target.'

Edwards then made his way to Copenhagen: 'We skirted the lighthouse at the top of Møn Island and headed due north to Stevns Klint, the lighthouse at the tip of Sjaelland. Soon we would be in Køge Bay with Copenhagen ahead.' The formation ploughed on relentlessly, and raced over the shore and across the bay, where they tucked into a close echelon to starboard formation. Despite the delay in arrival, there was only some opposition at first. Edwards described the scene: 'We got some intense and accurate flak as we flew into the neck leading to Copenhagen, then nothing until after the bombing when the flak ships opened up. As we ran into Copenhagen, not knowing what to expect, I cast my eyes over the navigator's head towards Sweden. There I saw the strange sight of twinkling lights as the evening was coming on. It was Malmö looking like fairyland. I switched my mind back to Copenhagen. After the initial flak bursts had petered out, the attack was plain sailing. The Burmeister & Wain works looked exactly as the briefing photographs had portrayed from this approach. Right behind was the spire of Christian's Church. We swept in over Christian, bomb doors opening, perfectly controlled with each crew aiming at their allotted target according to their own judgement. I was aiming for the test sheds, and between us we intended to cover the entire works. Bombs gone – I closed the bomb doors and turned steeply to port over the centre of the city, on the basis that any flak would be around the perimeter. No fighters seemed to be airborne. Our plan was to return to England singly, there being no advantage in formating since we had no firing power. As we flew westwards Tubby Cairns was extolling the quality of the raid. I was now happy enough to forgive him our route errors.'

So the leader had found and bombed the target from 50ft, despite flak hitting his starboard engine nacelle, and so did the other aircraft. 139's Sgt Leigh attacked from 300ft at 17.03 hours with unobserved results, followed one minute later from 200ft by Sgt Chrysler, who left the test shops with flames bursting through the roof. Sgt Clare was next in and let his bombs go at 17.05 hours at 100ft. Next, 105's F/O Wickham arrived but became caught in the slipstream of the preceding Mosquito and his bombs overshot. Meanwhile, F/L Blessing was braving the now intense light flak from 100ft as he ran in to drop his bombs at the same time as Gary Herbert, who described the attack as *he* witnessed it: 'When we eventually found the target, it was getting pretty dark, but we hit it good and proper. We attacked between two big chimneys and hit the machine shops and power station. Our bombs were delayed half an hour, 3 hours, 6 hours and 36 hours to disorganize the place for a while. The other kites had 11-second, as well as long-delay bombs. We got quite a lot of light flak as we left the target, but kept on the house tops and nobody was hit. When we were well away it was pretty dark, and one of the kites hit something and crashed in flames. The two sergeants in it were damn good chaps too.' This referred to Sgts James George Dawson and Ronald Harry Cox. At 17.30 hours, in poor light near Holbaek on the shores of the Holbaek Fjord, their aircraft, DZ407:R hit high voltage cables, crashed and exploded on the ground, resulting in a sheet of flame which rose 200ft in the air. Both airmen were laid to rest in the Tveje-Merløse church cemetery, in the south-west suburbs of Holbaek.

Gary Herbert continues: 'Petrol was getting short, so we throttled back to 230 mph, and as we passed the last island on the west of Denmark we went straight over a machine-gun post at 200ft. It threw up tons of light flak but I jinked and dodged it OK. We came back quietly, and landed in the dark at 8p.m.' The 139 Squadron crew of Sgt Richard Clare and F/O Edward Doyle were less fortunate though, as they had a starboard engine failure. Subsequently, at 19.50 hours their Mosquito struck a balloon cable and a tree. Both airmen died when their aircraft crashed near Shipdham, about 5 miles north-east of RAF Watton in Norfolk. It was concluded that their engine failure may have been due to shortage of fuel. Both airmen were laid to rest in Marham cemetery. The remaining two 139 crews landed at RAF Swanton Morley, as they considered that they were unable to reach RAF Marham (only 21 miles away), due to a shortage of petrol.

Edwards arrived home at 19.35 hours, with only 15 gallons of fuel left in his tanks, of which he was self-critical, considering that the dextrous use of pitch and throttle could have made an improvement. His arrival was not without incident: 'On leaving the runway, I taxied into some barbed wire. This was the first taxiing accident for which I was directly to blame since leaving Point Cook. I persuaded myself that I was tired and decided to leave the aeroplane where it was until daylight.'

In conclusion, Gary Herbert wrote of his return: 'We had a scare on the way back, as we were struck twice by lightning. Each time a ball of fire appeared on the wing and gradually died out. When I got back, I looked at the wing but there wasn't a mark on it. Seemed queer to me, but the weather man said it had happened before, so I couldn't have had the DTs. We invited the officers over to the mess in the evening to have a few drinks, and fight the battle again. Later, at the time the bombs went off, we drank a toast to them in the mess. It was a nice evening.' The raid had been an enormous success, and the following day reports from Stockholm stated that: 'The main assembly halls of the Burmeister & Wain shipyards at Copenhagen were destroyed by fire, and production of diesel engines brought to a standstill'.

W/C Edwards, on hearing this news, concluded: 'This was great and heartening stuff. Several bombs fell in the sugar factory, causing great combustion with a raging fire. It was probably these fires which our night bomber crews reported still burning in the subsequent 24 hours. Unfortunately, it is inevitable that the civilian population suffers in these raids. As a result of the devastation and the delayed-fuse bombs, 1,000 nearby inhabitants were affected and casualty figures revealed 8 dead and 17 wounded. This was a lousy war.'

CHAPTER 12

Listen – Mosquito Thunder!

The next operation was probably one of the most celebrated in the squadron's Mosquito history as an example of dash and initiative, winning the interest of the press. It was a propaganda coup that made the headlines. Reichsmarshall des Grossdeutschen Reiches (Reich Marshal of the Greater German Reich) and Commander-in-Chief of the Luftwaffe, Hermann Wilhelm Göring (born Rosenheim, Upper Bavaria, 12 January 1893), Hitler's heir-apparent and the military and economic leader of the Third Reich, and Dr Paul Joseph Göbbels (born Rheydt, Rhineland, 29 October, 1897), the propaganda expert of the Reich and Hitler's closest personal friend, were to address the nation at massed rallies in Berlin on 30 January 1943. It was planned that 105 Squadron would address the Göring rally in the morning at 11.00 hours, and later that afternoon, at 16.00 hours, 139 (Jamaica) Squadron would deal with the Dr Göbbels rally.

The 105 Squadron crews were to be led by S/L Reggie Reynolds and his excellent observer P/O Ted Sismore in DZ413:K. The other crews would be F/O A.T. Wickham with P/O W.E.D. Makin in DZ408:F and F/L J. Gordon with F/O R.G. Hayes in DZ372:C. Ted Sismore takes up the story:

> The raid on Berlin took place, as many did, on a day when we had been given a stand-down. We were about to go out for the evening when we were told to go to bed early, and to expect an early call. The early morning of 30 January 1943 was dark, cold, and very windy. It seemed quite unsuitable for any form of operations, but on the way to the ops room, in the flight van, Reggie stopped the conversation by saying, 'This is different, we climb after we cross the Elbe'. We walked into the crew room to see tapes stretching from Marham to Berlin. Everyone had the same question, 'Shall we have enough fuel?' We were told that the target was the radio station, and the aim was to prevent Göring from making his planned speech; a propaganda raid, but one which seemed to us to be fully justified.
>
> The weather forecast was good, low cloud and poor visibility over the North Sea and Holland with improving conditions further east in Germany. The navigation was relatively simple, provided the weather forecast proved to be correct, but the all-important factor was the timing; we had to bomb at exactly 11 o'clock to stop Göring's speech and demonstrate that his boasts about the security of the Fatherland were empty words. We took off under a low cloud base on a rough windy morning and this weather persisted until we were in Holland, when conditions slowly improved. The wind dropped off, the cloud lifted and the visibility improved, making the navigation easy but making us all feel very naked as we crossed into Germany, for what was our deepest penetration of enemy territory with the Mosquito up to that time.

The total distance was to be 1,145 miles, all to be flown on DR, with four way-points given for course correction before arriving at Berlin. The first was position 'A', about 35 miles west-north-west of the northern tip of the Frisian island of Texel. The formation took off at 08.49 hours and headed out over the North Sea in the usual open echelon-starboard formation, bound for point 'A'. The weather was turbulent with rain lashing down. The wind forecast at briefing was found to be correct at 190° true, and 31 minutes from leaving the English coast, position

DATE	SQDN	AIRCRAFT NUMBER	AIRCRAFT LETTER	CALL SICN	TARGET NO.	TARGET	CAMERA	CREW	TAKE OFF	S.C.	ETR	ACTUAL LANDING TIME	REMARKS
30/1/43	105	DZ.413	K	BU7		BERLIN	F.24 14"	S/L REYNOLDS / P/O SISMORE	0849	0851	1327	1325	
		DZ.372	C				F.24 14"	F/L GORDON / F/O HAYES	0849	0851	1327	1329	
		DZ.408	F				F.24 20"	F/O WICKHAM / P/O MAKIN	0849	0851	1327	1352	
	139	DZ.367	J	AR8		BERLIN	F.24 14"	S/L DARLING / F/O WRIGHT	1325	1327	1819	/	MISSING
		DK.337	N				F.24 14"	F/S McGEEHAN / F/O MORRIS	1325	1327	1819	1825	LANDED A COLTISHAL
		DZ.379	H				F.24 20"	SGT MASSEY / SGT FLETCHER	1325	1327	1819	1825	
	RESERVE	DZ.415	A										

The operations board in the Operations Room at RAF Marham, depicting the aircraft and crew status during the audacious daylight attacks on Berlin on 30 January 1943 carried out by 105 and 139 squadrons. (Via E.B. Sismore)

'A' was reached at 09.31 hours. The aircraft then altered course to another point, position 'B', located on the northern tip of the Zuider Zee causeway, about 13 miles west-north-west of Sneek, and north of the village of Makkum. The formation arrived over Eijerland on the northern tip of Texel at 09.36 hours, only about two miles south of track. From there they continued one mile to the starboard of Sneek, and flew towards the next point, position 'C', located about 16 miles south of Oldenburg and 2 miles west of Ahlhorn.

On the way, the crews had a little time to take in the surroundings and noticed the red and white sentry boxes as they crossed from the Netherlands into Germany. Church spires acted as good landmarks as they flew on over the cyclists and farmers ploughing their furrows in the fields. One horse took fright when the Mosquitos appeared overhead, overturned the plough and the worker followed. Another farmhand fell to his knees in fright with hands clasped over his hat. They flew on, avoiding flak posts by weaving around the towns until at 11.10 hours position 'C' arrived. Course was then altered for position 'D', to the north of the town of Nienburg on the river Weser. By 10.22 hours, they arrived at point 'D' to the north, nearer Drakenburg, in what by now was clearer weather. The formation then altered course and headed directly for Berlin, some 185 miles to the east. From point 'D', the Mosquitos began the climb at 1,500ft a minute, to the intended 25,000ft. The track to the southern edge of Berlin was set and the aircraft flew on with Hannover and the Steinhuder Meer visible to starboard. Cloud was met at 6,000ft, which didn't run out until they broke 13,500ft, when clear skies appeared again. On and on the Mosquitos flew, levelling out 77 miles away at 25,000ft and crossing the Elbe on the way. Continuous cloud obscured the way below and Ted Sismore remarked: 'It looked as if we would have to bomb on ETA, but a break appeared in the cloud just in time, revealing the lakes of Berlin clearly enough to define the target area [the lakes at Köpenick were ahead to

A clear view at 20,000ft from S/L Reynolds' Mosquito DZ413, GB:K, as they turn over the south-east area of Berlin near Köpenick on 30 January 1943, during the daring daylight operation to disrupt Commander-in-Chief of the Luftwaffe, Herman Wilhelm Göring's massed rally there at 11.00 hours. (Via E.B. Sismore)

starboard].' As the Mosquitos took careful evasive action, a steam train belching smoke was noticed first, but then the 'big city' came into view.

At exactly 11.00 hours, the bombs were let go in a long stick. Ted Sismore noted: 'The guns began to fire only after the bombs burst, so we had arrived undetected.' The formation photographed the activity and headed for the next way-point at position 'E', on the coast off Meldorf, at the Helgoländer Bucht. Sismore continued: 'Still, all seemed peaceful and quiet, no sign of fighters and then well below and behind us the black puffs of the shells from the heavy guns. We had turned and flown over the edge of the cloud before the bomb bursts could be seen, and now we had cleared the edge of the city before the guns had opened up. The three aircraft had split on the bombing run and now seemed to be alone in the sky. I could not imagine that they could have come to any harm in such a peaceful setting, but we still had the thought of fighters in our minds.' On course for the next position 'E' on the coast of Schleswig Holstein, Reynolds' crew spotted an aircraft below to starboard. A mad dive for the cloud base at 20,000ft revealed another Mosquito heading home. On they flew and dog-legged around Hamburg which they left about 7 miles to port causing no trouble, and so the formation climbed to fly through the tops of the broken cloud at 20,000ft.

At 11.46 hours, position 'E' was reached and they descended slowly to position 'F', in the North Sea, about 81 miles due north of the Dutch town of Dokkum. At 12.12 hours, and 15,000ft over position 'F', course was again altered to set a track for base. Ted Sismore concludes: 'Soon we were able to let down to sea level where we both felt much more at home. Once clear of the coast and back close to the water we knew that we had a good chance of reaching base successfully.' F/L Gordon was first to land in DZ372:C at 13.26 hours, followed by S/L Reynolds in DZ413:K, at 13.39 hours. Last home was F/O Wickham in DZ408:F at 13.52 hours, and he gave an account of the raid on BBC radio that night after the 9 o'clock news.

Sismore recalled that: 'After our return, we were able to listen to a recording of the broadcast, the announcement, an explosion, loud voices and then just martial music.' In their attack that afternoon, which was also successful, 139 Squadron lost a 105 Squadron Mosquito, DZ367:J, which was hit by flak and cost the lives of the pilot, S/L Donald Frederick William Darling DFC and his observer, F/O William Wright. Both were buried in Berlin's 1939–45 war cemetery.

The sounds of the bombs exploding during the morning raid were heard years later on a radio broadcast and were likened by the commentator to 'thunder' rumbling in the background. It was indeed 'Mosquito Thunder'!

The beginning of February saw little flying due to fog and snow. The crews relaxed and engaged in football and handball in the gym. An exception was F/L Bill Blessing, who travelled to London on the 4th, to make a BBC recording. On the 10th, W/C Edwards handed over command of the squadron to W/C Geoffrey P. Longfield. Edwards had been posted supernumerary to HQ Bomber Command before being posted to command RAF Binbrook on the 18th.

By now the principle of low-level and shallow-dive attacks had become well established with 105 Squadron usually engaged on the low-level work, backed up by 139 Squadron on the shallow-diving work. On the way to the target the combined formation of both squadrons would proceed at low level with the lead observer navigating for the entire formation. Time-delayed bombs, usually set at 11 seconds, were carried by the low-level boys. This meant that only about half a dozen or so aircraft would go in at low level for fear that the last in would meet the explosion of the leading aircraft's bombs. However, in order to maximize the number of aircraft that could attack, just before arriving at the target the follow-up formation of 'shallow-divers' would climb up to about 2,000ft. Then, when over the target, they peeled off and dived on to the target just as the 'low-levellers' were departing. The shallow-divers would then drop their instantaneously fused bombs, to explode on impact, by which time the diving aircraft had pulled away from the bomb release height of about 1,500ft and would head for a low-level route home. Exact timing was essential if the low-level bombers were not to be hit from above by the shallow-dive bomb-loads.

The next operation took place on Friday 12 February when four Mosquitos went to attack the railway marshalling yards at Rheine and railway workshops some 20 miles to the north at Lingen. By 16.27 hours, S/L Ralston was forming up his section of four in a new Mosquito,

No. 105 Squadron aircrews just before W/C Edwards handed over to W/C Longfield. Front row (left to right): S/L W. Blessing RAAF; F/L Syd Clayton; W/C Roy Ralston; W/C Longfield; W/C H.I. Edwards with dog Sallie; W/C R. Reynolds; F/L E.B. Sismore; Squadron M/O Dr Forbes. (Via H.C. 'Gary' Herbert/Pat Tennison)

DZ462:S, awaiting the arrival of the second section of four led by F/L Blessing in DZ458:J. The two sections closed up into formation and headed out at low level across the sea. The trip out was very turbulent as the formation hugged the wave-tops, and was lashed by heavy rain. Before making landfall, several Dutch trawlers were passed as the formation swept inland slightly off track as they arrived over Amsterdam without opposition. This was not to last long however. Soon four of the Mosquitos closed on Rheine, and anti-aircraft fire was flying at them from all angles; 40mm Bofors, 20mm Oerlikons and machine-guns blazed away at the marauding machines. All four Mosquitos attacked from 50–200ft. F/L Blessing suffered damage to his starboard wing and the Perspex canopy as he rushed in to drop his bombs into an engine shed which blew up, throwing up a large sheet of flame, following which a pall of black smoke covered the target. The others also dropped their bombs but could not see the results. W/O Herbert in DZ461:G noted, 'I got a good run at the engine sheds and released the bombs. I saw the leaders go into the target OK, and saw them go up – marvellous sight. The flak followed us for quite a long way before dying off. Then my observer [Sgt C. Jacques] got lost and we ended up smack over The Hague. It was dark by this time, and nothing opened up at us. Eventually, we got back to base and made a good landing.' The other section of four had also hit their targets at Lingen from 50–80ft. Brown columns of smoke and a dull red glow marked their presence, as well as a large sheet of flame belching from the northern shed. All aircraft headed home and landed safely, although F/L Blessing had a tyre burst on landing. W/O Herbert made an interesting discovery following his landing at 19.35 hours. He found that due to technical failure the bombs he thought had fallen over the target area had not, and were still sitting in the bomb bay. The next day, it was discovered that an oxygen bottle had broken loose during all the manoeuvres, and had fouled the bomb-release mechanism.

Continuing the relentless onslaught against enemy railway installations, Tours, about 100 miles to the east of Nantes, was next to receive the attention of the Marham-based Mosquitos. First, on the 14th, 139 Squadron's W/C Shand led an attack, severely damaging the locomotive repair facilities, despite atrocious weather which hampered the crews. The next day it was the turn of 105 Squadron to add to the damage, as S/L Reggie Reynolds led a full squadron effort of twelve aircraft. A low-level and shallow-dive attack was attempted. On reaching the River Loire, Bill Blessing took the shallow-dive formation up to 3,000ft and the others carried on at low level. The low-level formation attacked at 50ft. At 18.14 hours, flashes were seen in the target area but photographs later showed that the wrong target had been hit. The bursts had been on the goods depot and signal box instead of the engine repair shops. Huge blue sparks were observed from electrical flash-overs as the bombs struck. However, the 'shallow-divers' were more accurate.

Gary Herbert recorded: 'We were in no. 2 position. Everything went according to plan and as no flak came up we got a perfect run-up. I dropped in a salvo from 500ft, climbed, looked and saw my bombs burst on the corner of the building and other bombs burst all round the target. We dived over it again at low level, and saw that the roof was off about one quarter of the building, and the place was generally in a shambles.' All aircraft returned safely. A reconnaissance flight the next day by a 139 Squadron crew, F/L Mike Wayman with F/O G.S. 'Pops' Clear in Mosquito DZ465:E, made five runs at 4,000ft over the target area. The repair shops were clearly seen to have been severely damaged at the western end and most of the roof of the round-house was missing.

The weather worsened, and on Thursday 18 February 1943, W/C Longfield attempted his inaugural operation with 105, leading five aircraft on an attack on Liège. Severe frontal conditions resulted in the formation abandoning the task in nil visibility and 10/10ths cloud about 12 miles south-west of Gent. However, that same day, 13 Mosquitos from 139 Squadron, accompanied by 7 from 105 Squadron, headed back to Tours once again. In W/C Wooldridge's *Low Attack*, P/O W.E.G. 'Bill' Humphrey described the attack:

The whole force [20 aircraft] was led by Wing Commander Shand, with Reynolds and Blessing leading the two subsidiary sections. All aircraft but two bombed their primary targets. After forming up over the aerodrome, the formation flew down to the south coast [at Selsey Bill] at 1,000ft. Then it dived to 50ft for the sea crossing, and from the back I saw the marvellous sight of all our Mosquitos in echelon-starboard, skimming just over the wave-tops with their tails sticking defiantly up in the air. Over the French coast, we went in fine style, with only one machine-gun squirting at us as opposition, and then it looked as if the worst would happen. The cloud base came right down, first to 300ft, then to 100ft, and then on to the deck. It stayed like that for almost ten minutes but luck was with us. When we again emerged into brilliant sunshine the formation was still almost intact, with only two aircraft having lost themselves, and we were able to carry on, although the Wing Commander was a little surprised at finding himself back on the formation instead of leading it. He quickly took over the lead again.

Farther south we shot over three flak towers, where the German gunners were caught napping and just gaped at us in bewilderment. Then the River Loire loomed up ahead. Up climbed W/C Shand and his [seven accompanying] shallow-divers to attack the round-house in the centre of the town. Up [to 2,000ft], also, went F/L Blessing with a second section [of five accompanying aircraft] to attack the eastern round-house. Away to the left, low down on the river, went S/L Reynolds with the [five accompanying] low-level boys, making no mistake this time about hitting the repair shops. All three formations hit their respective targets well and truly, not a bomb being wasted. There seemed to be Mosquitos everywhere, and we shook up Tours thoroughly. Then, round to the north and a good fast trip back to England.

Unfortunately, one aircraft from 139 Squadron in F/L Blessing's section failed to return. F/Sgt Frederick Alfred Budden with Sgt Frank Morris in DZ420, XD:F, crashed north-west of Tours at Vengeons, about 8km south-south-west of Vire in France. Both airmen lie in Vengeons churchyard. Bill Humphrey concluded: 'For the price of that aircraft and its crew, Tours, for the time being at any rate, was put out of action as an important railway depot.'

There were no more attacks for a few days and this allowed time for a visit on Sunday 21st, by Sir Archibald Sinclair, who was able to meet the crews in person to congratulate them. The next few days were given to formation flying and low-level bombing practice, led by W/C G.P. Longfield in DZ365:V which had 'belonged' to his predecessor W/C Edwards. W/O Herbert noted in his diary on 21 February that the new Wing Commander had 'a bad habit of turning in towards the formation. As others turn away from him they lose sight of him and scatter a lot. It is a dangerous habit and leads to collisions.' These turned out to be very prophetic words, as we shall see.

On Friday 26 February, W/C Longfield with his observer F/L Millns led a formation of 20 Mosquitos in DZ365:V, to attack the naval stores depot at Rennes. The low-level section of ten 105 Squadron Mosquitos was split into two groups of armament. The leader in 'V' and another four aircraft, 'K', 'B', 'F' and 'P' were each armed with two 500lb GP TD (½-hour) and two 500lb GP TD (2-hour) bombs. The other five, 'Z', 'G', 'O', 'E' and 'Q', were each armed with four 500lb MC TD (11-second) bombs. It was to be a combined operation with 139 Squadron, who fielded 10 of the formation as 'shallow-divers', each armed with four 500lb MC TD (.025 second) instantaneous bombs. Just before 17.00 hours, the briefing was complete and the crews of both squadrons were jostling their machines, ready to ascend into the Norfolk skies to set course for France once more. As usual, the plan was that before reaching the target, the 105 Squadron formation was to continue at low level and plant their delayed-action bombs, followed by 139 Squadron who would rise up and further add to the damage by plastering the stores with instantaneously exploding bombs. Unfortunately, this was not to be the way things turned out.

On the way to the target all was quiet, as the 20 machines purred their way above the wave-tops. Eventually, landfall came and went and 139 Squadron reached the target first with no opposition; they had caught the defenders napping! Up they went to commence their shallow dives and the onslaught began. But where were 105 Squadron? W/O Gary Herbert was in the 105 formation and describes what happened: 'Our leader's observer got lost on the final run-up to the target and brought us to an aerodrome about 6 miles south of the target. They sent up a hail of light flak as we turned towards the target and then the leader, who had turned too much to the left, suddenly turned right again and collided with F/O Kimmel, a Yank [actually RCAF] who was formating on him [at 18.43 hours in Mosquito DZ413:K. The location was recorded as west of Rennes St Jacques at 48°06'N; 02°13'W]. Kim's airscrew chopped the leader's tail off just behind the wing. He went into a loop and dived straight into the deck. It wasn't a very nice sight. Kim lost height and disappeared below the trees at about 300 mph.' His aircraft was last seen losing height with a glycol leak from his starboard engine. W/O Herbert chillingly summed up the situation as he saw it: 'Four good men killed by a leader's inexperience.'

The remainder of the 105 formation carried on towards the stores depot. As they did so the bombs from the shallow-divers were beginning to explode. The low-levellers mostly pulled up to about 800ft before dropping the bombs to avoid the blasts the best they could, and bombs were dropped on the target when possible. F/L Bill Blessing took DZ489:B into the target area. On departure, he saw a 200ft pall of smoke rising from the area, as did F/O Wickham in DZ408:F. Experience told S/L Ralston to choose an alternative target and having climbed to 1,000ft, he threw DZ467:P at the marshalling yards and dropped his bombs. P/O L.T. Weston, a veteran who survived the Malta detachment also knew how dangerous the situation had become and decided to attack the double railway track at Vire from 50ft on the way home. P/O O.W. Thompson in DZ472:Z actually took his aircraft in for a second run and placed his bombs effectively on the target. Meanwhile, W/O Herbert was making decisions of his own in DZ461:G, as he recalls: 'By the time we reached the target, I could see the dive-bombers already starting their dive. We would have been blown up by their bombs if we had gone in. So I turned violently to the west, climbed to about 700ft, and dived below the other formation. I got my bombs on the target. "Mac" McCormick [P/O G.W. McCormick with Sgt P.E. Cadman in DK338:O], a young Aussie, only on his fourth [operation], didn't see the dive bombers till it was too late, and went in at low level [50ft!]. God knows how he got through, because photographs showed him right in the middle of the bursts. He came back with his radiators full of flock from bombed bedding stores. He used up a lot of luck that day!'

P/O F.M. 'Bud' Fisher, the American from Pennsylvania, USA, and his observer, F/O R.L. Reily decided that it was not possible to put their bombs on the target, and headed for home in DZ416:Q, leaving the smoke behind visible for the next 20 miles. On the way home, he jettisoned two of his 500-pounders in the sea, about 28 miles north-west of Le Havre, before landing, not at RAF Marham but about 30 miles away at RAF East Wretham, 4 miles north-north-east of Thetford in Norfolk.

Sadly, 139 Squadron had also lost a crew. On the way home, Lt T.D.C. Moe and his observer 2/Lt O. Smedsaas, both of the RNAF, who were last seen 60 miles from the target area, were killed when their Mosquito DZ481, XD:L crashed. As for the 105 Squadron crews, F/O Spencer Griffith Kimmel RCAF was laid to rest at Bretteville-sur-Laize Canadian war cemetery, about 16km south of Caen. His observer, F/O Harry Nettleton Kirkland, W/C Geoffrey Phelps Longfield and F/L Ralph Frederick Millns were buried in the Rennes Eastern Communal cemetery.

Yet another unfortunate incident took place the next day. F/O McCormick, who had 'used up a lot of luck' on the Rennes operation, was killed with a visiting Wing Commander, John William Deacon, formerly of the Worcestershire Regiment, of Army Co-operation Command, whom he had taken on a non-operational local high-level reconnaissance sortie to 30,000ft. The aircraft used by P/O Thompson the day before, DZ472:Z, suffered structural failure of a wing root and was last seen spinning out of control with smoke trailing from it as it dived into the ground a mile to the south-east of the aerodrome near Beachamwell, at Brick Kiln Wood. F/O McCormick was laid to rest in Marham village cemetery, where many other young airmen were also to find final peace. W/C Deacon was buried in Brookwood military cemetery.

The last attack of February was on the 28th, on the John Cockerill Steel works at Liège, Belgium, where Roy Ralston led six Mosquitos to bomb between 200 and 800ft. No aircraft were lost despite some light and heavy flak that flew up at the aircraft as they headed for home over the coast. Finally, on the same day, P/O Thompson paid the Stork diesel factory at Hengelo a visit. He led a formation of four Mosquitos, all arriving back safely at base some 3 hours later, having set out at 17.02 hours.

March started off quietly, with a visit to the station by Lord Trenchard, Marshal of the RAF, on Monday 1st. Gary Herbert wrote in his diary his general impression of the visit, commenting that 'he told us what good blokes we were'.

Standing against the fuselage of a 105 Squadron Mosquito are (left to right): Unknown; Danny Cooper; Cpl Bob Woodhouse and George Thornley. (Via Cliff Streeter)

Life at RAF Marham also had its lighter moments, and apart from keeping the Mosquitos up to scratch operationally, the groundcrew often made their own entertainment. Senior NCO of the Electrical Section, Bob Woodhouse, recalled: 'The Electrical Section had a dance band known as The Gremlins. If anybody was missing from the section, it was either rehearsal or a late night out.' Cliff Streeter also remembers: 'For relaxation we got together a small band, with George Thornley on accordion, myself on drums, plus others on guitar and trumpet. We went to play at various dances. Most of the place-names escape me, but I do remember playing at a USAAF dance somewhere and also a Canadian base where the Base Commander joined us, playing saxophone. I recall too, a civilian police dance at Swaffham. Indeed, our regular date was the village hall at Swaffham when we were free on a Friday night. It was usually a full house.' Woodhouse concluded: 'That damned band was a pain in the neck to me, although I was proud of them, especially when they put on a show at the Theatre Royal in Norwich!'

The aircrew also had some relaxation as Frank Templeton, P/O Hugh McCready's observer, recalls: 'We had fairly frequent ENSA shows at Marham, which were usually quite good, and helped pass the time in addition to a station cinema. We also had Norwich fairly close by which could be reached by public transport, or on occasions by station transport. The sergeants' and officers' messes each had quite good and well stocked bars, although I was not a great drinker.'

It was not long before ops began again, and on 4 March S/L Reynolds led an attack by six Mosquitos at low level from 50–200ft, on engine sheds and repair workshops at Le Mans. The target was plastered with bombs leaving the round-house smashed up as well as damaging the engine sheds. The weather held ops up for the next few days, until Reynolds was again airborne on the 8th, this time with three aircraft to carry out a very successful 'shallow-dive' attack on railway repair shops at Tergnier, 12 miles south of St Quentin in France. The same day, F/L Gordon led another two Mosquitos to attack the railway shops at Lingen, Germany. The low-level attack was successfully carried out with slight flak experienced over the target and over the coast on the way out. In the lead was F/L Gordon with F/O Ralph Hayes who took DZ518:A in at 100ft, leaving a column of dark smoke and flames shooting 200ft up into the air. P/O W.E.G. Humphrey and his observer Sgt Moore attacked in DZ379:H, and noticed that some of F/L Gordon's bombs had also hit home on some trucks. There was one casualty on the operation. Sgt W.W. Austin with his observer, P/O P.E. Thomas, were last seen leaving the target area in DZ460:W, apparently under control and in formation. However, the Mosquito was flak-damaged and crashed on the return trip at Den Ham, 27km east of Zwolle in Holland. Both airmen were taken as PoWs. The other aircraft returned safely.

Le Mans was again the centre of attention on the 9th. A combined 105 and 139 Squadron formation left RAF Marham at 17.14 hours ready for the usual dusk low-level and shallow-dive combination, to be aimed this time at the Renault works. Roy Ralston was in the lead in DZ489:B, accompanied by his expert navigator, Syd Clayton. He, and Ted Sismore, were considered by most to be the best in the squadron at navigation. Six low-level aircraft from 105 Squadron took part, accompanied by ten from 139. S/L Bob Bagguley in DZ469, XD-J, led the latter. Bagguley had transferred from 105 Squadron on 15 June 1942, as a newly promoted flight lieutenant. His observer, F/L C.K. Hayden, had transferred with him. The operation was highly successful. As 105 raced across the factory their bombs fell from the bomb bays from 100ft. One aircraft had a near miss; P/O L.T. Weston felt a concussion blast hit DZ461:G as one of the bombs detonated nearby. The Mosquito shook violently, but continued to fly. Now it was time to shut the bomb doors and get back to base. Not so for the 139 Squadron aircraft however, as the shallow-divers were met with a hail of flak, stirred up by S/L Ralston's boys. They survived, despite F/O J.H. Brown's aircraft DZ516, XD:O, being hit severely. He survived but sustained damage to the trim, rudder, and the wireless set. The hydraulics were also u/s and he had to crash-land back at base, which he did successfully. However, there was one final tragedy, as S/L Robert Beck Bagguley DFC and F/L Charles Kenneth Hayden DFC failed to return. They were lost without trace, and are remembered on the Runnymede Memorial.

The John Cockerill steel and armament works at Liège was next for punishment on the 12th, as S/L Reggie Reynolds, and P/O Ted Sismore led a combined 105/139 squadrons formation in DZ413:K. Six aircraft contributed from each squadron. S/L J.V. Berggren led the shallow-dive section. In W/C Wooldridge's *Low Attack*, F/O R.B. Smith (the Australian from New South Wales, who flew with Sgt P.E. Cadman in DZ467:P) gave this account of the operation:

We found at briefing that the target for our first op was to be the steelworks at Liège. Briefing lasted two and a half hours, and we were told about every possible detail concerning the target. When we were airborne we completed two circuits of the aerodrome, to let the whole formation pack up tight, and then we set course at nought feet across the hangars. We both noticed a lot of familiar landmarks over this country before we reached the English coast. The light was extremely good, and although this was to be a dusk attack, there was no sign of it deteriorating.

Flying low over the dead calm sea, we settled into a formation. It was slightly hazy over the water, and it would have been too easy to fly straight into the sea, as it was most difficult to judge our height right down on the wave-tops. The enemy coast came up rather quickly.

We increased speed and packed in almost to line abreast. I had a strange feeling inside me as we drew nearer. Then there were a few puffs of black smoke near the leader. This was the first flak I had ever seen. No one was hit, however. We were too fast for them.

We crossed the coast in a flash very low down. I nearly hit a large hotel on the front in my excitement. The landfall was dead accurate thanks to Sis, our leading observer. Once inside the coast we flew at tree-top height, making use of hills and slight rises for cover. It was terrifically exhilarating – just like a steeplechase. Every now and then we shot over farmers and their families working in the fields. We could tell they liked the look of us because they raised their arms in a 'V' and the kids waved excitedly. As we got nearer to our target we again tightened up our formation. We were now flying over very hilly country, full of deep ravines, at the bottom of which were picturesque villages with occasional large villages dotted about. When we were within a minute or so of our target I could see no sign of Liège and the light was steadily failing. I thought maybe we had missed it, when suddenly we passed over the brow of a fairly steep hill and there below us lay the town, with our target easily discernible close to the River Meuse.

We were so intent on looking for the target that we had forgotten about flak and fighters. Then somebody suddenly yelled 'snappers', over the intercom. We both found this very spine-chilling, and frantically searched the sky. We couldn't see any sign of fighters anywhere, and when we got back we found out that they had turned out to be specks of dirt on someone's windscreen.

By the time the flap was over we had started our run-up on to the target (we were in the low-level section). The bombing run was perfect. Squadron Leader Reynolds took us across in such a way that each of us could line up on our own particular section of the works. The target came up at such a speed that it was all over in a matter of seconds. Just before my building came up under the nose of my machine I pressed the bomb release, and as I did so I saw Sergeant K.H.N. Ellis's bombs just in front of me go slap through the roof. Then I shut my bomb doors and told Cadman to make sure that the camera was working.

Immediately after bombing, the formation split up and we set course for home. Shortly afterwards we passed very close to an aerodrome and saw four Focke-Wulf 190s going in to land with their wheels down. They were clearly silhouetted against the sunset. We swung sharply behind them and they did not see us – but the ground gunners did, and they put up a display of red tracer, which was not appreciated by us or the 190s. Crossing the enemy coast on the way out we got another bucketful of flak and shortly afterwards still more from a flakship. When we were at a safe distance from the coast we climbed as it was getting too dark to tell which was sky and which was sea. On landing we found only one hole in the tail. The raid was a great success, thanks to Squadron Leader Reynolds and Sis, who led our formation.

The result of the attack, in which 9.8 tons of bombs were dropped, was that numerous bursts were observed in the marine machine sheds in the centre of the works, and a huge flash was observed in the area of another engine shed. A two-storey building was left in flames and hits were also scored on the foundries and the power station. The raid had however cost the lives of a 139 Squadron crew. Sgt Robert McMurray Pace and P/O George Cook in DZ373, XD:B failed to return, having been hit by flak and crashed into the Ooster Schelde off Woensdrecht, on the return journey over the Netherlands. Pace and Cook are also commemorated on the Runnymede Memorial.

Engine sheds at Paderborn were next on the agenda. On the 16th, as usual, it was a combined operation with the sister squadron, 139, although this time it was led by their S/L Berggren.

W/O Gary Herbert recalled the operation, during which a total of 10.7 tons of high explosive were to be dropped from the 12 attacking aircraft: 'We went in low level. I was leading the second three and 139 Squadron went in right on our tails. It was quite a routine trip with quite a bit of flak over the target, and several kites were hit. None got us and we came out normally. We weren't fired at, at the coast, but we could see the guns a few miles to the north at Terschelling plastering somebody. Several kites came back on one engine. My own bombs were seen by the diving leader to lift the roof off the repair sheds, which collapsed completely. Photos confirmed this. It was a good trip and my eighth on Mossies.' Nevertheless, the raid again cost the lives of one 139 Squadron crew, as F/Sgt Peter John Dixon McGeehan DFM and F/O Reginald Charles Morris DFC failed to return in DZ497, XD:Q. Both airmen were laid to rest in Texel (Den Burg) cemetery in the Netherlands.

CHAPTER 13

New Leader

With effect from 10 March 1943, 25-year-old Acting W/C John 'Jack' de Lacy Wooldridge DFC*, DFM, AE, RAFVR was given command of 105 Squadron. He arrived on the 17th, having been sent from a signals depot, to which he was detached following a posting from Bomber Command HQ, where he had spent just over 3½ months actively engaged on attachment to the tri-Service PWD. Here he had worked on a fog dispersal system known as FIDO, of which we shall hear more later. He brought with him the nickname of 'Dim', but was in fact very much the contrary. Apart from having completed 73 operations on bombers, he was also a highly talented composer of music and an academic. However, it was time for Wooldridge to get operational again, and having persuaded Harris of this in person, it was not long before he would get his chance.

Meanwhile on the 20th, attacks continued on engine sheds. Gary Herbert recalls: 'Six of us went out on a low-level attack, to flatten the engine sheds and repair shops at Louvain in Belgium. Visibility was very poor and the leader [Reggie Reynolds in DZ492:K] led us in a couple of hundred yards north of our target. The outside men got on to the target OK, but the

W/C John de Lacy Wooldridge, sitting at the desk in his ground 'office' with awards lists, squadron crest and portrait of his actress wife Margaretta on the wall behind him. (Via E.B. Sismore)

leader and I bombed the railway yards. One of my bombs hung up, so I went round again and bombed the proper target. Then I went and had a look at the part of the target the other boys went for. There were fires burning in the yards and, in the middle of the bomb craters, was a Jerry squirting away at us with a cannon. We jinked and got away OK, and arrived back at base without further incident.'

The raid was followed by an assault on the St Joseph locomotive works at Nantes on the 23rd. W/C Peter Shand DFC, CO of 139 Squadron, led the raid. The five 105 Squadron, low-levellers followed F/L Bill Blessing who led the second section. Exhaust stubs coughed out blue smoke as the Mosquito engines came to life. The take-off was 13.50 hours for the ten 139 Squadron crews, and 105 Squadron followed nine minutes later. Not all the aircraft got off though, as DZ461:G had problems. Gary Herbert explains:

We developed a bad swing while doing about 100 mph on take-off. It became uncontrollable. The undercart collapsed and tore the wheels and legs off. The engine also caught fire but it was extinguished OK. We grabbed a reserve kite [139 Squadron's DZ465, XD:E] and chased the formation. We were a minute behind when we reached the coast and so had to turn back. The station photographic sergeant, 'Daddy' Knowles, was filming the take-off that day for publicity purposes. He was a friend of mine, and when he saw me prang, he left the camera running on its tripod and raced towards the aircraft in full view of the camera. Then the penny dropped! He realized there were 2,000lb of bombs on board and thought (wrongly) that they might explode. His reversal and speed back to the camera would surely have created a new Olympic record and his facial expression, as caught by the camera, could have been used as a classic example by any horror film producer. I later heard the comment that I was very brave to grab another kite and chase after the squadron after such a bad prang – not so! I was merely putting as much distance as possible between myself and the CO until he cooled down.

Meanwhile, the remainder of the formation flew on into worsening weather, which slowly improved as the Channel was crossed at Selsey Bill. Then, after landfall, the next half-hour was spent following the undulating French terrain, before meeting the River Loire. The sun was beginning to shine as the shallow-dive section began their ascent to commence the dive once the low-levellers were through. The 105 Squadron formation arrived at Nantes and proceeded to throw everything they had at the locomotive works, from 100ft. Then the shallow-divers added insult to injury from 50 to 1,200ft. Explosions were seen from every part of the works. Buildings disintegrated, leaving columns of black smoke billowing upwards. On the way home, enemy fighters had been seen circling St Nazaire, but all the Mosquitos made it back, the last landing at 19.00 hours.

The next operation was on 24 March, when three crews were given rail targets, the idea being that they should execute shallow-dive attacks. Reynolds and Sismore took DZ492:K (logged by P/O Sismore as DZ489:B) to attack the railway in Germany's Paderborn area on the line from Soest to Altenbeken with one 500lb MC TD (11-second) and three 500lb MC TD (.025 second) instantaneous bombs. They fell foul of ack-ack fire going in and the bomb doors would only open half-way. Consequently, they had to return and land 'bombs on' after three hours and five minutes, one hour and thirty minutes of which was flown in the dark. When they eventually arrived back at base, they had no hydraulics and the port engine had partially packed up. However, with skilful handling Reynolds managed to put the Mosquito down safely. The second aircraft away was tasked with finding rolling stock between Osnabrück and Bremen on the section of line from the Mittellandkanal to Bassum. P/O W.E.G. Humphrey, with Sgt E. Moore in DZ408:F, found two trains on this line and although the first two bombs from his dive

Wreckage of W/O H.C. Herbert and Sgt C. Jacques' Mosquito B.IV, DZ461, 'G'-George on take-off, bound for the St Joseph locomotive works at Nantes, France, on 23 March 1943. Both escaped unhurt and continued in another Mosquito. (Via Gary Herbert)

attack missed the first train, they demolished a section of track. The last two bombs stopped the other train, before the marauding crew returned to base. Herbert gives the following insight into *his* attack in DZ302:D: 'I had the line between Hamm and Bielefeld; a four-line track. We got a bit of light flak on the way in at the coast, and also east of Osnabrück, but we weren't hit. When I reached the line, I found plenty of trains and stooged up and down it, dropping one bomb at a time. We stopped two trains – I don't know whether they were derailed or not – and blew about half a dozen trucks of another off the line and down the embankment. We carried a vertical camera and also a ciné-camera in the nose. Six runs were made altogether and then we went down to the deck to get photos with the ciné. On the way back, we passed over a small village [Lathen] and all hell broke loose. Tracer came from all directions. I slammed everything wide open and jinked all over the sky, but they were good gunners and hit us with plenty cannon shells. They tore a hole a foot across in my port engine fairing. The starboard engine began vibrating badly, and so I shut it down. I tried it again later and it was OK. At the coast, again, small cannon and Bofors fire gave us a hot reception and we had to jink plenty to dodge being hit again. When we got back to base, we found that S/L Reynolds had done a belly-landing on the flare path and so I had to land at [RAF] Swanton Morley and came back to base by car. Groupie was pleased with our effort. Our vertical photographs were under-exposed and didn't come out.' The ciné film was sent away for processing, but unfortunately the low-level part over the trains failed to materialize, as the film had run out! However, for this action both crew were decorated. W/O Herbert received a DFC and Sgt Jacques a DFM.

Due to cloud base being down to ground level at the enemy coast, an abortive attempt was made on the 27th to go back to the marshalling yards at Liège. However, the month was not over yet, as one last operation was tackled the next day, and a costly one it was to be. Once more the weather precluded a further attempt on the marshalling yards. The light was very bad due to rainstorm clouds and visibility was down to half a mile. Nevertheless, F/L Gordon managed instead to lead a formation of seven in Mosquito DZ536:Z to bomb a factory north of Valbengit Bridge at Liège. The factory was duly attacked, however when the dreaded 'Butcher Birds' were encountered, the last two aircraft in the formation peeled off to starboard and 'failed to return'. F/O Jimmy George Bruce DFM, and his observer, F/O Richard 'Dick' Louis Reily, were last seen at 18.40 hours, about 18 miles east of Etaples. The aircraft in which they were flying, DZ416:Q, was being pursued by a FW 190 fighter. DZ522:W was also pursued at close range by two fighters and Sgt George Kenneth Leighton and his observer, Sgt Thomas Noel Chadwick, also perished. Lille Southern cemetery became the resting-place of all four airmen. So ended the month of March.

April began in a most auspicious manner. An attack on the 1st, the twenty-fifth anniversary of the RAF's formation, was launched by S/L Roy Ralston DSO, DFM and five other crews on the railway workshops at Trier. They were accompanied by a second wave of 139 Squadron Mosquitos led by S/L Berggren, who was briefed to attack the marshalling yards at Ehrang, a few miles further on to the north-east. It is interesting to note that they were the only two squadrons operating in the whole of Bomber Command that day.

It was to be a cloud-cover operation and for Ralston's expert observer, F/L Syd Clayton DFC, DFM, a most memorable one, as it was his hundredth operation. As leader, they set off in DZ462:S at 14.26 hours, and having departed the coast at Beachy Head, his formation settled down to sea level for the long haul to the target. The cloud base was at 3,000ft and the weather was very pleasant, which did not augur well for a cloud-cover attack. However, on arrival at the French coast, as forecast, the weather was to deteriorate. Some flak over the coast claimed a 139 Squadron machine and F/O R.A.V. Crampton had to return to base, where he successfully belly-landed his stricken Mosquito, DZ428, XD:K. Meanwhile, the formation charged on. Landfall was made in a downpour, with only 400 yards' visibility at first, decreasing by 200 yards at times. It was not until they reached a point 10 miles to the west of Luxembourg that the weather began to improve and the horizon stretched to about 10 miles. On and on the formation flew, south of Luxembourg and thereafter, over the German border. Soon the town of Trier identified itself by its smoky appearance. The Mosquitos prepared for the attack, as their flight path undulated among the hills. They made a northerly run up the Mosel (Moselle) Valley, and there lay Trier. Bomb doors on all 105 Squadron machines opened and soon twenty-five 500-pounders were falling with great accuracy on their target. No. 139 Squadron's crews kept on going to hunt out their quarry at Ehrang, some 10 miles further along the track. There they dropped 3.6 tons of bombs, leaving a rectangular building in the south-east corner of the yard damaged, and causing a huge explosion and flash from a coal container. Large explosions also demolished the coaches of two trains.

Back at Trier, large amounts of smoke rose up as a total of 5.4 tons of bombs detonated. The power station received its share as the middle of the railway workshops erupted in a sheet of flame, and debris was blown high into the air. Often, after an attack it was every man for himself, as the crews scattered to get back home by the most advantageous route possible. However, on this occasion formation was held as the Mosquitos sped for home. Fifty miles before the enemy coast, the weather cleared up. Consequently, the formation rose up off the deck to meet the cloud base, which was by now at about 4,000ft. While ascending to the relative safety of the clouds, flak rose up from the enemy aerodrome at Merville. Fortunately, it was a desultory attempt and the Mosquitos carried on through the cloud, before descending over the Channel for landfall back on the English coast. All of 105's crews arrived safely back at RAF Marham in the late afternoon, followed half an hour later by 139 Squadron. F/O Syd Clayton had survived his century after all, and apart from great celebrations in the mess that night in his honour, an official reward was to come in the form of a DSO. He subsequently left the squadron for training as a pilot and was ultimately to survive the war.

Two days later, on 3 April, W/C Wooldridge got his chance to lead his first 105 operation on the locomotive repair shops at Malines. It was dusk when he made the first run with his observer, W/O K.J. Gordon in DZ462:S, although he did not drop his bombs on the first pass. Next in was F/Sgt J. Little with Sgt A.E. Kitchen in DK521:V. Their bombs detonated successfully and left a 200ft pall of smoke, noticed by the Wing Commander during his second run at the target, when he also let go of his bomb-load. Somewhat unfortunately however, the primary target was missed and a brickworks had been bombed instead. Nevertheless, both aircraft returned safely. S/L R. Reynolds and P/O R. Massie attacked Namur's engine sheds and also returned home safely.

That same day, 105 and 139 Squadrons each lost four complete crews and aircraft to form the new 618 Squadron, based at RAF Skitten near Caithness, in bonny Scotland. They were to become a 'Highball' squadron, carrying a bomb similar to that used by 617 Squadron during the 'Dambuster' raids. Laurence Templeton, F/O McCready's sergeant observer at the time recalls: 'After a number of unspectacular operations with 139 Squadron, we and a number of other crews transferred to 105 Squadron, which had become very short of crews, owing to losses or completions of tours of operations. Shortly after this, at which time we had only flown two or three ops with 105, we and some other crews were taken up by 618 Special Duties Squadron to be trained, incidentally, to sink the battleship *Tirpitz*. In those days the Royal Navy was primarily responsible for the destruction of enemy naval targets. We were all set to take off from the Shetlands when we were stopped without explanation. We later heard that the Royal Navy had used their own special weapon [the midget submarine].' The RAF eventually sank the *Tirpitz* in Norway's Tromsö Fjord on 12 November 1944. Following the postings, several replacement 105 Squadron crews were received from 1655 MTU.

On the 6th, more low-level attacks were made on the railway workshops at Namur, Belgium. The raid was led by F/L Bill Blessing with Sgt A.J.W. Heggie in DZ483:R. The six 105 Squadron aircraft, accompanied by two from 139 Squadron, left engine sheds billowing black smoke up to 200ft in the air, and the marshalling yards received similar treatment. It had been a dusk attack and all aircraft arrived back safely. Two days later, as S/L Reynolds went to Stoke Orchard for a day's ATC liaison, his observer P/O Sismore amused himself with a flight in a captured Heinkel He111 bomber, in which he flew for twenty minutes. The next day, Elsdorf steelworks was attacked as well as a factory in the Eschweiller area.

On the 9th, a well-known face returned to RAF Marham. F/L Charles Patterson had returned for special photographic duties with observer F/L Jimmy Hill, with whom he had photographed the Eindhoven raid. Patterson had joined 8 Group's 109 (PFF) Squadron and had found it much to his disliking as, in his opinion: 'The whole attitude of everyone there was simply antipathetic to my outlook because they regarded themselves as the elite of the Air Force. None of them had done any ops anything like as dangerous, as daring or comprehensive as we'd been doing in 2 Group.' Subsequently, he had joined up with the RAF 140 Wing film unit having chosen his own personal Mosquito DZ414:E (later re-coded 'O' for Orange), which was to be his camera aircraft for the duration. Filming at high level at night proved fruitless, and so F/L Patterson found himself back with his film unit Mosquito as a pilot at station headquarters, RAF Marham, attached to 105 Squadron for low-level operations once more. The major disadvantage, in F/L Patterson's eyes, was that flying with the film unit meant always being near the back of a formation in order to be able to capture the action on camera. This is where the novices normally were placed, and tail-end Charlie often 'bought it' before the others. Furthermore, as

A dusk low-level attack on the engine sheds at Namur, Belgium, on 3 April 1943. P/O R. Massie and Sgt G. Lister's Mosquito DZ519, GB:U runs low (top left) over the sheds with its bomb doors open and bombs falling, illuminated by the flash of exploding bombs from S/L Reynolds' Mosquito DZ458, GB:J in front, from which the photograph was taken. (Via E.B. Sismore)

F/L Patterson was not officially part of 105 Squadron but on detachment to it, squadron promotions were not available. This would mean that he often had to follow a very much less experienced but higher ranking leader than he, which led to some considerable personal frustration, the apparent unfairness of which was a cross he had to bear.

The next operation was to the familiar Dutch target of Hengelo. On 11 April, four aircraft left RAF Marham at 19.10 hours for a low-level dusk attack. The leader was recently promoted S/L

Bill Blessing in DZ379:H, followed by F/O Bud Fisher in DK377:N, F/O N.S.B. Hull in DZ462:S and F/O Polgase in DZ536:Z.

The formation set out across the sea at 50ft for the journey to the target. About 20.37 hours, they were heading on a south-easterly course over the Vechte river, about 5 miles south-east of Nordhorn, ready to cross from Germany into Holland for the attack on Hengelo, lying some 18 miles to the south-west. The visibility was about 3 to 6 miles as the Mosquitos raced along under broken cloud some 3,000–4,000ft above them. Daylight was failing, when two formations of FW 190 fighters began to sneak up on them. When first noticed by F/O Hull, one enemy formation was flying in line-astern 500 yards behind but slightly to the starboard, and 450ft above the Mosquitos. The other was 800 yards behind at 5,000ft to port when F/O Fisher saw them. He immediately hauled his machine to starboard. The fighters fired a 2-second burst and then also turned to starboard to attack the two Mosquitos behind. Canadian F/O Norman Hull suffered an attack from the fighters from the starboard, and received fire from them at a range of 350 yards, which lasted for about 15 seconds as tracer flashed all around the Mosquito. Frantically, he turned into the attack, weaving, climbing and diving in a desperate life-or-death struggle, which rose and fell from 50 to 200ft. During this onslaught, one fighter wheeled round and went for 'Z' for Zebra, which was attacked at 20.36 hours, while still flying at 50ft. F/O David Polgase RNZAF and his observer Sgt Leslie C. Lampen, were now in a desperate predicament. The final blow came at 20.38 hours from Unteroffizier Wiegand of 2./JG1 [2nd Flight of the 1st Day Fighter Wing], who shot the Mosquito down at Metelerkamps Bauernhof 4, at Bentheim. Sgt Philip H. Brown, F/O Hull's observer, remembers the incident; 'They attacked from the starboard side and appeared to concentrate on the two end aircraft of our formation, of which we were one. F/O Polgase was the last and took the full force of the enemy fire. We saw his aircraft crash and explode. In the confusion, we lost sight of the other two aircraft and headed back to base. We escaped with a bit of luck, and a very good aircraft!' The two airmen were laid to rest three days later at Lingen, and now rest in the Reichswald Forest war cemetery. Of the others, the leader actually managed to attack the target, F/O Fisher bombed a train and F/O Hull brought his bombs back home.

By now the Bomber Command Battle of the Ruhr that began on 5/6 March was in full swing. In support of this, on 14 April, 105 Squadron was called upon to commence nuisance raids to Bremen, Hamburg and Wilhelmshaven. This was to be the beginning of what the Light Night Striking Force would continue in the future. The raids on each target were to be by pairs of Mosquitos and would be from high level. The attack on Bremen was remembered by W/O Herbert, who on this occasion flew Mosquito DZ458:D, and was accompanied by F/O R.B. Smith, in DK338:O: 'We went over at 26,000ft. We then dived to 18,000ft and let four 500lb screaming bombs go on the town. Each bomb had flutes on the tail to augment the noise. There was a terrific barrage as we went in, and then very accurate predicted fire as we came away. We dived down to the deck and covered the last 55 miles from Bremen to the coast in 7 minutes – about 480 mph. A bit of flak came from an aerodrome and light and heavy flak from Juist Island on the way out. The heavy flak followed us for about 6 miles without hits. The raid must have been demoralizing for the Jerries in Bremen.'

Apart from some low-level fighter affiliation with Typhoons on the 16th, the next operation was on the 19th, when a planned low-level on the engine sheds at Namur ended up abandoned due to poor visibility. Nevertheless, Aachen's marshalling yards, a motor barge in the River Waal and hydro-electric works on the River Maas between Maastricht and Roermond were all attacked.

Four days later, W/C Wooldridge was given the task of taking a formation at high level for a moonlight attack on the 'big city' – Berlin. Adolf Hitler was born on 20 April 1889. Nine

Mosquitos from 105 and two from 139 Squadron were told at briefing that they were to deliver a birthday present to him from the RAF, in the form of several tons of high explosive, smack on to the capital city of his beloved Fatherland. In fact, the operation was being flown in support of Bomber Command's operations by their 'heavies' that night, to Stettin and Rostock. 139 Squadron's W/C W.P. Shand was to lead their section in Mosquito DZ386, XD:H, accompanied by his observer, P/O C.D. Handley.

W/C Wooldridge was airborne at 22.08 hours that Tuesday evening, as the remainder of the Mosquitos formed up and headed out towards their target on this brilliant, moonlit night. The aircraft got as far as Helgoland (Heligoland) before a complete electrical failure in DZ483:R caused W/O J.F. Little to abandon the task. The remainder pressed on. F/L Patterson was in DZ414:E, and remembers the journey: 'It was a very long trip of course – over four hours of which about three hours would be over enemy territory. We had to constantly keep a look-out for fighters because the moon was so bright. It was a fascinating trip. As we wove and turned so that the navigator could look back for fighters, the moon would catch and reflect on the wings and on the Perspex. Looking down, all the lakes were lit up with the reflection of the moon. To go over Germany at high level at night in a Mosquito seemed almost as safe as flying over England, provided you kept out the way of any fighters. Then when we got to Berlin it came up very obviously; the great black city and the Potsdam lakes.'

The attacks were all launched between 18,000 and 22,000ft. First in was W/C Wooldridge at 00.24 hours, followed two minutes later by P/O W.E.G. Humphrey in DZ408:F. Both attacks were carried out without opposing flak. The defences were soon awakened however, as the next to bomb, F/O R.B. Smith in DK338:O, got a hot reception at 00.28 hours from moderate to heavy flak. The reception became even more awkward for DK337:N, as F/O F.M. Bud Fisher was coned in searchlights amid considerable heavy flak at 00.30 hours. DZ467:P was next in at 00.32 hours and P/O Ronald Massie met fairly accurate predicted flak. Two minutes later from 18,000ft, the next to bomb was F/L Patterson in his film unit Mosquito, DZ414:E. He had been included as an experienced squadron member, as the raid was to be a 'maximum effort'. He met intense and accurate flak and recalls: 'Suddenly there were flashes, black puffs and flak. I remember thinking that this is not what you get in a Mosquito; you're far too fast for this sort of thing. And then, just before I dropped my bombs, there was a sudden, violent thump. I still remember to this day the resentment and sense of outrage that one could be almost shot down at night in a Mosquito. It was just not done. It was unsporting – wasn't good form at all! Anyway, I just took it that it had been a fairly close burst and we turned round and wove our way back across northern Germany.'

After F/L Patterson, F/O Hull's DZ374:X bombed from 20,000ft. It too met inaccurate heavy flak. He was followed again, two minutes later, by F/O O.W. Thompson who was a little lower, between 15,000 and 17,000ft in DZ521:V. Again, moderate heavy flak unsuccessfully tried to pluck the raider from the sky. Now it was the turn of 139 Squadron's boys. W/C Shand bombed the target, as did F/O W.S.D. Sutherland, the Scot from Dollar, in DZ464, XD:C. He did so without much opposition from flak or searchlights, but did observe several small fires below him.

All aircraft were now heading for home. The first back was the leader, W/C Wooldridge, at 02.26 hours and the remainder at intervals thereafter. F/O Fisher was last back at 02.57 hours. All were home safely, except W/C William Peter Shand DFC with his observer, P/O Christopher Dinsdale Handley DFM. Those listening to German R/T noted that a night fighter had jumped them on the way back to base. Oberleutnant [Flying Officer] Lother Linke of IV./NJG1 [4th Squadron of the 1st Night Fighter Wing] sent the Mosquito to its end at 02.10 hours. DZ386, XD:H crashed into the Zuider Zee. Both airmen were subsequently laid to rest in Wonseradeel Protestant churchyard at Makkum, on the north-east coastal tip of the Zuider Zee.

F/L Charles Patterson remembers that once back at base: 'We were debriefed of course, and went to bed. The next morning when I went up to the flights, I was asked if I realized that I had been hit the night before. I said, "No, I had a bump and realized that there had been a burst fairly close. I didn't know that I'd been hit. It can't have been meant for me, I suppose there are just a few tiny holes in the wing or something." They said, "Oh, no. You'd virtually had it!" A piece of shrapnel had gone right through the tail of the Mosquito, where the elevator wires all link up with the tail plane and the rudder. All these wires had been severed and the only reason they were working was that one strand of wire was still standing. I'd never realized that anything was wrong at all; it had worked perfectly.'

It is of interest to note that the raids for which the Berlin operation was undertaken as a diversion proved successful, particularly at Stettin, where 100 acres of the city centre were laid to waste, destroying 380 houses and 13 industrial premises including a large chemical factory. Nevertheless, the death toll was 586 people in Stettin from the bombs of 339 aircraft. Eighty-six aircraft also attacked Rostock's Heinkel factory with uncertain results due to a smoke screen. The raid cost 30 RAF aircraft lost, comprising 8 Halifax MkIIs, 8 Lancaster MkIs, 5 Lancaster MkIIIs, and 1 Stirling MkI, all against Stettin, and 2 Stirling MkIs and 6 Stirling MkIIIs against Rostock.

On the 24th, F/O Norman S.B. Hull in DK337:N went alone to Trier with Sgt Philip H. Brown to carry out a dusk low-level attack on locomotive repair shops. They could not find Trier and decided to 'have a go' at a railway junction north of Maastricht in the Netherlands instead. Unfortunately, the bombs hung up and had later to be jettisoned. This was the last operation for this crew who were posted to 139 Squadron. Sgt Brown was eventually operating against Berlin on the night of 20/21 October 1943, when his aircraft DZ519, XD:U was brought down over the Netherlands. He recalls:

I was picked up by the Dutch underground and hidden in various houses before being taken to Brussels and Paris. In Paris, we became a party of a dozen or more, before being taken by train to Toulouse and eventually to the Pyrenees. Sadly, in crossing that range in February 1944, during snowstorms, we were spotted by a German patrol. We were split up and a small group, of which I was one, was captured and began our long journey back to PoW camp. I was kept in Toulouse jail for two weeks, then Fresnes prison in Paris for a month, followed by a long spell in Wiesbaden prison, before being taken to a PoW transit camp and then to Stalag Luft 7 at Bankau. Life there was like most RAF camps. Food became much scarcer but we managed to entertain ourselves and at the same time annoy the Germans. I played a lot of bridge, read many books and helped to run the camp clothing store for a while. Towards the end of the war, we were taken on a long journey (most of it in freezing cold conditions on foot) to a very large camp at Luckenwalde, and were eventually freed by the Russians. Life in a prison camp had its moments of laughter, but much of the time life took on a very serious aspect. It was an experience which has stood me in very good stead, but one which I would not choose to repeat.

Returning to 105's operations, on 24 April 1943, W/C Wooldridge had a 'shaky do' when he was intercepted during a low-level attempt on the railway repair shops at Tours. Flying DZ462:S, he led Australian from Brisbane, F/O D.C. Dixon, in DK338:O. They left at 19.22 hours, and when over the channel at 20.09 hours met an FW 190, first noticed one mile to starboard going in the opposite direction. The Mosquitos were speeding along at 245 mph on a course of 182° magnetic, at a height of 50ft above sea level. At 2,500ft there was 6/10ths cloud cover, with visibility of 5 miles. The fighter could hardly fail to see the Mosquitos. As they turned away to port, the enemy swerved in for the attack, and when about 400 yards away it let loose with its armament, sending a short squirt of green tracer at the Mosquitos, before miraculously disappearing out of sight. With the enemy in full knowledge of their whereabouts, both aircraft aborted the operation and returned to base. However, the day's activities were not in vain, as other crews flying in pairs attacked railway workshops at Jülich and Lingen with a high degree of success.

Duisburg was attacked in the dark early the next morning. P/O R. Massie in DK338:O bombed from high level through clouds. The month was finally rounded off by a taste of things to come. Six Mosquitos, two from 105 Squadron and one (DZ421, XD:G) borrowed from 139 Squadron with a 105 Squadron crew, armed with TI flares, attacked Wilhelmshaven at 21.48 hours. The other three, one of which was crewed by 139 Squadron, took off five minutes later and dropped instantaneously fused 500lb MC bombs in the target area between 22.48 and 23.00 hours from 20–25,000ft. The flares were also believed to have been dropped in the target area; however, one red flare fell in the water in the Jadebusen (Jade Basin), south-east of the town. One green flare fell south-east of the island of Alte Mellum and another south-west of the target. One crew reported having seen a green flare which they believed to be a dummy at the East Frisian island of Spiekeroog. On departure, a steady red glow was seen emanating from below the clouds. The reason for dropping flares was to create a diversion from minelaying operations going on nearby by part of a 207 aircraft 'gardening' operation.

May 1943 began with an attack on the 1st, once more on the Philips works at Eindhoven. S/L Reggie Reynolds was to lead five others in DZ467:P. All aircraft were ready for take-off at 14.07 hours. W/O Gary Herbert was in DZ483:R and recalls the unfortunate events that followed: 'During the formation form-up, F/O Thompson, a New Zealand lad, spun in and blew up. One of his motors failed and in his hurry, he feathered his airscrew on the other motor, thus killing both engines. He tried to turn into the aerodrome but stalled, flicked over on his back, and dived in. There was a terrific plume of flame and when it cleared about two seconds later, there was nothing except the tail plane and a few bits of debris.' The operation was immediately cancelled and all aircraft were recalled to base. F/O Onslow Waldo Thompson DFM, RNZAF and his observer, F/O Wallace James Horne DFC, had been flying DK338:O when they came down about a mile west of RAF Marham. The end was instantaneous. F/O Thompson was laid to rest close to several other young airmen, in Marham village cemetery, and F/O Horne in Norwich cemetery.

On Sunday 2 May, S/L Reynolds with F/O Sismore in DZ467:P led an attack by 7 Mosquitos on the railway workshops at Thionville on the Moselle river, about 12 miles south of the Luxembourg border. F/L Patterson, who went on the raid in the film unit Mosquito, DZ414:E, noted about the leader: 'He led this attack with a young officer who'd joined 105 not long before Christmas, who'd developed into a brilliant navigator called Sismore.' Ted Sismore recalled personally that the operation was, from his point of view, 'The perfect operation. The weather was just as good as forecast, and the winds were so accurate that I just followed the flight plan all the way to the target, on track all the way and arriving exactly on time. No flak, no fighters – quite remarkable.'

However, some flak *was* encountered over the enemy coast, as Charles Patterson recalls: 'As we came up over the cliffs, this flak came up: tracer. It seemed to me that it was getting very near to me so when I judged the moment was right, I did a quick little pull on the stick and went up about 50 to 100ft. Just as I did so the flak shot under me and went straight into the starboard engine of the chap on my left, which resulted in a big bang and a cloud of black smoke. He feathered his engine and went back home on the other engine.' Australian from Sydney P/O B.W. Coyle and his observer Sgt P.H. Harvey landed DZ521:V safely, at RAF North Weald.

Patterson continues: 'We flew across northern France, north-west of Paris right down to Soissons, mile after mile on this lovely summer's day, across the green fields of France. Then we made a turn to port towards Thionville, so that there was no chance of us missing the target by flying too far north or too far south. As a result we reached Thionville with no interception, without a shot fired. Reynolds, leading, opened the throttles and gained speed. He wouldn't go across the target flat out – the leader wouldn't do that – but he'd go up to about 300 [ft]. Then he'd give the order to open the bomb doors and the target comes up, and you're over it and gone in a flash.' W/O Herbert was flying DZ483:R and vividly recalls 'the leader's bombs smashing into the sheds. I was below and behind him. My kite was holed by flying glass and concrete. A good prang! Jake got lost on the way out and we came out over Vlieland, where we got a bit of flak, but it was inaccurate.' Charles Patterson continues:

We achieved complete surprise. The last pilot over said he thought he saw a gun open fire, but virtually after we'd gone. Then the really interesting part of the trip arrived. Instead of turning back north-west, to fly back across France and Belgium to the English Channel, the highly imaginative idea had been hit on of flying due north, knowing that the Germans would assume we must be coming back across north-west France and Belgium, or somewhere in that area. They would be sending in their fighters to meet us in that area before it got dark because, remember, we had attacked half an hour before dusk. This meant a very long flight indeed, right across Luxembourg, part of Belgium, and right across Holland from south to north, up the Zuider Zee and over the North Sea. I had a new cameraman with me who couldn't map-read for toffee; he had never done anything like this before in his life, and was completely bewildered. So, I had to rely on leaving him just to give me course and speed to steer according to the flight plan, and rely on my own experience and know-how to avoid flying over anything dangerous-looking, like a built-up area or an airfield. It was an extraordinary sensation, flying on across the mountains of Luxembourg, the Ardennes – all at low level and then down into Germany. It seemed endless. Then, in the gathering gloom, we suddenly shot over the banks of the Rhein. You could see all the barges – everything. Then up across Holland when it was getting quite dark and I felt fairly safe then. Of course I made for the Zuider Zee, over the causeway. Due to the experience I'd had on the Eindhoven trip, of coming out between Texel and Den Helder where the flak was just able to reach us, I went up to the next two islands and came out between Ameland and Vlieland [possibly either side of Terschelling], absolutely trouble-free.

Having been in the lead, F/O Ted Sismore had not noticed the flak behind him, as they had approached the enemy coast on the way in. When all were safely back at base, he then noted: 'Only after landing did the groundcrew point out that we had a bullet hole in the tailplane!'

A power station at Den Haag [The Hague] was next to be visited. On Tuesday 4 May, W/C Wooldridge was in the lead and Gary Herbert remembers: 'Three planes dropped bombs in a salvo in the middle of the target. There was only a little light flak on the way back. We saw gunners running for a heavy AA gun on the beach and dived on them. We scared them plenty. Wish I'd had guns on board – I'd have scared them more!'

The same day, an attack on Haarlem was thwarted due to seeing fighters over a convoy on the way over. The next day, six aircraft were to attempt a low-level attack on railway workshops at Tubize, lying about 12 miles south-east of Brussels. The intended leader, F/L Gordon, failed to get off the ground and the remainder found the target in poor light. Four overshot and returned with their bombs. A fifth, F/O W.E.G. Humphrey, dropped 30-minute delayed-action bombs on the target and tried to take photos. On the way back W/O J.F. Little

After the Thionville raid on 2 May 1943, G/C Digger Kyle (centre) is briefed in the Operations Room at RAF Marham by S/L Reggie Reynolds (to his left holding a ruler), watched by participating members of the operation. (Via E.B. Sismore)

was hit in the port engine by flak over the coast but managed, as did the others, to return safely, landing DZ467:P at 23.05 hours.

There were no operations for a while and in the interlude at least one Mosquito was used in making the film *Mosquito Raid*. However, operations were soon back on. Berlin was again visited on the 13th and 15th which heralded the beginning of a period of high-level night attacks, operating from 20,000 to 26,000ft, often amid slight flak and searchlights. Between 16 and 21 May, such attacks were made again on Berlin and also Köln, Düsseldorf, Münster and München (Munich). Of the operation of the 17/18th, Gary Herbert wrote: 'Three kites were sent to bomb Munich. We went over at 25,000ft without much trouble, apart from a bit of heavy flak at Mannheim. We dived to 20,000ft over the target and released our bombs [referred to in his logbook as 'four 500lb screaming bombs']. There was a bit of light flak over the target, and also searchlights, but we were not coned. It was an uneventful trip back, but searchlights coned us over London. We were later almost accused of bombing Zurich in Switzerland, but nobody could prove we did, no more than we could prove we didn't.'

On 22 May, W/C Wooldridge led an attack at low level to Nantes to add to the previous operations' destruction. Seven Mosquitos departed at 16.00 hours, crossed the aerodrome, crossed High Wycombe in thrashing rain and then flew south to Selsey Bill on the coast for the long flight to enemy territory. The weather had cleared up by the time they were over the Channel, and landfall was soon made over some cliffs, which the formation had to rise up 100ft to cross. A route adjustment to port at the railway line between Airel and Bayeux took the formation over hilly country until intercepting the Argentan–Flers railway. There, another change of track across the Leval to Le Mans road brought the Mosquitos over a hilly ridge. They observed a couple of twin-engined members of the Luftwaffe and a single-engined Fieseler Storch. Neither appeared to see the Mosquitos. As the formation flew down into another valley and headed east over a rise, two fighters appeared, closing in for interception about two miles distant. With only sufficient fuel for the operation and the impossible situation ahead, it was decided that discretion was the better part of valour, and that a northerly fast route home across the French coast between Bayeaux and Caen was in order. Accordingly, the formation was wheeled around and dropped into a steep valley to the east, and then when the fighters had hopefully been outwitted, a swing around to the north followed. The Mosquito formation had by now begun to split up and each was following its own track, hell-bent on getting back safely. The leader met some flak near Vitry. In *Low Attack* W/C Wooldridge described his way out: 'I approached the French coast flying due north with the arm of the Cherbourg peninsula stretching away some two miles to port. Away to my right there were three Mosquitos, well spread out and going like the clappers, while two more were just behind me on the same side. Where the rest of the formation were we could not tell for the moment. Then I saw two Hun fighters. They were flying along the beach dead ahead of us, crossing our track at right angles. Had I kept on straight I would have collided with the second one. It all happened so quickly that the Huns were as thunderstruck as we were. The two fighters were Messerschmitt 109s and I got a sudden view of their big black crosses neatly painted on the fuselages, their yellow spinners and numbers picked out in light blue. I could also see the pilots' heads, which were both intently watching the Mosquito over on my right. Then I banked a few degrees to port and shot behind them and carried on out to sea. They must have seen us, but made no attempt to follow us, for our speed was too great. If I had had a couple of cannon at that moment I could have done a useful job of work.'

W/O Herbert in DZ374:X noted that he 'didn't see any [fighters], but Jakey [Sgt C. Jacques] saw a couple inland and a couple nearer the coast. However, we got up speed and they couldn't catch us.' All arrived back safely for a landing at base, some with and some without bombs.

CHAPTER 14

Jena

Following the abortive raid on Nantes a period of intense low-level formation and bombing practice began. A big 'show' was looming, and the squadron was required to hone its skills to perfection for it. Both 105 and 139 squadrons were to be involved. This time the operation was to be on 27 May, at Jena, deep in the heart of Germany, about 45 miles south-east of Leipzig. For 105 Squadron, the target was to be the Zeiss optical instruments works, which was engaged in submarine periscope production, and the Schott glass works for 139 Squadron. This time, the whole raid was to be led by 139 Squadron.

Following the tragic demise of W/C Peter Shand DFC, newly promoted W/C Reggie Reynolds had taken over as C/O of 139 Squadron from the temporary custody of S/L J.V. Berggren. Reynolds was to lead the raid, with expert navigation by his observer, F/L Ted Sismore. It was to be the most ambitious operation attempted by low-flying Mosquitos to date.

The Mosquitos and crews were as follows:

Before the dangerous low-level Jena raid on 27 May 1943, F/L Ted Sismore DFC and W/C Reggie Reynolds stand in front of their Mosquito. (Via Pat Tennison)

Before the Jena raid on 27 May 1943, a confident W/C Reggie Reynolds stands in front of a Mosquito propeller (probably his DZ601, XD:B), sporting his Mae West. (Via E.B. Sismore)

105 Squadron

DZ591	GB:O	S/L W.W. Blessing DFC / F/O G.K. Muirhead
DZ337	GB:N	F/O F.M. Fisher / Sgt L. Hogan
DZ595	GB:C	P/O H.C. Herbert DFC / Sgt C. Jacques DFM
DZ521	GB:V	Sgt A.M. McKelvie / Sgt A.J.W. Heggie
DZ414	GB:E	F/L C.E.S. Patterson / F/Sgt L.A.K. Lee-Howard
DZ467	GB:P	P/O R. Massie / Sgt G.P. Lister
DZ483	GB:R	F/O A.J. Rae DFM / P/O K.S. Bush
DZ548	GB:D	F/O D.C. Dixon / F/O W.A. Christensen

139 Squadron

DZ601	XD:B	W/C R.W. Reynolds DSO, DFC / F/L E.B. Sismore DFC
DZ608	XD:D	F/L W.S.D. Sutherland / F/O G.E. Dean
DZ598	XD:N	F/O C.V. Pereira / F/O G.H. Gilbert
DZ593	XD:K	F/O A.B. Stovel / Sgt W.A. Nutter
DZ381	XD:W	F/L H.R. Sutton DFC / P/O J.E. Morris
DZ602	XD:R	F/O F. Openshaw / Sgt A.N. Stonestreet

The ordnance varied, with all aircraft carrying four 500lb MC bombs fused for 11 seconds' time-delay, except 105's Blessing and Fisher, and 139's Reynolds and Sutherland, who had 6-hour time-delay bombs on board. Charles Patterson recalls the start of the operational day:

When the briefing was over, we all went back to the hangars. Then there was always that extraordinary limbo; a time of waiting for the right time to go down to the aircraft and get in. There was the synchronism of watches and we would all settle into the aircraft a good ten minutes before we started the engines so as to ensure that everybody was in, and to allow time for somebody who might have forgotten something vital to dash back and get it. And then of course the vans arrived. I never seem to see the *Dambusters* film without thinking of Jena, when the crews were waiting at the flights and playing a game of cricket and so on. Well, we

Four 500lb tail-fused GP bombs with 11-second time delay being fitted into the bomb-bay of a 105 Squadron Mosquito. (Via Gary Herbert)

all got into our Mosquitos and it was time. We saw a flash of W/C Reynolds' exhaust and his engine started. Then all round the perimeter of the airfield, the engines started up. Again, on time, everybody gradually taxied out, formed up and took off. Forming up on these trips with a full muster of Mosquitos was a lengthy business, the leader circling slowly round and round the airfield for everybody to get airborne and catch up. Then the second formation had to go, and here I was with this damn film camera of course, going on another trip right at the end of my second tour, and flying near the back of not the first, but the second formation! So there I was, flying on this major trip behind a man who was leading me on his first tour, as the two formations settled down. The two formations each got right down to low level and swept across the hangars, and right across the centre of the airfield, which, if you were on the ground, was a very impressive sight and quite an exhilarating experience for the rest of the crew.

Ted Sismore recalled the trip out: 'Unlike Thionville, the weather did not accord with the forecast, and the defences were more extensive than we had been led to believe. In the usual way, we planned to attack just before sunset, so as to use the cover of darkness for the return. Outbound, we expected cloud cover over Holland and in the German frontier region, clearing over the hills and to the east of the Ruhr and in the target area. In the event, it proved to be the opposite, clear skies and good visibility on the route in. We were lucky there were no fighter interceptions.'

Patterson continued: 'We crossed the Dutch coast with no difficulty. Over the Zuider Zee we suddenly found ourselves flying slap into a vast fleet of little brown-sailed fishing vessels, and weaving in and out among them. At first we couldn't think what they were and I saw in front of me the whole formation break up and weave around: I thought something was wrong, but we settled down. Then my navigator drew my attention to something, and I looked across my starboard wing and had a clear view of Münster Cathedral just on my wingtip. The interesting thing was looking up at the towers of the cathedral, not looking down on them. We carried on towards Kassel, flying dog-legs to the east, never exactly on the same course for more than twenty minutes, when suddenly, we came across all the floods of the Möhne Dam raid, which had taken place only ten days before. We flew over completely flooded land for a good fifteen or twenty minutes; nothing but floods. It confirmed in our minds what an enormous success the raid must have been.'

The formation pressed on to the south-east, near the Diemelsee, where the flak became intense on approaching the mountain ridge before Adorf, at Helminghausen. Charles Patterson then noted: 'Just as I came to the mountain ridge myself, in the second formation, there was still a bit of flak. Right on the top of the mountain I saw an enormous ball of flame rolling down the mountainside.' W/O Herbert also saw the sad sight and noted: 'They sent up tons of light flak, and during the jinking which followed, two kites from the 139 formation collided and crashed down the mountainside. They broke into little pieces and rolled down the hill on fire, then the bombs went up.' [F/L Harold Ranson Sutton DFC with P/O John Ernest Morris in XD:W and F/O Frederick Openshaw with Sgt Alfred Newman Stonestreet in XD:R] Having been initially laid to rest in the nearby town of Rhenegge, all four airmen now lie in the Hannover war cemetery.

Herbert continued: 'A bit further on, another 139 Squadron kite [Pereira with Gilbert in XD:N] feathered its port airscrew and turned back. He got home OK.' All was not lost however, as Pereira bombed a railway bridge over the River Fulda at 51°04'N: 09°33'E on the way home, the results being unobserved as the bursts were in the water.

As the formation swept on, having crossed the River Weser just south of Kassel, Patterson recalled: 'We approached mountainous country. We were in the Thüringer Mountains. On the far side of the mountain, the front formation was just topping the far ridge.' Sismore continued: 'We approached the mountains in lowering cloud and poor visibility. We had to pull up into the clouds to clear the highest ridges and used careful timing to descend into the valleys.' Patterson: 'At one time, we were flying down a valley and there were houses on each side. Over my starboard wingtip, we saw a man open a door, and look out to see the Mosquitos passing. We saw the door suddenly slam as we whipped past. Suddenly the weather began to deteriorate, which had not been forecast, and I assumed as I think everybody was assuming that we would soon fly out of it. No, it got worse and worse. Blessing put on his navigation lights to try and enable us all to keep in formation, then everybody put on navigation lights. You got a rather lonely sort of feeling. Flying in cloud was something I was never particularly keen on. I was nervous flying on instruments in cloud, and although I did my best to keep the next aircraft in view, I'm afraid I lost him and found myself flying alone.'

Meanwhile, the remaining Mosquitos flew on. Ted Sismore continues: 'We let down on to the railway line leading to the target. The visibility was almost down to fog levels but the railway led us in successfully. The first shock was the sight of 40mm guns on towers on the side of the railway, firing with barrels horizontal. The second was the sight of close-hauled balloons, at about 200ft round the target area. We bombed successfully, and were immediately hit in the port radiator, propeller and front fuselage. I was calling for turns to miss the balloon cables, not knowing that Reggie's intercom had been severed, but miraculously, we missed them all and climbed into the cloud for the return.' Meanwhile, F/L Sutherland and F/O Stovel attacked the Schott works, where bombs hit the south, east and south-west corners of the factory, leaving flames soaring 100ft into the air.

Of the 105 section, Blessing, Massie, Rae and Herbert reached the Zeiss works. Blessing and Herbert bombed from 2–300ft. Bombs fell in the glass-grinding and polishing shops, leaving a cloud of smoke over the target. W/O Herbert described his run in to attack:

The fiercest crossfire of light flak I have ever seen opened up. I was last in the formation by this time and was free to go in how I liked. So I broke away and climbed up the mountain at the side of the town, hoping to fox the gunners and to dodge the balloons, which I expected would be spread across the valley. I didn't do either. As we went up the mountain, they poured light flak down at us and as we dived down the other side we got it again. The balloons were on the mountain as well as on the target. The only thing to do was to weave straight in, dodging the flak and praying not to hit a cable. As we screamed down, the flak poured at us and splattered all over the town. They put up a light flak barrage over the target, hoping we would run into it. Somehow, we dodged it and put our bombs fairly in the glass-grinding section – a sixteen-storey building. The heavy crossfire they put over the glass-grinding buildings was not directed at us, but obviously to deter us from going through it. They don't know how close they were to succeeding! I was absolutely terrified and did not think anybody could get through that and survive. I was sorely tempted to turn away and bomb an alternative target. The only thing that made me go through was that I could not face men like Hughie Edwards, Roy Ralston, Reg Reynolds, etc., and say 'I lost my guts and turned away'. I know that heroes are really cowards whose conscience would not let them hold their heads high in the presence of real brave men, but subsequent reports confirmed that I was not the only one tempted to turn away. We were hit in several places on the way out; however we managed to get away. We ran into a lot of flak on the homeward journey but dodged it OK. When we got back, we found that our hydraulics were out of action and had to pump our wheels and flaps down by hand. Then the throttles wouldn't close so I had to cut the switches to get in. There were so many aircraft pranged on the flare path when we got back that we were ordered to go to an alternate aerodrome – Swanton Morley. We came back by car, which took many hours in the blackout.

Of the other 105 crews who made it to the target area, F/O Fisher had tried to get to the target but was prevented from bombing it due to the balloon barrage. He dropped his 6-hour time-delayed bombs on the town from 200ft, and left them to explode later. F/O Alan James Rae DFM with F/O Kenneth Stanley Bush were seen over the target but crashed when landing on one engine at RAF Marham, killing both occupants. F/O Rae was buried in Marham cemetery and F/O Bush in Bath's Haycombe cemetery. P/O Ronald Massie with Sgt George Pearson Lister were missing after leaving the target area. They had crashed near Diepholz, again killing both crew members, who lie in Hannover war cemetery. S/L Blessing returned safely at 00.09 hours.

Of the 139 Squadron crews who attacked their target, F/O Stovel made it back safely and landed at 23.40 hours. However, F/L William Simpson Drysdale 'Jock' Sutherland made it back to England, only to crash at 23.57 hours at Wroxham railway station, having flown into high voltage overhead electrical cables when attempting a landing at RAF Coltishall in Norfolk. He was buried in Muckhart parish cemetery in Scotland, and his observer F/O George Ernest Dean was laid to rest in Harrogate (Stonefall) cemetery in Yorkshire.

W/C Reynolds successfully returned to base – a bit bloodied, as Ted Sismore describes: 'Reg was slightly wounded in the hand and leg, but one piece of shrapnel had ripped open his collar and just missed his neck. When I moved into the nose to make the bomb circuits safe, I found a piece of port propeller about five inches long had come through the side. In the dusk, we flew over two more defended areas before reaching the relative safety of the North Sea coast. Reggie did a great job of getting us home, although I do not think he was feeling too well. The doctor soon sorted him out and gave him a sedative so the next morning he was reasonably fit again.'

So what happened to the Mosquitos that got lost on the way to the target? Sgt McKelvie found a factory at Lobeda where bombs were seen to explode in the buildings, and F/O Dixon had tried three times to get on to the target but, frustrated by balloons and flak, had picked on a goods train at Lastrup at position 52°47'N; 07°52'E. His four 500-pounders fell and derailed the tail of the train, before he returned to land safely at 23.46 hours. Patterson also had an interesting trip:

I came out of the cloud and visibility was very poor. It was very grey and gloomy and my navigator had no idea where he was. So I decided the only thing to do was to turn for home and see if I could pick up something that was worth bombing. I could only tell where I might be within an area of 10 or 20 square miles. The only thing to do was to stick to the flight plan and steer north-east. The idea was to come up north of Hannover, by which time it was beginning to get dark, and fly due west across the Hannoverian plain.

I had only been flying a very short time when I found myself approaching the edges of what was clearly a very large town. In view of the low cloud base and limited visibility, I felt it quite safe to go up to the cloud base which was about 800–1,000ft. I wasn't worried about fighters, because if any appeared, I could pop into the cloud. When I got up to 800ft or so, I saw it really was a very large town, but I couldn't see any sign of a large factory or industrial buildings. It was just a great residential town with no flak around it. So I flew right down on the outskirts looking for something to attack. When I was on the south side, I remember seeing a lot of substantial-looking residences standing in trees in their own grounds. Then of course, we realized from the map, it must be Weimar. As I flew right round the outskirts nothing fired at me; nobody took any notice. I noticed there was a large railway station, which had two goods trains stationary in it in the centre of the town. So I thought, 'That's a very good military target, so we'll go for that.' Having done a complete circle, I turned towards the centre of the town, pointed the nose slightly down, and opened up to full throttle. Down we went in a steep dive straight at the railway station. I opened the bomb doors and dropped them [the bombs] straight into the station at about 200ft; I couldn't miss. At the moment the bombs left the aircraft and I leaned forwards to close the bomb doors, all hell broke out. Light flak came flashing and whizzing, and I was so busy twisting and dodging and concentrating on it that I really couldn't think of anything else. When we got to the edge of the town, I got right down over the rooftops. We flew up a valley with green hills on either side, which was the route I could see we had to take out. The flak went on; I thought it would never stop. It began to get very worrying, because one felt that if it went on like this they were bound to hit me eventually. As I went up the valley I found more tracer coming at me from the side of the hills. We were doing the usual evasive action when at last we emerged from this ordeal. I must say I do remember feeling rather shaken by it. I carried on up the valley and at last the flak stopped. Then of course, I no sooner got over the relief of that than I realized that I was in the middle of Germany, not sure where I was, having no clear idea of what course to steer to get home, but there was no use in panicking, you just had to get down to it.

I said to the navigator, 'What we must do is fly on long enough to get north of Hamlin [Hameln] which is bound to be defended, and looks very much as if it is in our path.' We got to somewhere north of Hamlin and all the bad weather evaporated. There I was in the familiar Hamburg plain, which I recognized, and knew that at least I was in the right area, flying in the right direction. Then of course one's spirit rose, in the clear weather; the forests, woods and trees and rivers flashing past. The light was beginning to fade and we were secure in the knowledge that before long it would be too dark for the fighters. I had no idea of where any of the others were and by the time we crossed the Dutch frontier, it was virtually dark and so one could come up to 300–400ft to avoid obstacles. I had a few minutes at low level and knew I was over Holland, because a very interesting thing used to happen over Holland – much more than Belgium. When they heard these low-flying aircraft coming towards them, the Dutch country people used to run to the doors of their little houses and cottages, and open and shut the door so that they signalled a flashing light of welcome towards us. It was a wonderful thing to see them doing, when one realized the terrible risks they were running in doing something that was purely a human gesture. I then made my way straight for my beloved Zuider Zee, taking no notice of the route set by the planners back at Marham for this stage, and went straight up to the causeway. Then, it was out between Vlieland and Ameland where there would be no flak, and then we landed.

DZ414:E arrived back safely, at four minutes past midnight. After the raid on Jena, Ted Sismore noted what happened on arrival: 'After debriefing, I had a call from intelligence at Bomber Command asking if I was sure that I had attacked the right target, as there were no balloons at Jena and no guns on towers. I remember saying, "Well, who was there, me or you?" He did call a week later, to say photographs showed the balloons and guns, but clearly, he hadn't believed me.'

Jena was to be the last joint low-level raid to be attempted by 105 and 139 squadrons. W/O Herbert noticed that on his return: 'Nobody of any importance except "Brooksie", our Senior Intelligence Officer, saw our report. By that time all the bigwigs from headquarters, who were there to decide whether we would continue as a low-level squadron or be switched to PFF had left.' There was, however, some considerable interest shown by the BBC. They turned up the next day to record the story of the raid, which survives to this day. In conclusion, Herbert noted in his diary on Thursday 3 June 1943: 'Quite a few gongs [medals] awarded today for the Jena trip. W/C Reynolds, who led, got a bar to his DSO. F/L Sismore, his navigator, got a DSO and also Bill Blessing, our leader. Bud Fisher got a DFC and his navigator got a DFM. Incidentally, they didn't reach the target that day, but have done good work before.' On Saturday 5 June, he finally noted what was expected: 'We have now changed our role. We will do no more daylight ops, but will be a Path Finder Squadron.'

After the raid on Jena, in RAF Marham's Operations Room. Observed by observer F/Sgt Lee-Howard (left), F/L Charles Patterson discusses the results with S/L Reggie Reynolds (right) who administers a 'steadier' to himself in the form of a tot of rum. (Via Pat Tennison)

Part Two – 8 GROUP

CHAPTER 15

Path Finder Force

Harris's area bombing concept had continued relentlessly since its inception in February 1942. Despite technical aids such as Gee, which was soon subject to German jamming techniques, the accuracy of navigation on these area raids was still subject to some debate. Therefore new ways of ensuring that the bombs struck home on the required targets were vital. It was to become a war in which brute force was more and more to be complemented by technical expertise. G/C S.O. Bufton, of the Air Ministry's Directorate of Bombing Operations, had been a great exponent of marking targets prior to the bombing runs by the 'heavies'. He experimented with several devices including barometrically fused flares, and came to the conclusion that it was essential to have a force of aircraft with specially trained crews to form a Target Finding Force. This was a technique which Bufton saw as being an aid to what he considered to be the vital principle of precision bombing, as opposed to the area bombing policy followed at the time. Bufton met the full force of Harris's wrath, who was absolutely against the idea of forming what he saw as a corps d'élite, which, in his opinion, would have a severely detrimental effect on the morale of his squadrons. Eventually, having received a direct order from the prime minister, Winston Churchill, ACM Sir Wilfred R. Freeman KCB, DSO, MC, Vice-Chief of the Air Staff, forced the issue and Harris had to accept the outcome. Nevertheless, he was insistent that the Directorate of Bomber Operations would not have it all their own way, and Harris vetoed the title Target Finding Force in favour of the now famous PFF.

To lead this new force, on 5 July 1942, Harris appointed a young officer whom he immediately promoted to Group Captain, Donald C.T. Bennett. Bennett was an Australian from Fairthorpe, Toowoomba, where he was born on 14 September 1910. He was of sterling character and had all the necessary forcefulness and single-minded determination necessary to make PFF a success. Bennett was well known to Harris, having been subordinate to him when operating flying-boats before the war. He subsequently joined Imperial Airways, which eventually became BOAC. Early in the war, Bennett had ferried aircraft across the Atlantic, and as a navigator was second to none. Command of 77 Squadron was given to him in December 1941, and then in mid-April 1942 he was transferred to command 10 Squadron, flying Halifax bombers from RAF Leeming in Yorkshire. It was from here that he was shot down when attacking the *Tirpitz* in a Norwegian fjord. He survived, and with great resourcefulness and displaying typical strength of character, found his way through the ice and snow to neutral Sweden.

Don Bennett was also a leader who had great knowledge of aviation technical matters and could lead by example, almost irrespective of the trade of those of whom he was in charge. He was extremely self-disciplined and expected the same of all under his command, which made him few friends but gained him enormous respect.

PFF became an entity on 15 August 1942, and became a separate group on 13 January 1943, designated No. 8 Group (PFF). Bennett was once again promoted, this time to air commodore, and he became the group's AOC.

By now, the technical war was developing and apart from Gee, the boffins came up with a 10 cm airborne radar called H2S. Reputedly, it got its name when Winston Churchill reviewed its use. He thought the idea stank and should therefore be called H_2S (as hydrogen sulphide, the 'bad egg' gas). It nevertheless turned out to be most effective and would give the operator a radar image of the ground below, even at night and in cloudy conditions. The system was far from perfect but gave the best chance available at the beginning of 1943 of accurate marking with flares.

However work was also going on apace with the latest bombing aid, Oboe. In 1940, the Germans had developed a system of bombing England guided by radio beams. It was called 'Knickebein' or 'crooked leg'. The system allowed the pilot to fly along a beam until it was intercepted by another beam. This caused a different note to sound in his earphones and then he would let his bombs go. It was not long before the British boffins came up with a counter-measure or 'jamming' capability. The accuracy of Knickebein was about a square mile. Oboe was really a refinement of the same principle but was much more sophisticated and hence far more accurate. From 30,000ft, Oboe could give a bombing accuracy of yards. The range was dictated by the curvature of the earth and was 300 miles from the fixed transmission points.

The aircraft would fly out on Gee to a point designated a 'waiting point'. Each pilot had his own personal call sign which would be called up when it was his turn to engage the Oboe track and start the Oboe run to the target. Oboe worked on pairs of ground stations, located around the coast. Initially, the stations were located at Hawkshill Down (Walmer), Trimmingham (Cromer) and Winterton (Norfolk), and soon thereafter at Sennen and Treen (Cornwall), Worthy Matravers and Tilly Whim (Swanage), Beachy Head and Cleadon (Newcastle).

As required, one station was designated the Cat and the other the Mouse. Most of the equipment for the Cat and Mouse were common. The transmitter was fully common, as was 95 per cent of the control console. The circuits which were different, depending on whether they were operating as Cat or Mouse, were switched in or out depending on the set-up for the raid. The ground stations sent separate signals to the transponder in the Mosquito, which automatically returned a signal of a few micro-seconds' duration to the station, where the range would show up as a blip on a CRT. The target range was calculated by the Cat, which set up an associated strobe on the CRT. When the aircraft was flying along the strobe signal, a steady note was sent to the pilot who heard it in his earphones. Reputedly, Oboe was so codenamed, as the steady note sounded like the tuning note given at the start of an orchestral concert. The target range signal was only 35 yards wide, and it was therefore necessary for the pilot to maintain his course along the centre of the track. Should he deviate and fly less than the target range, a series of Morse Code dots would be transmitted to him and conversely should he deviate to fly at greater than the target range a series of dashes would be sent. Hence there was an invisible corridor of plus or minus 17 yards either side to adhere to. The second or Mouse station also had its target range set up on the CRT as a strobe. However, on this screen, as the aircraft progressed towards the release point, so too did the return pulse on the screen. This station would transmit to the aircraft's observer, who received signals at four specified distances from the release point, designated 'A', 'B', 'C' and 'D'. 'A' would be sent at a point 10 minutes, 'B' at 8 minutes, 'C' at 6 minutes and 'D' at 3 minutes from the target. Navigator F/O Dennis Bolesworth pointed out: 'The letters were conveyed to the pilot by the scientific use of the index finger on the windscreen.' Observer Tom Wingham DFC also pointed out:

If the aircraft had been unable to be flying straight and level by point 'C', the mission for that aircraft had to be aborted. If the operation was cancelled, the signal was 'I-M-I'. There was no going round again as the next Mossie would be at point 'A' which was normally around

F/O S. Tom Wingham sits on the ladder of Mosquito B.XVI, PF518, GB:D. Note the stubby Oboe aerial hanging down half way along the fuselage. (Via Tom Wingham)

40 nautical miles from the release point. The following aircraft would not know that the earlier aircraft had failed [or not 'coped' as it was known]. Each crew had their own call sign from the ground stations, and the aircraft would be notified that it was under control from the call sign being transmitted. There was no communication between aircraft, although it would have been possible to call another aircraft on VHF, but radio silence was the order of the day. Obviously, if the aircraft was carrying marker flares then you could only drop at the release point if you were 'on the beam' and received the necessary signals [otherwise, the heavies would drop their bombs on the wrong target].

When the aircraft reached the point of intersection of the Cat and Mouse signals, the Mouse controller saw the blip on the CRT cross the strobe, and an automatic signal comprising four dots and a dash was sent to the aircraft. It then released its TIs. The Mouse computer, or 'Micestro' as it was appropriately known, made suitable corrections to the point of release. The trajectory was also carefully computed taking into account variables that would influence the descent of the TI such as wind speed, aircraft velocity and heading, weather conditions, instrument tolerances, and characteristics of the trajectory such as air resistance. Operating the type 9000/Oboe system was not all about the aircraft however, as Kenneth Kiely who was based at Hawkshill Down and Tilly Whim explains:

Life at an Oboe station was quite pressured. On the technical side, we were dealing with very new equipment, which was still being developed. Tilly Whim had two transmitters and four

Inside an Oboe ground station caravan. The Ground Controller looks on (left) as a WAAF checks the transmitting console upper long-range and lower shorter-range CRTs. (Via Geoffrey Parker)

consoles, all of which had to be serviced and be available whenever 8 Group required it. The operational staff had to train the new postings in, and the ex-aircrew arriving on the station had to have extensive operational training from the senior training officer. There was a very real discipline, from when the operational staff took over the consoles to the last of the releases. Although there was always complete silence, every successful release brought forth an audible sigh of relief and temporary relaxation before the next call-up signal was sent. Only technical and operational staff were allowed in the ops buildings, even the adjutant was only allowed into the main corridor, and then with an escort. The Army had the job of defending the site, and there was a system of passwords and numbers to get in. This meant that normal dress discipline was not in force. Some WAAFs could change into skirts and silk blouses, and some of the men would wear slacks. The general morale and team spirit was very high.

Kenneth Kiely describes the Oboe station equipment:

The equipment comprised a transmitter which operated at a wavelength of 10cm to give a very low and narrow beam, transmitted by a parabolic aerial mounted on a gantry. The console which controlled the output from the transmitter comprised a central unit housing a CRT, at a height of about five feet, and a second CRT at about sitting height. The controller managed the whole of the operation from this lower CRT display. The upper CRT had a long-range trace up to 600 miles, while the lower CRT could select any twenty-five, five or one mile section from the long-range trace and display it against a strip of paper about 11 inches long. The one-mile trace would be adjusted so that it coincided precisely with the 100 squares on the graph paper, enabling the range strobe to be set up to one hundredth of a mile. Either side of the central unit were vertical units containing control hardware, with many switches used to set up and modulate the output of the transmitter. A Morse key was plugged into the output so that the call sign and other messages could be sent via the transmitter output.

Prior to operations, the electronic equipment on some aircraft needed to be checked under flying conditions, and the Oboe stations received telex details of these navigation flying tests, which took place on the bombing range at Orford Ness. This was usually in the morning when the Mosquito would fly in at operational height of 30,000ft plus, and drop a marker into a six-yard circle. The impact was watched by an observer from a bomb shelter on line to the controller. When the controller had seen the release signal transmitted, he would warn the observer, saying 'On the way!' His reply very often was 'In the circle!' About 10.00 hours on the morning of operations, the tele-printer would start up giving data for the next targets: target range to two decimal places of a mile; call sign; waiting point; type of markers/bombs; aircraft height and speed; meteorological details; follow-up force if marking, etc. These details would be transcribed to a pro-forma, for later use in setting up the console.

Two hours before call-up the standby diesel generator would be run up. This was because the local electricity supply proved too variable for the sensitive equipment. When the diesel had been warmed up, the main switch would be thrown to 'standby', when the transmitter and consoles would be progressively switched on again. For the next hour, the technical staff would monitor the equipment to ensure it was operating satisfactorily.

This was the procedure for Tilly Whim. One hour before call-up time, the consoles would be handed over to the operational staff, who would set out the data from the pro-forma on to a sheet of Perspex mounted on a drawing board. This would show the approach tracks for the Cat and Mouse aircraft waiting points, warning letters for the Mouse, release point for the Cat and the target.

The console would then be set up using the upper CRT (to the nearest five miles), the lower CRT displaying the one-mile trace to the nearest two decimal places of a mile against the graph paper. The range would be checked and re-checked several times before handing over to the controller. He would verify the details on the drawing board, and the range (strobe) on the two CRTs.

Three minutes before call-up time, the parabolic aerials would be swung round to the required bearing and on time, the controller would key the call sign to the Mosquito. The aircraft blip would then show up on the traces, and the initial weaving of the aircraft could be seen on the trace, and heard through the transmitter output (dots/dashes). Very quickly the equi-signal (Oboe note) would be heard, followed by the four warning letters ['A' first, followed in sequence by 'B', 'C' and 'D'] and then the release signal. If there had been a successful run-in, and release by the observer, thereupon the aircraft would switch off its transponder. The Oboe station would then report a success. If the blip did not disappear (rarely) it showed that the aircraft had a problem, and the aerial would track it, while the controller would key a Morse message and await a reply. He would then decide if any action was necessary and proceed to set up for the next operation. I remember on one occasion, we had a flap when the transponder was not switched off after completing the run, but the Mosquito returned to base – apparently he had forgotten!

Although Oboe was a very useful bombing aid, its introduction was not as smooth as it could have been. Kenneth Kiely noted:

Two brilliant scientists, Alec H. Reeves of Standard Telephones and Cables (STC) and Dr Frank E. Jones of TRE [at Great Malvern], designed the Oboe equipment in theory. It was very difficult to get funds to make the equipment and test it. I recall going to the Air Ministry as a very young lad. I spent the morning telling them of the papers, which Reeves and myself had written, and trying to explain to them what Oboe was, and how it might work. On the whole I got a pretty fair reception, and they got rather enthusiastic about it. Funds were made available from the Air Ministry and eventually, after much development and testing, the transponders, etc., were installed in Lancasters. Then the Air Ministry was asked for the target, and it was to be Krupps in Essen. The Krupps site was very large, so a more specific target was requested – the machine shop. So the target was marked and there was a small follow-up force of Lancasters. The next day, when Photo-Freddie returned, the photographic interpretations showed that the machine shop had been blasted. Of course, all hell was let loose, and Oboe became top priority.

To mark his targets, Bennett's Path Finders started by dropping markers such as 'reconnaissance flares' and 'red blob fires'. The latter were 250lb incendiaries comprising a mixture of rubber, phosphorous and benzol, which glowed red when ignited. 'Pink pansies' were also carried by the 'heavies' which was simply a 4,000lb casing filled with the same as the red blobs but with added colouring which gave a brilliant pink colour when it exploded. However, true TIs were being developed and soon came to production as a 250lb bomb casing, housing 60 pyrotechnic candles, each candle 12 inches in length. The candles were ejected from the casing by a barometric fuse housed in the nose of the casing. The candles were to be produced in different colours, such as green, red and yellow. Initial trials were very promising with a 100-yd area being marked when the device was dropped from 3,000ft. However, there was a problem. As the Mosquitos were called up on Oboe, with a gap of several minutes between aircraft, it was necessary either to provide 'backers-up' aircraft or to devise a TI which would have a long burning capability so that it would not extinguish before the next Mosquito arrived to drop its markers. This was accomplished by manufacturing markers initiating an initial burst of 20 candles at one time followed, two and a half minutes later, by another 20 and finally five minutes later, by the last 20. Very long-burning target indicators were also devised to extend the overall burn time to 12 minutes, by altering time delays and the number of candles burning at once. Development of the TIs continued throughout the war and many complex configurations resulted. All were devised for one reason however: to mark the spot for the following heavy bombers to attack, and often to act as route markers for them to follow.

There were essentially three standard techniques of marking used by the Path Finders: Newhaven was the codename given to dropping TIs to mark the ground, thereby allowing visual recognition of the aiming point by the following bombers. Blind illumination or hooded flares were sometimes employed at intervals to light up the target, before the visual markers went in. Where Oboe was used to drop proximity markers, followed by illuminators dropping flares to ease identification of the target for the visual markers, the term Musical Newhaven was used.

Parramatta was a 'blind' ground-marking technique when H2S was used to locate the TI marking point, due to cloud or bad weather obscuring the target. The primary markers would then be dropped. This would be followed by 'backers-up' dropping a different colour of TI from the primary marker. Finally, the bombers would come along and bomb the secondary colour. If it was obscured they were to bomb the primary colour. As a refinement to this technique, there were two sub-divisions to the Parramatta technique. When the primary markers were dropped by Oboe-equipped aircraft such as Mosquitos, the term Musical Parramatta was used. These 'musical' markers were dropped at timed intervals throughout the raid and in this instance, the bombers dropped their bombs on the primaries in preference to the secondaries. When high-precision attacks were required, to take account of any error in Oboe marking, Controlled Oboe was employed. Here, a Master Bomber was allocated to the force, to visually assess the accuracy of the placing of the primary TIs. He would then call in either his followers with TIs to stoke the fires of the most accurately placed primary TIs, or advise the following 'heavies' how far from the target the TIs were.

Finally, Wanganui was the codename for a purely sky-marking technique. Flares were used; however, sometimes, due to lack of visibility in daylight, 'smoke puffs' were employed which were essentially marker candles on small parachutes. The following bomber force would then drop their bombs through the

The cockpit of an Oboe-equipped Mosquito, showing the observer's array of Oboe equipment. (Via Geoffrey Parker)

sky-markers to hit the target below. Musical Wanganui was the term used when the sky-marking was dropped by Oboe.

The names of the three principal techniques were chosen at random by Don Bennett, based on the names of the home towns of some of his staff. Cpl Ralph, Bennett's confidential WAAF clerk, came from Newhaven, Bennett suggested Parramatta in New South Wales, and S/L 'Pedro' Ashworth was a New Zealander from Wanganui.

CHAPTER 16

Music to the Ears

The first squadron to be equipped with Oboe was No. 109, which had been formed from the Wireless Intelligence Development Unit at Boscombe Down on 10 December 1940. It specialized in the highly secret development of radio counter-measures and radar aids until April 1942, when it assembled at RAF Stradishall and began to concentrate on Oboe development. The squadron moved to RAF Wyton on 6 August 1942, where it joined Bennett's No. 8 Group on its formation on 13 January 1943. Thereafter, 109 Squadron moved to RAF Marham on 4 July 1943 to join 105 Squadron. Before this, however, 105 were working up to their new role as Path Finders. There was a considerable amount of movement of personnel at the beginning of June, many of which were attachments to 109 Squadron at RAF Wyton to accommodate training on Oboe, and some to the NTU at RAF Upwood. High-level night bombing on ETA (and visually) commenced from the 13 June with Berlin, Köln, Düsseldorf and Duisburg being the centres of attention until the 24th, without the loss of any Mosquitos.

A major change was now in the air. During his time at 105, W/C Wooldridge put his personal mark on the squadron in several ways. Having attempted to bring a degree of levity to the proceedings, he had nose art painted on the Mosquitos' noses on the port side below the observer's observation window, just aft of the bomb-aiming nose blister. The artwork depicted, in clockwise rotation, the spade, heart, club and diamond as found on a playing card, to the right of which was emblazoned a well-known cartoon character with the aircraft nickname written close by. Examples of these included Donald Duck and the knave of diamonds; Goofy and the knave of spades; a gremlin and the Joker; the figure of Popeye simply entitled 'Popeye' and for the Americans, a gentleman in striped morning-wear carrying a bomb horizontally under his right arm, entitled 'Uncle Sam'. Examples of these can be seen in W/C Wooldridge's book *Low Attack*. However, following his relatively brief 3-month command, it was now time for Wooldridge to depart. On 25 June, he was posted to 82 OTU at Ossington, Nottinghamshire, as part of HQ Bomber Command's 93 (Bomber) OTU Group, but the posting was cancelled the same day in favour of an operational post as a Wing Commander to No. 3 Group at RAF Stradishall, 11 miles south-west of Bury St Edmunds in Suffolk. On 1 September 1943 he was posted back to the PWD. Wooldridge survived the war and devoted himself chiefly to composing, having studied with Sibelius. In addition he worked as a conductor, especially with the Philharmonia Orchestra. He wrote many plays, orchestral suites, incidental film music and film scores. One of these was the famous definitive film about Bomber Command, *Appointment in London*, for which he wrote the music and the squadron song as well. Tragically, his career ended on 27 October 1958, when Wooldridge died in a car accident. Following his posting in 1943 came his replacement, in the form of 109 Squadron's W/C Henry John Cundall AFC, who had been newly promoted for the post (ultimately to become G/C Cundall CBE, DSO, DFC, AFC, psa, pfc).

With their new change of role, 105 Squadron also had to be equipped with Oboe Mosquitos, which started on 5 July 1943. Oboe Mosquitos were initially provided by 109 Squadron in the form of modified B.IV series iis and a batch of B.IXs. Whereas the B.IV Mosquitos were equipped with 1,280hp Merlin 21s or 1,390hp Merlin 23s, the B.IXs were powered by the larger two-stage 1680hp Merlin 72 engines with an increased range and high-altitude capability,

American pilot F/O Bud Fisher DFC with observer, Sgt L Hogan, in front of their Mosquito 'Uncle Sam', probably DK337, GB:N in May 1943. (Via Cliff Streeter)

although they were not pressurized. Two extra 500lb bombs or alternatively, two 100-gallon fuel drop-tanks could be carried. These were mounted under the wings, outboard of the engines.

S/L Jack V. Watts DFC (later Brigadier General Watts DSO, DFC*, CD) remembered the early association of the two squadrons:

> In the early days of Oboe, when 105 joined the newly formed 109 Squadron at RAF Marham in Norfolk, it was a major change for the members of 105 who had been operating with 2 Group until that time. Right from the start there was great rivalry between the two squadrons, each attempting to prove their superiority over the other, in timing and bombing accuracy. This even extended to the rugger field where we played some vigorous games in which I was the lone Canadian amongst the mixed bag of English, Scottish, Australian and New Zealand youngsters. Our [109] Squadron Commander, 'Hal' Bufton who had been a Harlequin rugger team member before the war, was an enthusiastic participant, which boosted squadron morale in the field as well as in the air.

No. 105 Squadron aircrews in 1943. Front row (left to right): Squadron M/O Dr Forbes; F/O E.B. Sismore; S/L W. Blessing; S/L R. Reynolds; W/C Wooldridge; S/L R. Ralston; F/L S. Clayton; F/L J. Gordon; Unknown Engineering Officer. Second row: P/O H.C. 'Gary' Herbert, RAAF; F/O W.A. Christensen, RAAF; Unknown; F/O Don Dixon, RAAF; F/O R.G. Hayes; F/O R. Massey; Unknown; Unknown; Unknown; Unknown. Back row: Unknown; Unknown; Unknown; Unknown; Sgt A.W.J. 'Jock' Heggie; Sgt C. Jacques; Unknown; Unknown; Unknown. (Via Gary Herbert/E.B. Sismore)

The 109 Squadron CO, W/C 'Hal' E. Bufton DFC, AFC, was the brother of G/C S.O. Bufton, of the Air Ministry's Directorate of Bombing Operations. Hal Bufton and his observer, F/L E.L. 'Ding' Ifould, were also the first crew to drop Oboe-guided bombs from a Mosquito, which fell on Lutterade in the Netherlands on the night of 20/21 December 1942. Meanwhile, on 4 July 1943, 109 Squadron moved into RAF Marham to join 105 Squadron, and 139 Squadron swapped places and moved to RAF Wyton. They too were now part of 8 Group and were to be used as a squadron in support of the Oboe markers. As well as nuisance raids, they would be required to go in with the early markers and carry out diversionary attacks, acting as bait for the enemy fighters to keep them at bay during the main Oboe raids. No. 139 Squadron were to become part of the Light Night Striking Force.

No. 105 Squadron's first Oboe operation was carried out on the night of 9/10 July 1943, when S/L Bill Blessing with F/O G.K. Muirhead flew to Gelsenkirchen in 'Musical' Mosquito DK333:F, accompanied by F/O W.E.G. Humphrey with F/Sgt E. Moore in 'Musical' Mosquito DZ485:W and 12 other Mosquitos flown by 109 Squadron crews. For 105 Squadron, S/L Blessing was first away at 23:59 hours, followed by F/O Humphrey three minutes later at 00:02 hours. They successfully 'coped' and attacked the primary target with one yellow TI and three 500lb MC bombs. Oboe or 'the precision device', as it was recorded in the squadron record book, due to the highly secret nature of its identity, had worked perfectly and a month of training at RAF Wyton for both crews had paid off. MkI Oboe was not without technical difficulties however, as it soon became common to have crews return having had a 'failure of the precision device'. This happened to the same crew during the subsequent operation to Köln on the 13th.

Training continued apace, but nearly ended prematurely for one crew. P/O C. Prentice RNAF and observer P/O J.L. Warner were injured on the 25th, when their 1655 MTU Mosquito DZ318 crashed on approach to RAF Marham, and the next day 105 Squadron's DZ595:H had an undercarriage retraction on the ground at Foulsham.

On the night of 24/25 July 1943, Bomber Harris commenced his Battle of Hamburg, which was to last until 3 August 1943. The Battle of the Ruhr was not yet over, but Harris decided that Hamburg was to 'reap the whirlwind' as well. Hamburg itself was beyond Oboe range but Essen was not. 'Window' comprised strips of black coarse paper with one side made of aluminium metallic foil, each strip being 2cm wide by 25cm long. German 'Würtzburg' radar was the control tool for flak-guns and night-fighters, and research had indicated that if Window was dropped by bombers, both Würtzburg and the airborne-radar 'Liechtenstein' could be completely confused, and hence should not be able successfully to intercept our aircraft. The theory had not been put into practice yet, due to the misguided viewpoint that if the Germans understood the technology they would also use it. With the Luftwaffe depleted due to its presence over the Russian front, it was considered time to try Window. This was attempted for the first time on Hamburg on the first raid, proving a very effective counter-measure. An attack on Essen on the night of 25/26 July was to attempt a major raid while the Window dropping of the previous night would hopefully still have the enemy in disarray. This was to be 105 Squadron's next Oboe operation. That night four Mosquitos were despatched to Essen, where they successfully marked the target for a force of 705 bombers comprising Lancasters, Halifaxes, Stirlings, Wellingtons and Mosquitos. Twenty-six aircraft were lost but Essen also suffered heavily. The Krupps works was severely damaged, as were many other industrial buildings. Five hundred Germans were killed that night, mostly civilians, including forty-two PoWs.

On the 26th, during a night flying test for ops that evening, F/O W.E.G. Humphrey and F/Sgt E. Moore of 105 Squadron experienced a port engine failure on take-off in a 139 Squadron Mosquito, DZ597, XD:H, and crashed at Fincham. F/O Humphrey recalls the incident: 'It was just over the boundary from the airfield. The engine stopped, and the only thing to do in such circumstances is to shut down and go straight ahead. I remember quite distinctly, I was about 80 or 90 knots and one thinks one did it nice and coolly, but one is talking literally about a split-second decision, and I just shut everything down and pulled the undercarriage up. We were all right. We went charging along for about a mile and went straight through a stone wall and came out all right. You were in a very strong box in a Mosquito, with two engines stuck out each side and in front of you. The main spar was behind you and you had a very strong little place to be in if you hit something straight in front of you, and so we survived going through the wall. Well, everything came to pieces and one shook oneself, but there wasn't any aeroplane, it had broken up. Nobody really complained, for if I hadn't done that we wouldn't have been alive.' So the crew survived, and Humphrey subsequently entered in his logbook, what must be one of the shortest flights on record, clocking up a mere 15 seconds!

The month ended with an operation by three 105 Squadron Mosquitos in the company of six from 109 Squadron. No. 105 Squadron fielded F/O J.R. Hampson with P/O H.W.E. Hammond in LR508:G and F/O Kenneth Wolstenholme with S/L J.F.C. Gallacher DFC in DZ550:A. F/L A.W. Raybould DFM with F/L I.F. Tamango DFC in LR506:E acted as the reserve 105 Squadron aircraft which, as it transpired, was not required to attack. All departed on the night of 30/31 July to mark Ramscheid, with each of the Mosquitos carrying four red TIs, to mark for a force of 273 heavy bombers. They destroyed 83 per cent of the town, which had never before been the centre of Bomber Command's area bombing attention. This brought Harris's Battle of

F/O William Ernest Gifford Humphrey RAFVR in flying kit. (Via W.E.G. Humphrey)

the Ruhr to an end, after having flown 18,506 sorties, dropping 58,000 tons of bombs for a loss of 872 aircraft, i.e. 4.7 per cent of his force.

August started inauspiciously, as the Battle of Hamburg also came to a close. No. 105 Squadron had not been deeply involved, but Bomber Command had caused havoc. In the raid of 27/28 July, 40,000 people were killed as a firestorm swept the city over a 3-hour period. However by 6 August, the battle ended and 75 per cent of the city had been laid waste. Two-thirds of the population, about 1.2 million people, fled the city in terror. Harris's attentions were soon to turn to Berlin.

No. 105 Squadron had a quiet start to August, as Bomber Command concentrated their main efforts on Italy. Milan, Genoa and Turin all received attention in an attempt to hasten the decision of the Italian government to negotiate an armistice.

G/C Percy Charles Pickard DSO**, DFC, soon to be hero of the now-famous raid on the prison at Amiens, was the CO of RAF Sculthorpe, situated 14 miles east-north-east of Kings Lynn. He came to RAF Marham to familiarize himself with the Mosquito, which was soon to take over from the Venturas flown by 464 (RAAF) and 487 (RNZAF) squadrons. As CFI of 1655 MTU, S/L E.A. Costello-Bowen had been with 105 Squadron since its early Battle and Blenheim days. He had recovered from having evaded capture as a Flight Lieutenant following his crash with W/O Tommy Broom back in August 1942, and was now to show G/C Pickard the ropes. He took Pickard up for two very successful flights. However, on the 9th, F/O S.B. Abbott RAAF, a pilot on the Oxford Flight of 1655 MTU who had previously been a member of 464 Squadron, requested of Pickard that he might be permitted to take his 487 Squadron Ventura AJ454, EG:G up for a short sortie. Permission was granted and S/L Costello-Bowen and Cpl F.R. Magson went along as well. It had stopped raining, and the weather was overcast with good visibility as they turned on to final approach at 15:30 hours, in a moderate to fresh westerly breeze. Tragically, during this manoeuvre, at Larch Wood, 1½ miles to the north-east of

Beechamwell, Norfolk, the aircraft stalled and hit the ground, killing all on board before it burned out. Four days later, on 13 August, the unit stood down as S/L Edgar Alfred Costello-Bowen AFC (46332), F/O Sydney Charles Bertram Abbott DFC, RAAF (Aus. 400404) and Cpl Frank Richard Magson (1165126) were all laid to rest in the local cemetery in Marham village. Cpl Magson's wife and relatives attended, as did S/L Costello-Bowen's friends. Officers from the various courses acted as pall-bearers, following which a bi-denominational service was conducted by the Church of England chaplain, the Reverend D'Arcy-Hutton and Roman Catholic Father O'Meara.

Returning to operations, on the 22/23rd it was back to marking again, and Leverkusen and Brauweiler were attacked. Leverkusen was attacked by 462 aircraft but of the four 105 Squadron Mosquitos, part of a force of thirteen, F/L Raybold in LR507:F had a 'technical failure' and was unable to bomb so F/O Wolstenholme took over in reserve aircraft LR506:E. Each Mosquito dropped two red LB TIs and two red TIs but Oboe was not operating perfectly that night. Düsseldorf and a dozen surrounding towns were hit, instead of the intended I.G. Farben factory, which received only minor damage from the few bombs that did hit Leverkusen. At Brauweiler the Mosquitos were also having difficulties with their MkI Oboe. Consequently, of the six 105 Squadron Mosquitos despatched to accompany the seven from 109 Squadron, two returned early due to engine trouble or failure and the remaining four dropped their loads of three 500lb MC TD .025 and one 500lb GP LD bombs visually. F/O Humphrey was with F/Sgt Moore in DZ408:H, and in frustration after the raid Humphrey simply recorded in his logbook the statement 'Ops: Brauweiler – What A Shambles.'

Oboe redeemed itself the next day, however, as a force of 727 heavies droned their way across the skies to Berlin. Three 105 Squadron Mosquitos and five from 109 Squadron were earmarked to mark their route. The first away from 105 were Wolstenholme and Gallacher in LR507:F, taking off at 20:37 hours. Unfortunately, they had to abandon the task as a flock of birds got in the way and smashed into the ascending Mosquito. It landed safely, and then it was up to S/L Blessing with F/O G.K. Muirhead in LR508:G who left at 20.52 hours, followed 15 minutes later by F/L F.R. Bird with F/O T.L. Hildrew in LR506:E. Red LB TIs fell at 52°50'N; 06°50'E between the Dutch towns of Westerbork and Zweeloo, and green TIs at 52°35'N; 07°02'E just over the German border at Georgsdorf, some 270 miles due west of the 'big city'. The attack by the heavies was partially successful with much of the bombing falling to the south of the city and other areas where villages were hit. However, the attack did cause the most serious damage of the war so far, with the loss to the enemy of 2,611 buildings destroyed and 854 people killed, including two PoWs. It was a costly night for the RAF as well, as some 57 of the Bomber Command 'heavies' were lost due to enemy action, falling foul of a mixture of night-fighters and flak.

The month continued with an operation on the 30th to Duisburg which was marked and bombed by Lt Bud Fisher DFC, USAAF (previously referred to in the records as F/O F.M. Fisher) in DZ550:A. He was accompanied by F/L R.W. 'Bob' Bray DFC in DZ548, previously coded 'D' for Dog but now re-coded 'J' for Jig. Mönchengladbach was also marked that night by four 105 Squadron Mosquitos and eight from 109 Squadron, for a wave of 660 aircraft which also attacked the neighbouring town of Reydt. At Bomber Command, the marking was considered to be excellent and the new 105 Squadron CO, W/C Cundall AFC with S/L A.C. Douglas DFC recorded a 'cope' from LR507:F of only 40yds error.

Ammunition dumps in northern France were the centre of attention on 30/31st, and on the night of 31 August/1 September three of the squadron joined six from 109 Squadron, taking off at 15-minute intervals to route-mark Berlin. The weather was cloudy with moderate visibility as the red TIs fell on a point 50°23'N; 05°45'E near Damvillers, north-east France and green TIs at 50°34'N; 06°10'E near Luxembourg town, for 622 aircraft to follow. The TIs over Berlin were dropped to the south of the city but the main bombing was up to 30 miles away, as some could not see the flares from a distance. This was due to cloud and enemy interceptions by night-fighters, many of which followed the Germans' own flare marking of the bomber stream routes into which the night fighters swarmed. The death toll was high: forty-seven RAF bombers failed to return, but the Mosquitos got home safely.

The early part of September was spent marking 'special targets'. On the 2nd F/O D.C. Dixon and F/L Tommy W. Horton DFC, along with four 109 Squadron Mosquitos, marked ammunition dumps in the Forêt de Mormal near Englefontaine in France, about 40km south-east of Valenciennes. The 105 Squadron crews dropped two red LB TIs and two red TIs from 26,000ft for a formation of five Lancasters. The next evening the operation was repeated, as Horton and Lt Bud Fisher joined another four 109 Squadron Mosquitos to mark another ammunition dump, again with two red LB TIs and two red TIs. This time it was hidden in the Forêt de Raismes, some 10km north-west of Valenciennes, and received the attention of six Halifaxes. There were more 'special targets' on the 8th, when German long-range gun batteries were the target near Boulogne. One target, at 50°43'N; 01°34'E, escaped 105 Squadron Oboe marking when they failed to 'cope' but another at 50°48'N; 01°34'E was marked by two green LB TIs and two red TIs. Altogether, 257 aircraft attacked and were joined by five American B-17 Flying Fortress bombers, on night operations for the first time in the war. However, from a marking and bombing perspective the results were poor and little damage was done to the gun batteries.

On 22 September, six 105 and six 109 Squadron Mosquitos went to Emden, where most bombed on DR due to failure of the Oboe system. The operation was a diversion for the main raid of 711 'heavies' on Hannover that night. On the 23rd, two 105 Squadron Mosquitos route-marked at a point near the Belgian/German border near Simmerath, about 12 miles south-south-east of Aachen. About a quarter of an hour later, three more of the squadron and three from 109 Squadron successfully bombed Aachen itself. As it was realized that it would not be long before the MkI version would be jammed, trials with a new version of Oboe had now begun. W/C Cundall with F/L C.F. Westerman had tested it on 11 September in LR512:O, and for the next two days Aachen was to be the proving ground. Codenamed 'Penwiper', Oboe MkII used a Klystron CV170 tuneable valve and a new IF [Intermediate Frequency] amplifier but failed miserably on both occasions and therefore most of the bombs were dropped on DR.

Operations continued with marking of Bochum for a 352-aircraft musical Parramatta on the 29/30th. Three 105 Squadron Mosquitos set off at nine-minute intervals from 18.36 hours. The first away was F/L F.R. Bird with F/O T.L. Hildrew in LR508:G, followed by F/L C.V. Pereira with F/O Geoffrey H. Gilbert in DZ441:D and lastly Bud Fisher and F/Sgt Leslie Hogan DFM in LR506:E. The aircraft reached the target and marked with red TIs, all except F/L Charles Vernon Pereira's machine, which was held as reserve aircraft. No. 109 Squadron fielded six Mosquitos as well, and Bochum was accurately bombed, with many bombs falling in the old part of the town. The Mosquitos departed for home, two landing safely. Sadly, the third, Fisher's aircraft, crashed one mile north-west of RAF West Raynham in Norfolk, killing both crew members. F/Sgt Hogan was laid to rest in Lancaster's Scotforth cemetery. Meanwhile, back in operations, four other crews were attacking Gelsenkirchen, where three 500lb MC bombs and one 250lb GP LD bomb were dropped from each aircraft. All arrived back to base safely, but S/L Peter Channer DFC and his observer, W/O Kenneth Gordon, landed at RAF Coltishall due to inclement weather.

October saw a vast increase in operational requirements. On the 1st, Witten was ground marked with red TIs for a force of 243 aircraft. Hagen was also bombed, which successfully put many industrial installations out of action, including a manufacturer of U-boat electrical batteries. Areas south of Aachen were again route-marked on the 3rd and 4th, while Aachen itself was the target for Oboe II trials yet again on the 3rd and 7th, with mixed results, until success on the 17th when three Mosquitos of 105 Squadron attacked it successfully with the 'precision device'. Moderate and heavy flak was met over the cloud-covered target and F/O J.R. Hampson with P/O H.W.E. Hammond DFC sustained flak damage to the port wing of ML902:S, but made it back home safely.

The oil target of Castrop-Rauxel was the subject of attention on the 8th and on the 18th Stolberg, Düsseldorf and Duisburg were attacked with mixed results from the Oboe equipment. On the latter raid, F/L R.B. Smith with F/O P.E. Cadman had a narrow escape when Mosquito DZ441:D swung on take-off, resulting in the undercarriage collapsing and the aircraft crashing to the ground. Mercifully, the crew were uninjured. F/L R.W. Bray DFC, whose PFF call sign was 'Peter–Willie' (PW), had a dual Oboe and Gee failure in LR510:N on the 21st. He therefore dropped three 500lb MC bombs and one 250lb GP LD bomb on Aachen as a 'last resort' target, instead of the intended 'primary' target of Büderich. Good fortune was lacking on the 22nd, when having been attacked on the 3rd, 4th and 20th, the last raid of the month on Knapsack power station took place. Six Mosquitos from each of 105 and 109 squadrons left in the early evening. No. 105's DZ591:K was sixth in to attack, but F/L Gordon Sweeney DFC and F/L William George Wood failed to return to base. F/L Sweeney and F/L Wood are commemorated on the Runnymede Memorial. The month ended with attacks on Rheinhausen and Büderich on the 24th and Oberhausen on the 31st, all with a mixture of successful and unsuccessful Oboe operation and bombing on DR.

A ground-marking of Düsseldorf occurred on 3 November for 589 aircraft, during which Lancaster pilot F/L William Reid of 61 Squadron was awarded a VC. The same day, a Krupps factory at Rheinhausen was bombed by 13 Mosquitos, 6 of which were from 105 Squadron and the remainder from 109 Squadron. Three 500lb MC and one 250lb GP bombs fell from each aircraft, except Bray's. He brought back two 500-pounders which had failed to leave the bomb bay. Cliff Streeter recalls: 'When an aircraft returned from an op, it opened its bomb doors, and when the engines had stopped the armourer would remove the fusing links from the bomb racks and show them. It was then known that the bombs had been dropped "live". Sometimes, it happened that the bombs were brought back and if the pilot said that they had been unable to drop them, the bomb doors had to be pumped by hand to the "open" position (not having been opened when the engines were running). Then, with the pilot present, an attempt had to be made to drop them "safe" (unfused). If they did drop, the electrician and armourer who had signed the Form 700 were very relieved; the aircrew presumably were not.'

Returning to operations, Thursday 4 November saw attacks on Aachen and Leverkusen and next day Bochum was the target. Channer in LR508:G and Blessing both dropped six 500-pounders. F/L John Gordon DFC and F/O Ralph Gamble Hayes DFM were returning in DZ587:B, when at 21.10 hours, it crashed into a field at Road Green Farm, Hempnall, about 10 miles south of Norwich, killing both occupants. F/L Gordon was buried in Kileanan burial ground and F/O Hayes in Wandsworth's Putney Vale cemetery. This veteran 105 Squadron crew was the first loss of the month, but sadly there were more to come.

As there were no major targets to be marked, the majority of the month was spent bombing targets at Dortmund, Bochum, Essen, Duisburg, Krefeld and Düsseldorf, mostly with a full complement of six 500lb MC bombs on each Mosquito. Many of these were performed on DR due to failures of the Oboe system.

The 11th saw an attack on Düsseldorf by four of 105 Squadron as well as eight Mosquitos from 109 Squadron. F/O Angus Caesar-Gordon DFM was flying DZ550:A, with his second tour navigator, F/O R.A. 'Dick' Strachan. They had on board 500lb MC bombs to be dropped on an Oboe attack. In Chaz Bowyer's *Mosquito at War* Dick Strachan describes what happened on this, their first Mosquito operation, as they were called up on Oboe and the run to the target began:

The flak started about four or five minutes before the target and immediately it was apparent that it was intense and extremely accurate. Oboe entailed the pilot flying dead straight and level for 10 minutes on the attack run. Suddenly a tremendous flash lit up the sky about 50 yards ahead of our nose and exactly at our altitude. Within a tenth of a second we were through the cloud of dirty yellowish-brown smoke and into the blackness beyond. I shall never forget the spontaneous reaction of both my pilot and myself. We turned our heads slowly and looked long and deep into one another's eyes – no word was spoken – no words were needed. Despite continued heavy flak, we completed our attack run and dropped our bomb-load on the release signal, within a quarter of a mile of the aiming point and, with luck, some damage to a German factory. Turning for home and mighty glad to be out of the flak, I glanced out of the window at the starboard engine and immediately noticed a shower of sparks coming from the starboard engine cowling. A quick glance at the oil temperature gauge showed that it was going off the clock. Only one thing for it, and the pilot pressed the extinguisher button and then feathered the engine. The sparking ceased but we now had 300 miles to go and only one engine to do it on. I remember thinking this wasn't much of a do for our first operation, but at least we had a good deal of altitude and still had a fair amount of speed, even with just one engine. The danger was interception by a German night fighter and I spent a lot of time craning my neck around to check the skies about our tail. The other thing I remember was a terrible consciousness of our own weight, sitting as I was on the starboard side. However this feeling wore off and the remainder of the flight home to base was uneventful. Then came the strain of a night landing on one engine . . . again that awful awareness of how heavy I was . . . but after one anti-clockwise circuit, a superb approach and magnificent landing. I recall the great feeling of relief as the wheels touched the runway. I also remember the urgent desire to get my hands round a jug of beer to relieve the dryness in my throat and to celebrate a safe return from what was to prove my worst experience on Mosquitos. Needless to say, the beer was not long in forthcoming.

On the 15th, a specific target, the Rheinmetall Borsig AG ironworks at Düsseldorf, was bombed. Two aircraft bombed the primary with the others bombing 'last resort' (secondary) targets in the Duisburg, Krefeld and Düsseldorf area. On the operation to Düsseldorf, it was a clear night as ten Mosquitos of 105 Squadron plus one from 109 Squadron were routed over Krefeld. Blessing was flying ML913:E with his observer, F/Sgt D.T. Burke, when the enemy realized their track and 30/40 searchlights scanned the skies and flak poured up in reprisal. Soon shrapnel burst all round and some thudded into the aircraft. One piece scythed up through F/Sgt Burke's navigation board and through his hand. Meanwhile, in ML919:V, F/L Humphrey was having his own problems. He recalls: 'Suddenly, everything came at us. A flak shell went off a few feet under the aircraft and turned us upside down. We went into a spin but survived, however I had been hit in the foot and leg. The Germans were extremely good with flak, especially when you were flying down a beam. Fortunately, they didn't have enough of it. We landed all right, at an American airfield [Hardwick], and although the flak didn't hit our engines, one stopped on return. There were two things about operational flying: low-level had been extremely dangerous but not very frightening, as one was working so hard – Oboe was terrifying; flying dead straight and level along a beam and letting them shoot at you!' One other aircraft, ML904:T crewed by F/L J.R. Hampson and F/O H.W.E. Hammond DFC, RCAF, went missing and it transpired that the crew had been shot down and taken as PoWs ending up for the duration, as several others of the squadron, in Stalag Luft 3.

The August Thyssen AG foundry in Duisburg and the semi-finished products of the Bochumer Verein in Bochum were the targets for 17 November. On the 18th, Harris's Battle of Hamburg finished, and his Battle of Berlin began. The same day, Aachen was specially marked by two 105 Squadron Mosquitos, but F/L R.B. Castle with P/O J. Griffiths in DZ489:D had to abandon the primary and bombed a 'last resort' target before returning to base, where they overshot the landing area and crashed at 23.31 hours without serious personal injury. The aircraft was damaged beyond repair.

The IG Farbenindustrie AG chemical works at Leverkusen was the subject of an abortive sortie on the 19th due to technical failures but received four 500-pounders on the 22nd from Channer in LR508:G. Meanwhile, five others of the squadron attacked 'last resort' targets in the Leverkusen area and Köln. On the 23rd, the Goldenbergwerke power station at Knapsack was to be attacked by three of 105 Squadron. The first away was S/L J.S.W. Bignall AFC who attacked a 'last resort' target in LR507:F, followed by F/L C.F. Boxall who managed to hit the primary target with four 500lb MC bombs from ML913:E. The target was clearly visible and despite 100 searchlights probing the sky, the flak was light. Nevertheless, LR477:B returned early and P/O Eric Wade BEM with F/O Alfred Gerald Fleet joined the circuit. At 19.50 hours their Mosquito crashed 5 miles north-west of Swaffham in Norfolk, at Narborough's Contract Farm. Tragically, both occupants were killed. F/O Wade was buried in Keighley (Utley) cemetery and F/O Fleet in Bowling cemetery in Bradford.

Thereafter, on the 28th, F/L Wolstenholme returned safely from an attack on the Fried Krupp AG foundry at Essen when his aircraft DZ429:B started to vibrate viciously over the North Sea, about 50 miles east of Great Yarmouth, where he jettisoned his bombs. Angus Caesar-Gordon with Dick Strachan in DZ408:H and S/L J.S.W. Bignall DFC with F/O G.F. Caldwell DFM in ML913:E bombed the target safely, although DZ408:H received some flak damage.

The month ended with attacks on the Rheinmetall Borsig AG ironworks at Düsseldorf and the steel producers Vereinigte Stahlwerke AG at Bochum. During the latter, the CO, W/C Cundall AFC, met problems, as he explains: 'Tommy [S/L I.F. Tamango DFC] and I had just made a successful run to the Target Release Point at some 30,000ft and −30°C, when the cabin suddenly filled with steam from the heating system. Up to that point, the flak had been about normal for the Ruhr Valley and Bochum. The fumes came in from the port side of the cabin and I feathered the port airscrew. While this was happening, all the cold surfaces inside the cabin were quickly coated in ice: windows, instruments, the lot. Tommy cleared the escape hatch ready for use. The weather was good and by removing some ice from a patch of windscreen, it was possible to re-orientate and level the aircraft. Some more urgent scratching at flight and engine instruments showed it was the starboard engine that was really in trouble so that had to be feathered too. The port engine looked OK although it had already stopped. As soon as the starboard feathering was complete, I started the port engine again and all went well for our return to base in good weather, from a height of about 19,000ft. The forecast risk of fog at base did not materialize and we thanked God also, for an aircraft which hardly needed a second engine in these circumstances.' So ended November 1943.

December began with a visit by Marshal of the Royal Air Force, Lord Trenchard, who addressed the aircrews in the afternoon. As recorded in the ORB, 'He congratulated the squadron on the excellent work they had done leading the heavy force during the Battle of the Ruhr, and also on their present role of precision attacks on special targets.' The remainder of the month saw a return to many targets attacked previously, such as Hamborn, Leverkusen, Krefeld, Düsseldorf, Liège, Aachen and Bochum. However, on the 12th tragedy struck. The Krupps works at Essen was the target. No searchlights were seen due to 10/10ths cloud, but flak, nearly absent on arrival, was encountered towards the end of the attack. Sadly, F/O Benjamin Frank Reynolds with F/O John Douglas Phillips in DK354:D crashed in the Netherlands at Herwijnen, on the north bank of the Waal river. The two airmen were subsequently laid to rest in the Herwijnen General cemetery.

Other targets of vital interest to the RAF were the Germans' V-1 rocket sites. The V stood for *Vergeltung* – German for reprisal. Nicknamed the 'doodle-bug', the V-1, or Fiesler Fi103, was a flying bomb propelled by a pulse jet engine mounted above its fuselage. Some 8 metres long, it flew on an integral automatic pilot guided by a gyroscope. The pulsing, low-frequency throb of the engine could be heard as it flew along its trajectory before, at a predetermined range, the engine cut and the bomb would glide silently to earth where its 1,875lb warhead would explode. Since the famous RAF attack on the experimental station at Peenemünde on 17 August 1943, it was known that the Germans would try to erect rocket sites in northern France. Concrete structures were evident from PR sorties in the Pas-de-Calais and Cherbourg peninsula areas. By December 1943, it became certain that the structures were, in fact, V-1 sites and consequently ops referred to as 'Crossbow' began to the sites, which were codenamed 'Noball' sites. They were to be obliterated before the Germans could start to get the weapons in the air. The attention of 105's Mosquitos was drawn to the V-1 sites, and special ops were flown to mark them for the 'heavies' following on behind.

On 16/17 December, sites near Abbeville were attacked. S/L Channer in LR508:G led the first 105 Squadron wave of three Mosquitos. Three from 109 Squadron also took part, to mark a point 50°03'04''N; 02°05'35''E, at Tilley-le-Haut, each dropping two green TIs and one yellow TI. Twenty-six Stirlings were to have bombed the site, but they were let down by the Mosquitos' Oboe which failed. This was followed by S/L Blessing in LR507:F who was to mark a point 50°05'15''N; 01°59'10''E, a wood at Flixecourt, with the next wave of three 105 Mosquitos. Again, they were accompanied by the same number from 109 Squadron. One failed to mark due to Oboe failure, but Blessing and W/C F.A. Green DFC in ML911:U both marked successfully, each dropping two green TIs and two green LB TIs. Subsequently, nine 617 (Dambuster) Squadron Lancasters dropped 12,000lb 'Tallboy' blast bombs which missed by 100 yards. This was put down to the inaccuracy of the Oboe marking, which was unfortunately some 350 yards from the required point.

On the 21st an unusual operation took place as seven Mosquitos of 105 Squadron and five of 109 Squadron were despatched to bomb Aachen and then to carry on to a second site to route-mark Berlin. Thereafter, 397 heavies followed the markers as they droned their way to the 'big city'. Jack Watts noted in *Nickels and Nightingales*: 'Navigation of the Oboe aircraft on this dual operation was much more demanding than usual. The need for accuracy was just as great at both target locations, and there was no slack to compensate for any time lost on the first operation. It required a high standard of crew discipline over a longer period than we had faced on any of our earlier Oboe sorties.'

The last ops of the year were on the 30th, when Bochum was attacked and a further attempt was made to mark a V-1 flying bomb site at Cherbourg. The Vereinigte Stahlwerke AG steelworks at Bochum was attacked by S/L Bignal in LR507:F. W/O I.B. McPherson returned in DZ589:C without having dropped his bombs as he had reached the target but could not identify the primary, and S/L Channer returned early with an engine problem. On the V-1 operation, of the two that went out, one Mosquito found the target. F/O Humphrey with P/O L.C. Poll dropped four 500lb GP bombs from DZ408:H on target through 3/10ths low cloud. Blessing, who was first away from base, attacked a 'last resort' target in DZ548:J.

And so ended 1943, a year that saw heavy losses initially during the daylight operations with 2 Group and thankfully saw the losses diminished somewhat in the night operational 8 Group PFF role.

CHAPTER 17

The Heat is On

In 1944, the number of sorties required of 105 Squadron rose dramatically. It would not be practicable to describe all of them in this book but we shall give consideration to the more notable operations and events which occurred as the year progressed.

The first ops of the year were largely industrial, with attacks on steel producers at Ruhrstahl AG at Witten, J.A. Henckels Zwillingwerke AG at Solingen, Fried Krupp AG works at Essen, Verstahlwerke at Duisburg and Deutsche Edalstahlwerke AG at Krefeld. It was not all plain sailing however, as during the attack on the Krupp Stahl AG works at Rheinhausen on 14 January, F/L Castle in ML921:X met with flak which damaged his port engine nacelle and stabbed into the starboard side of the fuselage. Fortunately the result was not fatal and the crew returned safely at 06.25 hours.

The Rheinmetall Borsig AG ironworks at Düsseldorf and the Mannesmannröhrenwerke AG iron and steel tube plant at Rath were attacked on the 20th. On the latter attack, S/L J. Comer and observer P/O E. Jenkins DFM had a narrow escape when their Mosquito DZ408:H was returning from what should have been an attack on Mannesmannröhrenwerke AG, but a 'last resort' target had been bombed. The two airmen had to take to their parachutes at 20.43 hours, when their Mosquito became uncontrollable and ploughed into the ground 3 miles east of Kings Lynn at Waveland Farm, Grimston. Happily both airmen survived, with S/L Comer receiving a strained left knee.

The Gutehoffnungshütte AG foundry at Obershausen was also attacked, as was the ironworks of Rheinmetall Borsig AG at Derendorf on the 23rd, following which F/L Wolstenholme and P/O V.E. Piper crash-landed LR508:G at RAF Manston due to lack of elevator control. Again the crew, and this time the aircraft too, survived.

Also receiving attention throughout January were the Chemische Werke industrial chemicals plant at Huis, and the Mannesmannröhrenwerke AG iron and steel tube plant at Untererthal. The 25th saw a full squadron effort with 14 Mosquitos sent to bomb the Nazi HQ at Aachen. In the event, 10 found the primary and 40 bombs were despatched through the cloud on to the target despite light accurate flak. Two days later, 8 of 12 aircraft were despatched, again to bomb Aachen and to drop green TI 'spoof' route markers just north of the town. All got back safely, although F/L J.W. Jordan in DZ550:A noticed his starboard engine overheating and made a precautionary landing at RAF Manston in Kent.

Airfields at Gilze Rijen, Venlo and Deelen were also the subject of attention at the close of the month. For a while thereafter, one target became the centre of concentrated attention: the G&I Jager GmbH ball-bearing factory at Elberfeld. It was the subject of the last attack of January and into February was to be attacked on a further eight occasions. Although the attacks were without loss, after the third visit on 5 February, an NFT took the lives of F/L John Fosbroke Slatter and observer F/O Peter Oscar Hedges. They had taken off in the afternoon in DZ548:J. Once airborne, the Mosquito hit a USAAF Boeing B-17G of the 96th Bombardment Group's 337th Bombardment Squadron from Snetterton, Norfolk. The Mosquito came down near St Ives, killing both its occupants. F/L Slatter was laid to rest in Salford (St Matthew) churchyard and F/O Hedges in Crystal Palace District cemetery. The Fortress, AW:B serial 42-97480, landed safely with minor damage. However, the 96th Bombardment Group was not always as fortunate, as they were destined in the first four months of 1944 to become the group to have the highest number of losses in the whole of the 8th Air Force.

RAF Marham was visited by HRH the Duke of Gloucester on the 11th. Wearing the uniform of an air marshal, and accompanied by AVM D.C.T. Bennett CB, CBE, DSO – AOC 8 Group, he inspected the aircrew who were presented to him by the Station Commander, W/C H.J. 'Butch' Cundall DFC, AFC.

Throughout the remainder of February, airfields at Gilze Rijen, Deelen, Volkel, St Trond, Twente, Venlo and Leeuwarden were attacked with 500lb GP, 500lb GP SD and 500lb GP LD bombs, all without loss. While the airfields were pounded, the V-1 sites in northern France were not forgotten, with attacks on the 19th and 21st. The only casualty came on the 23rd when F/O L. Holiday DFM was briefed to attack Düsseldorf in ML902:S. The aircraft received damage to the fuselage on the starboard side and the navigator, F/O C.L. French, was wounded in the thigh. They made it back nevertheless, having attacked the primary target. Both crew members were temporarily awarded the PFF badge on the 26th. There had been no operational deaths on the squadron this month.

March started with an operation on the 1st, in support of an attack by heavies on Stuttgart. In all, 557 aircraft took part, comprising 415 Lancasters, 129 Halifaxes and 13 Mosquitos. No. 105 Squadron were to field 12 Mosquitos out of a diversionary force of 18, to harass the enemy aerodromes and keep the fighters occupied, away from the main stream of bombers. Airfields at Volkel, Florennes, St Trond and Venlo were to be attacked without cloud cover over the Netherlands and only broken cloud to the west. At Florennes however, Oboe let the attackers down and a 'last resort' target was bombed instead. The other targets all received due attention and 500lb GP and GP SD bombs rained down. The Mosquitos arrived back safely but a heavy snowstorm at base made things increasingly difficult and some aircraft had to wait, to land when the storms momentarily abated. Three Lancaster MkIIIs and one Halifax MkIII were lost to enemy action, accounting for 0.7 per cent of the force.

On the 2nd, Australian F/O R.B. Smith was flying alone in DZ372:C. Despite managing to write the aircraft off when coming in to land at 19.45 hours at RAF Marham, he survived. The same day saw a milestone in 105 Squadron operations, with the first operation using the new B.XVI 'high-altitude' Mosquito. This aircraft, an adaptation of the B.IX, had a pressurized cabin and Marshall's blower, and was equipped with the more powerful two-stage Merlin 72 (starboard)/73 (port) engines. (Later versions were equipped with Merlin 76 (starboard)/77 (port) engines.) The first B.XVIs could carry four 500lb bombs in the aircraft with one 500lb bomb on each wing station or alternatively, a useful ordnance of four 500lb bombs with two 100-gallon wing-mounted drop tanks. These were modified early in 1944, to carry the 4,000lb 'blockbuster' in a bulbous bomb-bay with two 50-gallon wing-mounted drop tanks, giving an altitude limit of 37,000ft. Some were fitted with paddle-blades to increase the performance and allow the ceiling to be stretched to 40,000ft, however there was a consequential loss of performance at lower levels.

For the operation, six Mosquito crews, four from 105 and two from 109 Squadron were led by W/C H.J. Butch Cundall and his navigator S/L I.F. Tamango. They were to attempt to ground-mark an aircraft assembly plant of SNCA du Nord, at Meulan-Les Mureaux, about 15 miles north-west of Paris. The plant, which originally turned out Potez aircraft for the French, had since occupation produced 15 Messerschmitt Me108s each month, as well as components for Bf 109s and Dornier Do24s. The plan was that the Mosquitos would drop red and green long-burning TIs for a force of following Halifaxes, 54 from 4 Group and 63 from 6 Group.

The leader had taken his new aircraft ML938:D for a 1 hour 20 minute height test on 29 February, and a 40-minute navigation flight test (NFT) during the day to ensure the Oboe set was operating in conjunction with the ground stations. The operation opened with their Oboe run at 03.05 hours but, much to their dismay, there was a complete failure to 'cope', which the crew put down to ground station 'fingers'. Butch Cundall explains: 'Great pressure was on to use new equipment as early and as much as possible. Dr F.E. Jones and his boffins were in residence with us from TRE at Great Malvern, at all times, doing what was effectively development work and technical training of our groundcrews. The ground stations on the coast were in a similar state and there were inevitably a number of abortive sorties.'

Consequently, five minutes later than expected, two 109 Squadron aircraft, F/L Hunter with F/L Crabb in HS:A and F/L Jacobs with F/L Tipton in HS:N started the innings, each dropping four long-burning red TIs. Trouble dogged 105's S/L L.F. Austin DFC with S/L C.F. Westerman DFC in LR508:G, and F/L D.C. Dixon with F/L W.A. Christensen, the Australian from New South Wales, in ML914:K who failed to 'cope'. Consequently, neither dropped their four green long-burning TIs. The 105 Squadron side was nevertheless kept up by the reserve aircraft ML913:E, when Wolstenholme and F/L V.E.R. Piper dropped four red long-burning TIs at 03.18 hours before returning to land at 04.33 hours. The raid was nevertheless successful and the following 'heavies' inflicted considerable damage. The squadron ORB noted: 'The main assembly shops, the factory testing hangars and the sea-plane base have all been completely wrecked. Extremely severe damage, amounting almost to destruction, has been done to the electrical power plant, while in the machine shops, the four largest bays forming one building have been wiped out. The stores and paint shops have suffered blast damage to the roof in the centre section and there are numerous direct hits on the extreme western and eastern ends of the long narrow extension. An auxiliary building to the south of the stores and paint shops are completely gutted and were still on fire over 12 hours after the attack. Blast damage has been done to the final assembly hangars and the maintenance shops, and one quarter of the building to the east of the machine shops has disappeared. Immediately to the east and adjoining the factory is the airfield, and extensive damage has been done to the hangars.' It seemed that the facility would not be operational for some time.

The temperamental nature of the Oboe equipment showed up further on the 5th when two of each of 105 and 109 squadrons were to mark Duisburg for three Mosquitos carrying 4,000lb 'blockbusters'. S/L Peter J. Channer DFC had to abandon the task before reaching the target as his Oboe equipment blew up, leaving a strong burning smell inside the cockpit. He returned safely to land ML920:W at 03.31 hours. They met slight but accurate flak on the run-in to the target, hitting F/L C.P. Gibbons' 109 Squadron Mosquito ML939 at 30,000ft, fortunately without fatal results, but also menacing his colleague, F/L E.M. Hunter in ML960. However, 105's F/L G.W. Harding in ML508:G also 'coped' and reported a cloud of smoke and a red flare hanging over the target. The same target was attacked the next night. Three of 105's Mosquitos went out and ML913:E, flown by F/L Wolstenholme, sustained flak damage to the starboard undercarriage door and starboard flap. He returned safely nevertheless.

The 'blockbuster' bombs, sometimes referred to as 'cookies', brought their dangers for the groundcrews as well as the enemy, as L.W. 'Wally' Fennell, who was a 105 Squadron armourer, recalls:

We [armourers] were known as the Mad B——s. Some time in early '44, the sergeant in the bomb dump phoned me to say there had been a mishap with a 'cookie', a 4,000lb bomb. A winch had slipped (two were used) when lifting an unfused bomb. On one of the bars, the hook had slipped under and taken all of the strain. One bolt had sheared, and he asked 'could I fix it?' I told him to send the trailer to the armoury and I would personally put it right. I was sitting on a sack as the bombs were cold, with a cow-mouth chisel and a hammer, and started to tap away to unscrew the stud of the bolt. It did not dawn on me that there was no one walking past the armoury. Suddenly, the Chiefy and the Armaments Officer arrived and asked what I was doing, or words to that effect. I told him and we all had a good, and I mean good, laugh. It seemed that the Station CO had phoned to say that an officer had phoned him to say that a bloody maniac was sitting on a f——ing great bomb, hitting it with a f——ing hammer. A few phone calls from the Armaments Officer put the station at ease again. I was known as the 'mad Corporal' ever after!

As the RAF began to prepare for the 'Second Front', further attacks began in a campaign of depletion of communications within the Normandy area. This started on 4 March, under a directive issued by the Air Staff to ACM Harris to see if precision bombing could work sufficiently well on railway networks, ammunition dumps and airfields. Harris drew up a list of marshalling yards, seven in all, at Trappes, Aulnoye, Le Mans, Amiens, Courtrai, Laon and Vaires-sur-Marne, all of which were to be visited. Consequently, 105 Squadron sprang into action and those at Trappes were marked on the 6th and at Le Mans on the 7th. The latter in particular was of great importance as they served western and north-western French communications. On the same day, an attack was made on the road and rail junction at Aachen. Three 500lb GP and one 500lb GP LD bombs were to be delivered by two aircraft. The first Mosquito, DZ429:B flown by F/O C. Chadwick, failed to 'cope' and returned with the bombs. The other aircraft, a modified B.IV Mosquito, DZ550:A, flown by W/O Grenville Eaton, had an exciting time, as he explains:

Crossing Holland at 28,000ft, with a clear sky, we could see the distant Zuider Zee, now converted into polders of dry land. We switched on Oboe, and found we were early, so guided by the navigator [W/O J.E. Fox] I wasted a precise number of minutes and seconds until finding and settling into the 'beam' towards the target, about fifteen minutes flying time away. We noticed we were leaving long white contrails behind us – frozen water vapour crystals in the exhaust of each engine. Suddenly streams of cannon-shells and tracers enveloped us from the rear, hitting us in numerous places, but luckily missing Jack, me and the engines. I immediately dived down to port, then up to starboard several times, then resumed height and regained the beam. The only protection was a sheet of steel behind my seat. Most instruments seemed to work, so we continued. Half a minute later, a second and noisier attack came from the rear, so I again took evasive action, more violent and longer and again gained height and beam. Now there was considerable damage to dashboard, hydraulics, fuselage and shells had missed us, truly by inches. However, engines and Oboe still worked, so being so near we had to continue to target, deliver the load, and turn for home, changing course and height frequently, and assessing the damage as far as we could. Certainly hydraulics, flaps, brakes, airspeed indicator and various other instruments were smashed – but we were OK.

At Marham, landing in pitch darkness was a problem, but for safety I landed on the grass, starboard of the main runway [which was also grass] by feel, I suppose, at about 150 knots, with no brakes. We hurtled across the aerodrome, just missing two huge armament dumps, straight on through the hedges and violently into a ditch. Jack was out of the emergency exit like a flash. I could not move, nor could I undo the safety belt. Jack leaped back, released me, and we scampered away to a safe distance in case of exploding petrol tanks, and emergency services were quickly there. Debriefing was interesting, as not only was our run 'seen' on the cathode ray tube, but our bombing error was calculated and we wondered whether all operations were to be like this one!! [his second on Mosquitos] Incidentally, we

Pilot F/O J.W. Grenville Eaton DFC.
(Via Cliff Streeter)

never saw the attacking fighter. Soon afterwards, I was privileged to be awarded an immediate Distinguished Flying Cross [DFC] – I believe the first for a Warrant Officer on 105 Squadron – but Jack deserved one too. Our aircraft, 'A' for Apple, was a write-off, but my engine fitter carved a model which I still cherish.

W/O Eaton's immediate award of DFC was announced on 17 April 1944.

That same night, F/L Caesar-Gordon took the squadron's first 4,000lb 'blockbuster' to the Reich itself, to the Verstahlwerke steel production in Hamborn. The target could not be identified so the bomb was dropped on the Duisburg area instead. One limitation of operating with the 4,000lb bomb was the risk of an engine failure on take-off, which could result in a huge explosion, whether the bomb was fused or not. Maximum speed was given to the aircraft on take-off by keeping on the runway as long as possible before lifting off, often to about 200 yards from the end. The theory was that should an engine fail, the heavy aircraft might have more chance of maintaining flying speed. Should there be a problem on return, the jettisoned bomb would almost certainly explode and so there was a jettison area designated for this purpose in The Wash. For the former reason, this operation was flown from RAF Graveley, 5 miles south of Huntingdon, home at this time to nos 35 and 692 PFF Squadrons. Graveley had a solid runway, as opposed to the rough grass at RAF Marham, which was not satisfactory for this type of operation. Graveley was also the first base to be equipped with the fog-dispersing FIDO system, an acronym for 'Fog Investigation and Dispersal Operation'. Trenched piping feeding

143

burners ran in parallel for 1,000 yards of the approach and the same length and 50 yards from it, along either side of the runway. The burners heated the feeder pipes and therefore would emit clean burning vaporized petrol along their length. This locally evaporated the fog on a 150-yard wide strip, allowing the aircraft to descend into the corridor and land safely. The device worked well and saved many lives. RAF Woodbridge emergency landing ground on the Suffolk coast was also equipped with FIDO, and Dennis Bolesworth described landing there: 'It always reminded me of flying into the jaws of hell, with the fire tender and blood wagon [ambulance] chasing up the runway and stopping. The hatch was flung open and the dulcet tones rang out, "How many dead and how many wounded?" to which we replied "none" – thank God!'

At last, on 12 March, the first 'blockbuster' reached its primary target. Bignal and Caldwell took off from Graveley in ML938:D, accompanied by two Mosquitos of 109 Squadron, and had the satisfaction of witnessing, amidst moderate flak, a huge flash through the cloud from where the bomb struck the Verstahlwerke steel works at Hamborn. Throughout the month marshalling yards were still being targeted, in accordance with the Air Staff's directive. Trappes, Le Mans and Amiens were attacked with good results. In the latter, 605 tons of bombs had laid waste to several parts of the north-east and southern areas of the yards. Railway workshops, storage buildings, tracks, sidings, rolling stock, a road bridge, roundhouse, engine sheds, and lines under construction were all severely molested.

Diversionary raids on airfields at St Trond, Venlo and Deelen were flown in support of Bomber Command 'heavy' attacks by 863 aircraft on Stuttgart on the night of the 15/16th. However this did not sway the fighters entirely, and they attacked the main force, which lost 37 aircraft (4.3 per cent) with many of their bombs falling in open country south-west of the city due to poor Path Finder marking. Some bombs did hit Stuttgart however, and eighty-eight people were killed.

Further support operations were flown for attacks on Frankfurt. On the night of the 18/19th airfields at St Trond, Volkel and Venlo were attacked and on the 22/23rd Leewarden, Venlo, Deelen and Juliandorp were to be the targets. The heavies bombed Frankfurt with 846 and 816 aircraft on respective nights and caused massive damage due to the much-improved PFF marking. The first time 2.6 per cent of the heavies failed to return and 4 per cent on the latter attack.

There was however one tragic incident for 105 Squadron as well. On the 22nd, F/L Charles Frank Boxall with F/L T.W. Robinson DFC were flying LR476:T. They had taken off at 19.55 hours, accompanied by two other aircraft, to attack the airfield at Deelen, which they did successfully through 5/10ths cloud. One of the 500lb MC wing-mounted bombs hung up and refused to drop off. The Mosquito had to return with this appendage until arrival back at RAF Marham. At 22.50 hours they came in to land, when the starboard wing-bomb jarred itself free and exploded, causing the wing to disintegrate and the aircraft to burn out. The pilot died and was laid to rest in Cambridge City cemetery. F/L Robinson, the observer, was injured but survived. He was taken to the RAF Hospital at Ely, suffering from shock and severe burns to his left foot and minor burns on the right foot. In addition, he had a fractured left clavicle and facial abrasions. Cliff Streeter of 105 Squadron's Electrical Section recalls the tragedy: 'The first time wing-bombs were carried, the grease from the bomb release froze and hung up a bomb until the aircraft landed when it dropped and blew up causing casualties, leaving us wondering what the heck was happening. This was only one of quite a few tragic accidents.' It is of interest to note that on the same day as the Venlo operation, F/L J.H. Ford with F/L L.W. Millett also had a wing-bomb hang up on LR508:G, though thankfully the crew returned safely.

CHAPTER 18

Bourn's Second Front

The limitations of RAF Marham were now becoming apparent, such as the requirement to use other aerodromes such as RAF Graveley when operating with the new 'blockbusters'. It was soon decided that RAF Marham should be upgraded for use by the largest bombers and concrete runways should be laid. The work would take 18 months to complete. Therefore, on the morning of 23 March 1944, propellers were turning and Mosquitos were lining up on the runway ready for departure, but this time for permanent departure from RAF Marham as the squadron, along with 9105 Servicing Echelon, was being transferred to RAF Bourn, 6 miles west of Cambridge. Before they left, however, RAF Marham was given a traditional low-level 'beat-up' for old time's sake before the Mosquitos flew off to RAF Bourn. The sky was covered with 9/10ths cloud at 3,500ft, with a visibility of 5 miles and a 2-knot south-south-easterly breeze as the new base controllers waited for their new incumbents. Soon runway 192 was alive with incoming Mosquitos for over an hour. The first in was ML902:S at 11.08 hours, followed one minute later by ML938:D, then LR503:C, ML916:L, LR507:F, ML964:J, ML914:K, ML922:Y, LR508:G, MM237:M, LR512:O, ML913:E, ML919:V, LR504:H, ML920:W and lastly ML911:U at 12.11 hours: 105 Squadron had arrived.

The new station was, in F/L Bill Riley DFC and bar's eyes: 'A wartime-built station and not nearly as comfortable. We lived in [Nissen] huts. People tended to go into Cambridge if they were free in the evenings. There were often pick-up games of football, cricket and baseball. I remember that the Aussies not only usually won at cricket, but were also capable of beating the Canadians at baseball!' Doubtless the football would have been well coached and commented on, as pilot P/O Ian B. McPherson, a Scot from the Glasgow area, played professionally for Glasgow Rangers pre-war and thereafter for Arsenal, and pilot F/L Kenneth Wolstenholme became a well-known television and radio sports commentator after the war. Electrician Cliff Streeter also remembers the station:

When we were at Bourn, the local pub was The Fox. Quite a few hectic evenings were spent there and many RAF-type songs were sung. It was also close to the Old North Road station, handy for a quick rail return after hitch-hiking when off duty for a day or two. The Fox landlord was quite happy for us to leave our cycles in his yard ready for a quick dash back to the billet in the early morning, before work started at the flight and the hope that you hadn't been missed. Sometimes, while waiting for the aircraft to return from ops at night, we would do a repair on one of the aircrew's cars while he was away. It gave one something to think about while one waited. I well recall one night, after doing a repair along with Len Ellis, we decided to take it for a test run around the perimeter track which was well defined all the way round by dim blue lights. As we blasted round at goodness knows what speed, the lights went out, resulting in complete and utter darkness and complete and utter panic on my part. However, we made it back to the section – very slowly. The navigator never did know how close he had come to having his car bent.

Despite this, F/L Riley made the following comment: 'I feel strongly that a tribute should be made to the groundcrews. They worked in all conditions, and the aircraft were always ready. A

Mosquito B.IX, LR504, GB:H, 'The Grim Reaper' at Bourn in August 1944. Standing in front of it are (left to right): AC2 Smeaton; F/L Riley (pilot); F/L Chadwick (navigator) and Corporal Tout. This aircraft passed to 109 Squadron and was struck off charge on 14 September 1945. (Via A.W. Farrell/Bill Riley)

few holes in the woodwork were repaired very quickly, by glueing bits where they were needed. The engines and technical equipment were serviced by hard and sustained work.'

Cliff Streeter amplified this: 'Working at dispersal was great in fine weather but on a hot, sunny day, the cockpit of a Mossie could become almost unbearable. Sometimes in the summer we would find a bird's nest in the grass filled with eggs, and they would be marked so that hopefully moving aircraft would avoid them. When working outside an aircraft on an icy, snowy winter's day, there would be a few curses flying around, especially from engine fitters, as frozen fingers grappled with small screws, nuts and bolts. However whatever it was, it had to be done and usually was.' Conditions could be very severe and required improvization, as he further describes: 'One cold winter, our water at the billets froze up, so we made a lethal water heater from a large jam tin, with a wooden slat clipped across the top, and a carbon rod from a torch battery hanging down from it. A lead was soldered to the tin, and another to the brass top of the carbon rod and "hey presto!" with some water begged from a nearby house, and some ice added – hot water! I go white thinking about it now.'

Having arrived at the new station, there was initially little time to spare and the first operation started immediately, as marshalling yards at Laon were visited by six crews from both 105 and

109 squadrons. The latter squadron were also to leave RAF Marham (on 2 April), to commence operations from RAF Little Staughton in Bedfordshire, situated between Bedford and Cambridge. Out of 143 aircraft only the first wave of 72 'heavies' bombed Laon. They were aiming for the marshalling yards, which half the force managed to hit, the remainder landing on housing in a 3km radius, killing seven people.

Attacks continued to build up for the remainder of the month on railways and marshalling yards and the usual supporting airfield diversionary attacks on Twente, St Trond and Venlo. On 25 March, Aulnoye marshalling yards were the subject of attention of six Mosquitos and two reserves. A total of 192 aircraft were to bomb on their markers. The ORB records: 'The marking was so accurate that S/L Bird reported the reds and greens as being in one big cluster with bombs bursting right across them.' The next night Essen was the target and in particular the Krupps works. A force of 705 bombers were preceded by six 105 Squadron Mosquitos, one of which was a reserve aircraft and one, LR507:F flown by F/L Jordan, lost an exhaust stub and returned early. The weather to the target was clear on the way but 10/10ths (complete) cover over the continent. The Mosquitos were loaded, each with two red long-burning TIs and one ordinary red TI. The visual backers-up were to drop the green TIs. Over the target there was a great deal of haze with thin cloud, the top of which was about 10,000ft. F/L Bob Bray DFC was in ML911:U with F/L T.W. Pierce DFC and started the attack. Testimony to the accurate marking came in the form of a large red glow emanating from the ground, visible through the haze, accompanied by a large explosion just north of the aiming point. So intensive was the glow of the burning fires that it was visible as far as the Dutch coast. Following the marking the squadron dropped 'spoof' markers over Bochum to confuse the enemy before returning to base. Due to the switch of target back to the Ruhr, the Germans were taken by surprise. Not only was there a lack of the usual searchlights, but flak was mild and as a result, of the 705 aircraft that went out to bomb the markers, only 1.3 per cent of the main force were lost, amounting to nine heavies, comprising six Lancasters and three Halifaxes. All Mosquitos returned safely to RAF Bourn.

That same night, three aircraft of 105 Squadron, accompanied by four of 109, also visited the marshalling yards at Courtrai to mark for a force of 109 heavy aircraft. Again accurate marking with four long-burning red TIs allowed the bombers to drop their loads. F/L Ford and F/L Millett in LR497:A did two runs, dropping two markers each time and reported that 'the bombing of the first wave was very good but the last two waves produced little further effect'. Further, they noted 'a good concentration of fires spreading to the north-east and others to the south-east and south-west. A number of explosions were seen.' There was no defensive flak and no aircraft were shot down. The accuracy of the bombing was nevertheless in question as built-up areas were hit. *The Bomber Command War Diaries* notes that it was stated in a detailed report on the bombing by local historian José Vanbossele that: 'It is obvious that the bombing spread to many built-up areas beyond the railway targets. Three hundred and thirteen buildings in the town were destroyed, including the gaol, where five prisoners were killed, and a Catholic school, where nine nuns died. When the gaol was hit, several prisoners escaped including a local butcher who had been caught helping airmen to evade capture. The total number of civilians killed was 252; of these 79 people were not local inhabitants, but visitors who had come to Courtrai for the celebration of a religious feast.' The marshalling yards had nevertheless been plastered as PRU photos showed. Engine sheds and a turntable were hit in the reception sidings. Hits were scored in the forward sidings, passenger stock and the marshalling yard, where thirty sidings tracks were cut and wagons damaged. Furthermore, direct hits were scored on multi-bay shops alongside the reception sidings, and damage was done to a factory just south of the yard. Despite the damage outside the railway area, the operation had been a complete success.

At Vaires-sur-Marne, 16 miles east of Paris, the marshalling yards were the subject of the operation on 29 March. Four markers from 105 and 109 Squadrons took off to drop red TIs. As they left, the 76 Halifaxes from Nos 4 and 6 Groups went to work. Due to the accuracy of the marking, they were able to drop their bombs smack on target. Minor explosions and a large orange flash with flames 600ft into the clear night sky resulted. Aircraft at 12,500ft felt the blast and were rocked as black smoke billowed upwards and polluted the sky above them. It was a successful attack which left two ammunition trains blown to pieces and 1,270 German troops dead, for the loss of one Halifax MkII, HR912, VR:F and its seven crew members from 419 Squadron.

That night, however, Bomber Command were to meet much heavier losses, as 105 Squadron supported a main attack on Nürnberg, by launching diversionary attacks on Oberhausen, Aachen, Köln, and airfields at Gilze Rijen, Twente and Deelen. The main attack by the heavies was a disaster. The Germans ignored the diversionary attacks and concentrated their night-fighters on the main bomber stream. Due to badly forecast winds, in addition to those who did get to Nürnberg, some 120 aircraft bombed Schweinfurt, 50 miles to the north-west. In all, of the 798 aircraft despatched, 95 bombers were lost that night: 10.1 per cent of the total force.

The ORB recorded at the end of March: 'It is doubtful whether the squadron has ever contributed so much to the bombing offensive as it has this month.' Despite the Nürnberg debacle, this was amplified by a communiqué from the AOC-in-C Bomber Command, who stated: 'Please convey to all operational squadrons my congratulations on their outstanding achievements in March. They may well be proud of the tremendous blows, which they have dealt the enemy during this vital period. All previous records for sorties and bomb tonnages on objectives in Germany have been broken, in spite of difficult weather conditions and in the face of the bitterest opposition at the lowest casualty rate for the last thirteen months.' The Path Finders and Bomber Command had now shown that the precision required by the Air Staff could indeed be achieved.

The preparations for the invasion were now to commence and the softening up of the German war machine around the Normandy area was to be the priority. Railways were to receive further attention in France and Belgium and ammunition dumps and explosives factories in the two countries were to be hit as well. Later, coastal gun emplacements were to be annihilated before the offensive. However, bombing the Normandy area was not to be unique, as the Germans would then surely guess where the invasion was to start. Consequently, in an attempt to deceive the Germans into believing that the attack was to be in the Pas-de-Calais area, bombing operations were to include attacks there as well, dropping a similar tonnage as in the Normandy operations. German cities were to be attacked otherwise.

So for 105 Squadron, April began with attacks on communication centres at Aachen on the 1st, 4th and 6th of the month, interspersed with attacks on Köln and Krefeld. During the attack on Köln on the 4th, F/L Angus Caesar-Gordon's Mosquito MM237:M had a lucky escape when searchlights and accurate heavy flak nearly got him, blasting a hole in his main petrol tank. Fortunately, the aircraft did not catch fire and the crew returned safely. Not so fortunate, however, was the crew of Mosquito ML921:X on an air test on the 9th. F/L Robert Barnsley Smith DFC, RAAF, with observer F/L Peter Eric Cadman DFC commenced take-off at 14.53 hours on RAF Bourn's runway 252. When they were only just airborne, the aircraft swung to starboard and headed straight for the control tower. Smith attempted to pull up and, in doing so, appeared to stall and crashed behind the tower where he hit a hangar. Sadly, the pilot was killed and, although rescued, the observer died the following day of his wounds. Both were buried in Cambridge City cemetery. Bill Humphrey recalled the fair-haired F/L Smith, who was often picked on by the photographers for publicity shots: 'He was very photogenic, and they were always looking for Australians and New Zealanders to photograph. Smithy was my closest personal friend. I was very sorry to see him get the chop, all because he had an engine failure on take-off and didn't close everything down; he tried to do the noble thing and take it off.'

On the night of 9/10 April, the squadron was to mark Villeneuve-St Georges on the southern outskirts of Paris, with green long-burning TIs for a force of 225 aircraft. Although there were 400 houses damaged or destroyed with the loss of 93 lives, the raid was a success operationally, with 240 hits in the target area. The squadron also marked Lille for an attack on the Lille-Déliverance goods station by 239 heavies. Despite F/L Humphrey's adverse report that the red markers burst at different heights and so fell some distance apart, the main force reported concentrated marking. A 'huge explosion at 00.52 hours, which settled into a bright red fire, belching smoke up to 10,000ft.' was subsequently reported, and 2,124 of the 2,959 goods wagons were destroyed. However, bombs were dropped outside the target area, and 456 French people met their deaths. Many of these were from the town of Lomme, where the toll was 5,000 houses destroyed. Perhaps F/L Humphrey's assessment of the marking was more correct than was accepted at the time.

The month continued with more attacks on marshalling yards at Aulnoye, Aachen and Osnabrück. Airfields at Juvincourt and Florennes were attacked on the 11th and then it was back to railway yards again with attacks on Osnabrück, Düren and Dortmund. On the 18th Juvisy was marked for a successful attack by a formation of 202 aircraft, the S/L of the main force describing the attack as the finest example of precision bombing he had ever seen. The same day Rouen was marked by 105 Squadron's newly formed third flight: C-Flight, or Bar-Flight as it was affectionately known. Due to the fact that having an additional flight used up the aircraft code letters, and to distinguish C-Flight from A and B flights, a bar was painted above the aircraft identification letter. The first Bar-Flight aircraft was ML974:B-Bar, flown successfully on this occasion by F/O L. Holiday DFM with F/O E. Jenkins DFM.

Marshalling yards at La Chapelle were attacked on the 20th and a good concentration of bombing was obtained. Additional damage was done to the Societé Général des Cirages Françaises, SA Anc et Luchaire and the Dupas iron foundry, all lying outside the target area. That night Düsseldorf was marked for 596 aircraft, with 2,150 tons of bombs being dropped. The marshalling yards were left ablaze, as was the city. Düsseldorf was considered to be 'an extremely important industrial and transport town connecting the Ruhr and the Rheinland. It housed the headquarters and administrative offices of the large Ruhr factories as well as having important industrial plants of its own.' That night it lost 883 of its inhabitants from 2,000 houses with 593 injured and left 403 in the rubble. In addition, 56 large industrial units were destroyed.

Railway targets continued to be hammered and on the 26th Villeneuve-St Georges was again the target. The next day F/L E.L.D. Drake was on return from a bombing exercise in the reserve aircraft from the night before: LR496:K. On landing, the aircraft swung before the landing gear gave way. The Mosquito eventually came to rest at 13.24 hours, on the port side of the runway about one-third of the way up. An ambulance and fire tender raced to the scene but fortunately there was no fire and crew were without injury. The busy groundcrews had some substantial work to do nevertheless. The month concluded with more attacks and marking of railway targets, with Aulnoye and Achères being visited on the 28th. This was followed by a repeat attack on Düsseldorf on the 30th, where severe damage was done to the Rheinmetall Borsig AG ironworks, the Scheiss Defries AG machine-tools plant, Mannesmanröhrenwerke AG iron and steel tube making plant, the Preß-und Walzwerke AG steel and pressed/rolled goods plant and railway marshalling yards. Moderate damage only was done to the Deutsche Röhrenwerke AG tubing plant and Deutsche Metallwerke AG. In all, 152 sorties were carried out in April 1944, with the squadron having completed 992 PFF sorties to date.

No. 105 Squadron C-Flight groundcrew in front of their Mosquito, LR503, 'F-Bar' for Freddie at Bourn, April 1945. Left to right: Unknown; Lofty Donaldson; Unknown; Tom Harpham; Sgt Jones; Joe Leighton; Unknown; S/L H. Almond DSO, DFC; Cliff 'Slash' Streeter; Paddy Lee; Flight Sergeant Sargent; Chas Dentith; Unknown; Titch Clayden; Ron 'Bill' Channon (above, under nose art); Unknown; Unknown; Sgt Jarman (hand on propeller); Unknown; Corporal Patterson; Unknown; Unknown; Corporal Jock Fraser; Unknown. (Via Ron Channon/Cliff Streeter)

May saw the final run-up to the invasion, with railway targets on the night of the 1/2nd again receiving attention from the heavies in three Musical Parramattas. Each was to be directed by a Master Bomber, backed up by a 'Deputy' operating on the 'Darkie' radio frequency of 6,440 kc/s while flying at 8–9,000ft at Malines, at 7,000ft at Chambly and at 5–6,000ft at St Ghislain. The latter was last visited by W/C Edwards during the squadron's low-level days. The Master Bombers used call signs 'Robin Hood' at Malines, 'Little John' at Chambly and 'Friar Tuck' at St Ghislain. Four crews from 105 and 109 squadrons marked the targets with Oboe control from four stations at Hawkshill Down, Trimmingham, Winterton and Worthy Matravers. This time severe damage was done to locomotive sheds and carriage/wagon repair shops. At Chambly, the goods depot was destroyed and damage inflicted on the sidings and storage buildings.

On the 3rd, in addition to ground-marking Montdidier airfield for 46 Lancasters, munitions depots at Mailly-le-Camp and Châteaudun were ground-marked and bombed respectively. On the 4th, the IG Farbenindustrie AG chemical works was attacked with a 4,000-pounder dropped by F/L Bob Bray DFC with F/L T.W. Pierce in ML973:A-Bar. Flak over the target smashed into his port engine and the Mosquito lost height rapidly. F/L Bray wrestled bravely at the controls to arrest the swing and skilfully managed to get back to RAF Manston at low height and airspeed, where, with one engine on fire and the other unserviceable, he put down. On landing the wheels came down satisfactorily but there was no brake pressure. The aircraft stopped safely and the occupants survived to fight another day.

That 'other day' was in the mind of ACM Sir Arthur Harris, AOC-in-C Bomber Command, when he wrote on the 5th:

The work which you have done in the past two months has been outstanding in quantity and what is far more important in quality. No one outside Bomber Command would have believed such an extraordinary accuracy and concentration possible in night bombing. The US Air Forces who specialise in precision visual attacks by day, are, in particular astonished at the results which you have achieved. You have, in fact, wiped their eye for them at their own game. Such friendly rivalry is all to the good. You are aware of what portends. The success of vital combined operations will rest largely in your hands. I know that you will do all in your power to achieve even better than the remarkable best which you have attained in March and April. The work of Bomber Command during the last 14 months has got the German enemy reeling on his feet and has provided the Allies on all fronts with the preconditions of victory. Your continued and intensified efforts will be the major factor in putting him down for the count. Go to it, rightly proud of your past efforts and determined to surpass them by fulfilling our contract with the other arms and services in full and overflowing.

Ammunition dumps and gun batteries now became the most pressing pre-invasion targets for the month. Ammunition dumps were attacked with 'blockbusters' at Châteaudun on the 4th, marked at Morsalines and bombed again at Châteaudun on the 9th. At Châteaudun, highly experienced S/L Peter Channer DFC was flying ML982:E-Bar with F/O B.W. le Sueur DFC. Le Sueur was a Rhodesian who allegedly was aged 42 in 1944, and had knocked off 5 years to get into the RAF. S/L Channer remembers him as being 'a very good navigator', and vividly recalls the result of dropping the 4,000lb bomb on the dump: 'Never in all my life have I seen such an explosion, it really went up!'

Gun batteries received attention at St Valéry-en-Caux on the 7th, at Cap Gris Nez and Berneval on the 8th, as well as at Morsalines, Bernville, Calais and Mardyck on the 9th. The next day, batteries at Dieppe were ground-marked for a force of Lancasters. During this softening up of gun emplacements, communications were not ignored and railway centres at Boulogne, Louvain and Hasselt were marked. There was however one tragedy on the night of the 12/13th. Having returned from dropping a 4,000lb bomb on the ammunition dump at Châteaudun, F/L Norman Clayes DFC and F/O Frederick Ernest Deighton were in the circuit, 2 miles due east of the airfield, prior to landing ML978:C-Bar. A Verey pistol somehow discharged in the cockpit and control was lost. The Mosquito crashed and burned 200 yards south of Madingly Church at 01.13 hours. A fire tender was despatched to the crash and the Cambridge police attended, but sadly the two occupants were dead. The pilot was laid to rest in Crompton cemetery in Lancashire, and the navigator at Edmonton cemetery, London.

Airfields and 'special targets' such as the radar jammer at Mont de Couple were visited. The radar site was to be marked on the 19th, but the two Mosquitos were unable to mark the target which was bombed on a timed run by a force of 30 Lancasters. When they left the area, it was emitting bright blue electrical flashes. Doubtless, the jammer had been jammed.

Possibly the remnants of General Major Dietrich Georg Magnus Peltz's Fliegerkorps IX, who made a desultory attempt to blitz London from January to March and were by now only a token force roaming around the home counties, visited on Tuesday 23 May. At 03.10 hours, a 'purple warning' was sent out at RAF Bourn, as an intruder had been detected over the Huntingdon area. The airfield lights were dipped to quarter strength, and ten minutes later, a hostile aircraft machine-gunned the base and dropped three bombs, which exploded, leaving craters 20 yds from the perimeter. Cliff Streeter recalls the event and the numbing effect it had: 'One night, after our aircraft had all returned, I was talking to Sergeant "Timber" Wood on the perimeter track, when a German plane dived in dropping bombs and machine-gunning. I fell flat on the concrete and Timber, who had his bicycle with him, ran for the long grass alongside. He told me afterwards that he couldn't understand why he had difficulty in running, until, when all had quietened down, he found he still had his bicycle in his hand and had been dragging it behind him as he ran.'

The month concluded with many more attacks on gun batteries, railway targets and radar sites. By the end of the month and after 285 sorties, the communications systems in the Normandy area were in complete disarray.

June started with a crescendo of 'spoof' attacks in the Pas-de-Calais area to continue the invasion deception. It was not until the night of the 5/6th that coastal batteries all along the Cherbourg peninsula were attacked. They ranged from west to east, from La Parnelle, Crisbecq, St Martin-de-Varreville, covering what would soon be the Utah beach landing area, flanked by Grandchamp-Maisy then St Pierre-du-Mont and Longues-sur-Mer covering the Omaha beach landing area. Further east is Mont-Fleury covering the Gold beach landing area and Ouistreham, Merville and Houlgate, flanking the Sword beach landing area. The first wave to attack was led in ML902:S by F/L W.E.G. Humphrey DFC with S/L J.F.C. Gallacher DFC, who left at 22.04 hours for Crisbecq, about 3.5km south of Quinéville. F/L Humphrey marked the occasion with a note in his logbook stating 'Ops. Crisbecq – Dropped first TI on night the second front started.' In the process, out of 946 aircraft, 3 heavies were lost. Nevertheless, more than 5,000 tons of explosive rained down on the gun emplacements, putting all but one gun out of action, ready for the Allied assault.

In the early hours of 6 June, Operation Overlord began, under command of General Dwight D. Eisenhower, Supreme Commander, Allied Air, Naval and Ground Forces for the Normandy landings. Around 176,000 men and machinery, of General Montgomery's 21st Army Group landed on the beaches of Normandy. The United States' 1st Army landed Major General J.L. Collins' 7th Corps at Utah beach, and Major General Leonard T. Gerow's 5th Corps at Omaha beach. The British 2nd Army landed Lieutenant-General G.C. Bucknall's 30th Corps at Gold beach and Lieutenant-General J.T. Crocker's 1st Corps, comprising Canadian troops at Juno beach and British troops at Sword beach. The Second Front had begun at last.

Geoffrey H. 'Taffy' Gilbert DFC*, who flew as a F/L navigator with W/C F.A. Green DFC, remembers the night Overlord began: 'I flew on 5 June [ML916:P for an NFT] and went to bed early, in preparation for another flight that night [to Maisy in ML916:P – take-off 01.55 hours]. I was woken up by my batwoman to say my leave was cancelled and that the Second Front was open! The remarkable thing about the invasion was that I knew nothing about it until it happened. It was obvious from pre-invasion targets that something was happening. Things got a bit more hectic once we reached D-Day.'

In praise and appreciation of the recent softening up efforts for Overlord, the AOC-in-C of Bomber Command signalled PFF that: 'You did famously last night in the face of no mean difficulties. Fire from the coastal batteries, which were your targets, has been reported as virtually negligible. All four radar targets were put right out. The next few days will necessarily be the critical period of this operation. Calls upon you may be heavy and the weather may not be easy. I know that you will do your damnedest to meet all assignments with that efficiency and determination which has characterised the whole of your share of Overlord to date.'

No. 105 Squadron were therefore assembled that afternoon at 14.00 hours and addressed by the CO, G/C Cundall DFC, AFC, who recently recalled: 'The meeting of 6 June was organised on a squadron basis, with all available aircrew in the Squadron Briefing Room. It was mainly to clear the air on what was happening. For the past 2–3 months the media had expected D-Day at almost any time. Our target patterns in that period often suggested "today could be the day".' In fact, I was not informed that it had happened until we returned after the operations of 5/6 June. At our flying height and with much broken cloud lower down, we mostly saw little of remark on the 6th.'

The squadron ORB recalls G/C Cundall's address: 'He told them that their work of the preceding night had put nearly all the coastal batteries in the invasion area out of action. As far as the squadron was concerned the invasion would mean a tremendous amount of extra work. All leave would have to be suspended and 6 crews would be required to stand by at 30 minutes readiness, 24 hours to the day. The normal working day for aircrew not at 30 minutes readiness would start at 16.00 hours. No aircrew would be allowed away from the flights for more than 3 hours and then only on condition that they remained at the end of a telephone. All officers and airmen were ordered to carry [side-]arms at all times.'

Trevor Walmsley DFC recalls a story, allegedly the result of the issue of revolvers: 'One night, our orderly officer got a so-called invasion alarm and rushed into where the Station Commander was sleeping. "Sir" he said, "the Germans are coming – what shall I do?" The CO opened one eye, said "You shoot the buggers, Dickie", and went off to sleep again.'

On the night of the 6th, nine railway centres used by the enemy to bring reinforcements to the beachhead areas were marked for 1,065 heavies. On the 7th, tanks and fuel dumps of the German VII Army were marked for 112 Lancasters, south-west of Bayeux in the Forêt de Carisy. Communications such as railway targets, airfields and bridges were the subject of sustained attack for the first half of the month in support of Allied forces in Normandy. Enemy shipping in Le Havre was marked on the night of the 14th for a force of 221 Lancasters, as were troop concentrations at Aunay-sur-Odon. A return to synthetic oil targets began on the 16th with a visit to Sterkrade-Holten, north of Duisburg and Gelsenkirchen, on the 17th.

At 04.20 hours on Tuesday 13 June, the first V-1 'doodle-bug' fell on London, killing six people. It was to be the first of a further 2,420, which were destined to reach their targets throughout the remainder of the war. Thereafter, the gradual move began back to V-1 rocket sites. Such targets as Oisemont, Watten, St Martin l'Hortier, Siracourt, Marquise, Les Hayons, Noyelle-en-Chaussée, Bonnetot-le-Faubourg, Flers, Rimeux, Le Grand Rossignol, Bamières, Middle Straete (Lederzeele), Pommeréval, Prouville, Ligescourt, Gorenflos and Montorgueil were all visited. However, on the 30th, a cry for support was received from General Montgomery, due to an immense concentration of enemy tanks of the 2nd and 9th Panzer Divisions, having massed on the road just west of Villers Bocage. Despite the distraction of two Spitfires, which closed on F/L Wolstenholme DFC's ML928:E-Bar, engaging but not opening fire, four other Mosquitos from 105 successfully marked the target for a force of 266 aircraft. They dropped 1,100 tons of high explosive, leaving the five-road junction completely devastated, and cancelling the German attack. The cost: one Halifax MkIII of XV Squadron and a Lancaster MkI of 514 Squadron over enemy territory and one Lancaster MkIII of 514 Squadron, which collided in the air with a XV Squadron Lancaster. In all, in June, 105 had flown 380 sorties without loss. This was not to last through the next month, however.

At the end of June there was an arrival from 109 Squadron. Under direct orders from AVM Don Bennett, a 23-year-old Canadian, S/L Jack Watts DFC had arrived to take up the post of Squadron Navigation Officer. He was officially posted to this position later, on 13 July. Bennett had seen the percentage of 'copes' for the squadron consistently within the 50–60 per cent band, for some months prior to D-Day. He felt there was need for improvement on the navigation front, and S/L Watts had been hand-picked to improve matters. As mentioned, Watts was known to the Station Commander, G/C Hal Bufton DSO, DFC, AFC, as Bufton had been his

Portrait of S/L Jack Watts as a Flight Lieutenant, taken for his mother at the Curzon Studio, London, having attended an investiture at Buckingham Palace to receive his DFC from HRH King George VI. It also depicts a bracelet of Canadian nickels, his lucky charm. (Via Jack Watts)

109 Squadron CO. Having effected a smooth transfer from the previous Navigation Officer, it was not long before he was accepted and became an integral part of the squadron.

On 1 July 1944, a grateful General Bernard Law Montgomery wrote of the bomber contribution at Villers Bocage: 'It was a most inspiring sight for all Allied soldiers in France to see [the] might of Bomber Command arriving to join in battle. The results of your actions will not, repeat not, be forgotten by us or by the enemy. Please thank all crews.'

V-1 sites, marshalling yards and oil targets were again the priority this month. But tragedy struck on the night of the 5th. A-Flight's F/L George Kenneth Whiffen and F/O Douglas Knight Williams DFC went to Scholven-Buer, to attack and mark an oil target in ML913:E. They took off on runway 192 at 23.29 hours and although their bombs and TIs were seen to go down successfully in the target area, the aircraft disappeared without trace, and the crew were never seen again. They are both commemorated on the Runnymede Memorial. Once more, on the 7th, General Montgomery called for assistance, as the enemy were providing a formidable opposition in the northern suburbs of Caen. It was the eve of his intended frontal assault on the 8th, codenamed Operation Charnwood. Consequently, two waves of heavies attacked; the largest force of RAF daylight bombers yet. A total of 2,276 tons of bombs from 467 aircraft fell on the German positions and Caen, which was almost razed to the ground. However, whether by divine intervention or merely good fortune, amidst all the destruction the 1,000-year-old church at Abbaye-aux-Hommes, containing the tomb of William the Conqueror and the temporary home of 2,000 refugees, survived untouched. The German defences were left a mass of rubble. No. 105 Squadron had sent 10 Mosquitos to Caen to mark the target: one of them was ML964:J, flown by the Australian Officer Commanding A-Flight, S/L William Walter Blessing DSO, DFC, RAAF, with P/O Douglas T. Burke. The crew had attacked Caen from 32,000ft.

S/L Peter J. Channer (left) with S/L W.W. 'Bill' Blessing RAAF. (Via Pat Tennison)

Shortly thereafter, the navigator had leant forward to pick up his chart when from behind, out of the sun, came a fighter which opened fire. The cannon shells exploded, as S/L Blessing pushed the nose down into a dive. Having evaded the fighter, the starboard wing was missing a 3ft section and the starboard engine was over-revving. The pilot saw a landing strip and radioed RAF Biggin Hill at 21.45 hours to say that he would not be crossing back over the Channel and that he was at a rough position between Fécamp and Le Havre, at a height of about 14,000ft. Tragically, however, control was lost and the aircraft went into a spin. S/L Blessing ordered P/O Burke to take to his parachute, which he did, just before the aircraft broke into pieces. Blessing died in the crash and was buried in La Déliverande war cemetery in Douvres. Burke awoke on a stretcher behind allied lines and survived.

The AOC-in-C, Harris, wrote: 'The efforts by your chaps witnessed over Caen tonight made us all feel very proud to belong to the RAF.' The attack was also well received by the land forces, and subsequently General Montgomery courteously thanked the RAF for their assistance, as did Lieutenant-General Sir Miles Dempsey, C-in-C of the British 2nd Army, who wrote: 'Your magnificent operation yesterday evening was the greatest assistance to us. Second Army sends Bomber Command its thanks and congratulations.'

Next, it was back to flying-bomb sites again and on the 10th, Nucourt was ground-marked for 213 Lancasters which were to target the flying-bomb storage dump there. One of those involved was P/O John William Grenville Eaton DFC, who takes up the story: 'At 4a.m. on 10 July 1944, quite elated, we took off on our first daylight operation in Mosquito ML919 [V-Victor] with a full load of target indicators and, of course, at full throttle. As we reached the end of the runway, the port engine blew up, an event that was usually fatal. I do not know how, but somehow I was able to circuit and land again on one engine – just – and switch off the ignition.' Then the most tragic thing happened as, prematurely, P/O John Elton Fox left the aircraft. At 04.50 hours, Flying Control received a transmission from V-Victor, to say that an ambulance was to be sent immediately as a navigator was injured. The ambulance and a crash tender were despatched and the navigator, P/O Fox, was taken to station sick quarters. The medical report describes the sad outcome: '177086 P/O Fox J.E., navigator of Mosquito MkIX, ML919 sustained fatal injuries on alighting from the aircraft whilst the engines were still running. He was admitted to station sick quarters at 04.55 hours and died 20 minutes later from the injuries sustained'; he had been struck by the propeller. P/O Fox was laid to rest in Roundhay (St John) churchyard in Leeds. Thereafter, P/O Eaton was crewed with F/O Dougie Burke, the late Bill Blessing's navigator. It is of no surprise that Grenville Eaton remarked: 'We both needed several trips before regaining our confidence.'

On the 13th there was another aircraft loss, as C-Flight's B.XVI Mosquito, ML987:C-Bar, was returning from having attacked an oil installation at Schloven-Buer. Hit by flak over enemy territory, W/O A.Y. Lickley's aircraft was returning on one engine. When on the outer circuit, about 5 miles south of North Walsham, Norfolk, it crashed. The crew survived however, suffering from minor injuries and shock. They were picked up by the CO of the Army's Lancashire Regiment, and taken to RAF Coltishall sick quarters. They were detained there for five days, before W/O Lickley and F/Sgt J.F. Cameron were allowed to return to the station sick quarters at RAF Bourn. Both were discharged to duty on 28 July.

Three days later, on the 16th, a new concept was tried out. Jack Watts, who flew with Peter Channer on a raid to the V-1 rocket site at St Philbert-Ferme, recalled what happened in his memoirs, *Nickels and Nightingales*: 'This attack introduced a novelty in our way of operating. There were 3 Oboe' Mosquitos involved, and each Oboe aircraft led a loose formation of 10 Lancasters. The target was cloud-covered, and the Lancasters were briefed to close up formation on the bombing run and to drop the bombs simultaneously with the leading Oboe aircraft. With the accuracy of Oboe and the pattern of the bombs which would fall, the chances of hitting even such a small target as a launching platform would be optimised. Unfortunately, because of the cloud, we had no way of knowing how successful we had been.' Although some difficulty had been found in keeping a low enough speed to enable the heavies to keep a tight formation, attacks of this nature were deemed a success and were to be repeated.

Two further appeals for assistance were received, one on the 18th and the other on the 30th, requiring marking for forces in support of the land offensive. Oil and steel producers, ammunition dumps, flying-bomb sites and a U-boat at Le Havre were also attacked before the month concluded. It was satisfying to all concerned, and no doubt to S/L Watts, that the month's 'copes' had risen to 73.2 per cent; a 'marked' improvement.

August 1944 saw similar operations to those of July, with railway centres and oil installations all receiving attention. V-1 supply depots and dumps were also visited such as those at Forêt de Nieppe and St Leu-d'Esserent, which were marked on the 5th by three and four Mosquitos respectively of 105 Squadron. At Forêt de Nieppe, for absolute pinpoint accuracy the attack was a 'controlled visual' type, where the TIs were dropped by the Mosquitos and the Master Bomber visually identified the aiming point for 268 out of a force of 273 Halifaxes that attacked. Several fires were started and marking was well concentrated, although the target was soon smothered in smoke. At St Leu-d'Esserent, the attack was split into two phases, with 2 Mosquitos marking each phase. The first was by 189 Halifaxes and 59 Lancasters and bombing was a little scattered. In the second phase, 182 Lancasters bombed from an alternative track, but

The flying-bomb storage site, marked with four (either red or yellow) TIs by each of four of 105 Squadron's Mosquitos, at the French village of St Leu d'Esserent. Photograph taken at 29,900ft on 5 August 1944 from F/L C. Chadwick's Mosquito B.IX, LR503, GB:C, which dropped red TIs. (Via Bill Riley)

4–6/10th cloud up to 14,000ft caused inaccuracy. Halifax LL594, KW:U of 425 Squadron was shot down by flak and crashed near the Lille–Paris railway line. Another, 433 Squadron's MZ828, BM:H crashed preparing to land at Skipton-on-Swale, killing two, plus a little five-year-old boy called Kenneth Battensby, who was hit by the bomber as it gouged its way across the village square.

At this time the Normandy battle was drawing to a close, and the last pocket of major resistance lay in the area between Falaise and Argentan, where the enemy were all but surrounded. General Patton's 3rd US Army and the French 2nd Armoured Division turned north from their positions at Le Mans, and stopped at Argentan on the 12th. In the north, battling southwards from Caen, was the Canadian 1st Army under Lt-Gen Harry Crerar. The 4th

Canadian and 1st Polish Armoured Divisions met fierce resistance and were halted on the 9th. They decided on a charge of 750 tanks, which started along the Caen–Falaise road on the 14th. Further troop support operations were flown that day when the area around Fontaine-le-Pin, on the Caen–Falaise road, about 9km from Falaise, was marked by 22 Mosquitos of 105 Squadron. One of the veteran crews, F/L Pereira DFC with F/L Gilbert DFC left at 12.47 hours in ML920:W. Geoffrey Gilbert noted what for him was a special operation: 'One of the marking requirements was the marking of the battle zone. I had the privilege of opening the attack on the Caen–Falaise gap for 805 heavies. It turned out that this was my last trip – the powers that be said I had done enough [81 operations].'

By the 16th, the Canadians and Poles reached Falaise, but there remained a gap, the Falaise Gap, through which the surrounded German Army tried to withdraw eastwards. At least 40,000 men escaped before it was sealed on 20 August, trapping the Germans, 10,000 of whom died in the ensuing fight; 50,000 were taken prisoner. Here ended the Battle of Normandy, and the drive to cross the River Seine began.

On Saturday 19 August two Mosquitos acted as reserves to mark the railway centre at Connantre. In the event they were not required and on return F/L Geoffrey W.A. Parker with F/O V.W. Gordon Musgrove DFC were returning at 00.50 hours in B.XVI Mosquito ML966:N, when they experienced undercarriage trouble coming in to land. They were able to lower the main wheels by using the emergency gear, but the retracted tail wheel refused to lower. Eight minutes later they made a safe, flapless landing and were told to stop at the end of the runway where a tractor arrived to tow the stricken aircraft off for repair.

The squadron carried out marking for a major daylight raid on Homberg on the 24th and attacked more V-1 sites, airfields and storage depots. The final operation of the month took place on the 31st. It was to mark for an attack on nine rocket storage depots in northern France, this time believed to be housing the Nazis' new terror weapon, the V-2. This was a 12-ton, 14-metre-long rocket, carrying a one-ton warhead that could be propelled over 200 miles by an alcohol and liquid oxygen-fuelled motor. The device was launched from a truck-towed platform, and was therefore highly manoeuvrable. By the end of the war a total of 1,115 were to reach their targets in England. Dennis Bolesworth recalls the method they used to determine the source of the rocket: 'At the time of the V-2 blitz, we were requested to pinpoint the launching pads for the missiles. At 30,000ft we could see the rockets streaking up towards us and then going higher than us into the stratosphere, and so could pin point the sites for the Intelligence Officer at debriefing. The following day a flight of Lancasters would be sent out to pay them their respects, destroying the pads and any spare rockets there.'

At the end of the month the 'copes' were up to a much-improved 81.2 per cent! This would not last, however, as in September Oboe MkII was formally introduced and testing of new Oboe stations was required. With the Allied assault deepening into Europe, it was now possible to increase the range of Oboe, by introducing ground stations on the continent. Increase in range had been attempted by repeater facilities in two high-flying aircraft, one acting as the Cat and the other the Mouse, but the prospect of using ground stations held much greater appeal.

The month began with attacks to mark enemy airfields in the Netherlands, such as Venlo and Steenwijk, as well as supporting attacks on troop positions and transports by 344 aircraft at Le Havre on the 6th. The next day F/O J.A. Ruck and P/O L.B. Winsloe were in ML902:S. Their operation was to Emden, but during the bombing run the starboard engine stopped. They feathered it immediately and jettisoned their bombs. Four 500lb MC bombs lighter, they turned for home. After three minutes, the other engine also stopped and windmilled, as the crew prepared to take to their parachutes. The squadron ORB explains what happened next: 'At 25,000ft the port engine was feathered. At 15,000ft the pilot decided to unfeather the starboard engine which began to fire intermittently, and eventually picked up at 12,000ft. The port engine was then unfeathered and continued to fire intermittently. A successful landing was made at base on the starboard engine. The trouble was due to extremely low temperature, −73°C at 36,000ft, causing the petrol to freeze in the carburettors': a useful lesson learned.

Support continued around Le Havre coastal batteries on the 10th, when 3 of the squadron's Mosquitos attacked in the morning, for a force of 50 Halifaxes. The marking was accurate and well backed up, and a vivid explosion was seen in the target area. This was followed in the afternoon by 14 out of 20 Mosquitos successfully dropping four TIs each, for a force of 935 heavies. They made a well-concentrated attack, causing large explosions from the gun-sites. Further oil targets and airfields were marked thereafter. On 25 September, following his

German gun positions near the port of Calais marked for heavy bombardment on 26 September 1944. Photograph taken at 21,900ft from F/L Cyril Muller's Mosquito B.IX, ML922, GB:Y. (Via Cyril Muller)

No. 105 Squadron groundcrews with G/C Keith J. Somerville, September 1944, at RAF Bourn. (Via Cliff Streeter)

promotion on 1 June to G/C, Henry John Cundall DFC, AFC, left the squadron on a posting to 28 Group's 14 (War) Staff College. In his place came the also highly respected Oboe pioneer, the then W/C, Keith J. 'Slim' Somerville DFC, AFC, posted in from 109 Squadron.

The month closed with attacks marking gun batteries at Cap Gris Nez and Calais, and more army support on defended positions on the 28th in the same areas. The 30th saw a return to oil installations at Bottrop, Sterkrade and an attack on Aschaffenburg. For reasons already stated, the 'copes' were lower this month at 69.1 per cent for 397 sorties.

October's targets were little different from those of the previous month, but with many flying-bomb sites now inhabited by Allied forces attention was turned once more to oil installations; however support for the Allied advance was naturally given priority.

There was an incident on the 4th, when C-Flight had the 'experimental' targets of Pforzheim and Heilbronn to attack with 4,000lb 'blockbusters'. F/L W. Baker with F/O R.F. Lewis were in ML986:G-Bar, when they lost an engine on leaving the target area and headed back for base, fighting through cumulus cloud on the way. On arrival at the aerodrome, the aircraft settled into a right-hand circuit, where it began to side-slip, and the propellers on the dead engine started to mill. Side-slipping caused loss of height, which resulted in a crash on approach at 23.39 hours, short of runway 012. An ambulance and a fire tender were immediately despatched to the scene, where the crew, both injured, were taken to hospital. The aircraft was destroyed in the fire. Less fortunate still were F/L John Edward Brook with Sgt Woodrow Wilson Bowden in A-Flight's ML996:K. They took off at 18.47 hours on the 6th acting as reserve crew, to mark Dortmund for a force of 523 aircraft. The Mosquito failed to return and nothing was ever heard from them again. Both airmen are commemorated on the Runnymede Memorial.

The port of Antwerp had been captured on 4 September, but until the Germans had been cleared from the Schelde estuary supplies could not be brought in. A pocket of resistance to the Canadian 1st Army existed north of the Leopold Canal, controlling the Wester Schelde across to Vlissingen, about 10 miles south of Breskens. It was necessary to silence the gun batteries of Fort Frederik Hendrik at Breskens and on the 11th, 105 Squadron participated in their attempted destruction by marking for 160 Lancasters.

Towns and cities were also marked for the heavies, the 12th being a particularly hectic day when Wiesbaden, Wanne-Eickel, Düsseldorf, Schwienfurt and Köln were all visited. On the 14th Duisburg was heavily attacked as part of Operation Hurricane, Harris's attempt to demonstrate Allied air superiority in the area. This involved two waves of 1,013 and 1,005 heavies respectively, backed up by the American 8th Air Force which contributed 1,251 aircraft, 1,000 of which hit the Köln area. No. 105 Squadron marked both raids, the first in the morning with 10 Mossies, including Slim Somerville with the Squadron's Navigation Officer, Jack V. Watts in ML982:E-Bar as reserve. The second wave of 14 Mossies left in the late hours of the 14th and early hours of the 15th. Destruction was massive, as the ORB summarizes: 'Marking was punctual and accurate and bombing concentrated in the marking areas in both raids. PRU photographs prove the damage to be very severe and widespread, and most of the large steel plants have been very heavily damaged, by direct hits or blast. The built-up area around the old town, the old town itself, and the main railway station have been almost entirely destroyed.'

On the 19th the squadron lost another two fine airmen. F/O Leonard Priestley Whipp with P/O Clifford Bertenshaw had been detailed along with three other crews to drop 4,000lb 'blockbusters' on Düsseldorf. That evening around 19.00 hours they lined up for take-off in Mosquito ML993:H-Bar. Shortly after the aircraft rose up into the sky the crew had some type of problem, allegedly with their astro-emergency homing equipment. In any event, the pilot jettisoned the bomb – a fatal act at such comparatively low height. The resulting blast blew off the tail-plane, and destroyed the flaps. The Mossie then fell to the ground at 19.01 hours, about half a mile to the west of Great Staughton village, 10 miles south-west of Huntingdon. F/O Whipp was buried at Chatburn (Christ Church) churchyard and F/O Bertenshaw in Cheetham Hill (St Luke's) churchyard.

October closed with further attacks on the gun positions at Walcheren Island on the 28th and 29th and attacks on Köln and Saarbrücken on the 31st.

Operation Anvil had started on 15 August 1944, when the US 6th Corps and French 2nd Corps landed in southern France and fought northwards to meet up with the Allies. By 12 September they had met, and the thrust continued in an Allied north–south advance towards Germany. Aachen was captured on 21 October and the drive towards the Rhein continued. November was therefore taken up by attacks on the German supporting industries such as oil, and communications targets. Further attempts were made to attack targets under control of the new continental Oboe ground stations, but there was still a lot of work to be done, and the results were less than satisfactory. On the 2nd, Düsseldorf was marked for the last major Bomber Command attack there of the war, when 13 Mossies dropped TIs, flares and bombs. It was a bad night for starboard engines, as both S/L Tommy W. Horton DFC with F/L B.L. le Sueur returned in ML982:E-Bar from a point over the North Sea at 3° East, for a successful emergency landing at RAF Woodbridge. Similar problems beset F/L Peter Sleight with F/L D.L. Moher DFC, when PF385:K also lost its starboard engine near Orford Ness on the way out, but returned safely to RAF Bourn. A total of 992 aircraft attacked the industrial areas that night as fierce fires raged and large explosions resulted. Seven industrial premises were destroyed, but so too were around 5,000 houses, mainly in the northern sector of the city. Over 1,000 people were injured and 678 died on the ground.

The first sighting by the squadron of a jet fighter, possibly an Me262 or He162, occurred on the 3rd, when F/L J.A. Buck with F/O L.B. Winsloe DFC were attacked in MM237:Q. They returned early to land back at base at 21.21 hours.

Marking for attacks on oil production continued. The Nordstren synthetic oil plant at Gelsenkirchen was hit on the 6th, followed by a refinery at Wanne-Eickel on the 9th. F/L Ronnie Plunkett recalls another event he had logged that day: 'An "Experimental Exercise" on 9 November 1944 on Lancaster PB369 [as 2nd navigator] was to prepare me for operating the Oboe equipment which was then installed in this aircraft. I flew with S/L Hildyard who had some experience flying Lancs – up at 12.45 hours for 2.55 hours. This was really for familiarization on a different type [of aircraft] and I believe to give me some practice for the raid on Cologne which was to come on 23 December, when Bob [Jordan] and I were to lead the Lancaster formation. I was instructed to enter this exercise [in his logbook] as "experimental" – obviously, it was to be kept quiet.'

The Hoesch AG synthetic oil plant at Dortmund suffered on the 11th and Schloven and Wanne-Eickel again on the 15th. The US Army were assisted on the 16th when their 1st and 9th Armies were about to attack three towns between Aachen and the Rhein. No. 105 Squadron was allocated Düren, where they dropped red long-burning TIs for over 485 heavies. Due to shortage of ammunition and wet ground hampering their tanks, the American advance proved slow and expensive.

A return was made on the 18th to Erfurt, when three Mosquitos were compelled to drop 'last resort'. The fourth, ML914:C, crewed by F/L D. Tidy with F/L Gavin H. Barr DFC were unable to get above 17,000ft. Worst of all, they were unable to jettison their 4,000-pounder in the Zuider Zee, due to lack of hydraulic pressure which prevented the bomb doors from opening. The only way out of their predicament was to return to the emergency landing ground at RAF Woodbridge and perform a very careful belly-landing, which they did at 20.06 hours – and survived!

G/C and Mrs H.E. Bufton (front) lead S/L Tommy W. Horton (right at rear) and his navigator F/L A. Haworth to attend the wedding, on 23 October 1944, of S/L Jack Watts to his wife Norma. (Via Jack Watts)

As the month drew on, the winter weather began to bite. Consequently, despite the difficult conditions, on the 26th RAF Woodbridge and RAF Downham Market were very busy. On the 27th Sleight and Moher in ML999:B-Bar made a successful emergency landing with the port engine feathered, and assisted by FIDO at RAF Woodbridge.

The last operation of November was on the 30th. In the morning, W/C Slim Somerville with F/L R.E. Jordan as reserve, and S/L J.D.G. Bishop DFC with F/L D.C. James as reserve, left with another two 109 Squadron Mosquitos to mark the Meiderich AG Tar and Benzol plant at Duisburg. Jack Watts was Somerville's navigator and recalls in *Nickels and Nightingales*: 'We were one of three formations of Mosquitos, each led by an Oboe Mosquito, and each targeted on the plant. This was the first time our Oboe aircraft had been used in cooperation with Mosquitos from other commands. It turned out to be a bit of a farce as two of the three formations failed to link up and our single formation was inadequate for the job. Since the target was just as important as it had been when we made the first attempt, we had to repeat it on the following day, though I flew with Bishop not Somerville. The experience of the previous day must have been a learning one, because the three formations linked up in good time and we were able to make the attack in good form. But it was not without a great deal of nervous anticipation that we flew at the head of our nice tight vee formation, straight and level, over heavily defended territory of the Ruhr. It felt even more like a live turkey shoot in daylight than it did at night – and we were the turkeys!'

Meanwhile, the land battles raged on, as the squadron was engaged in attacks on the 3rd on the Erft river Heimbach Dam in the Eifel region. It was important to demolish it, to protect the advancing US troops from drowning at the hands of the Germans, who it was anticipated might open the floodgates to flood the area of advance. The attack was made in three formations, each led by an Oboe-equipped Lancaster with an Oboe Mosquito in reserve. Each formation was followed by nine more Lancasters, briefed to bomb on their leader. F/L I.L.T. Ackroyd DFC with F/L J.P.H. Carrere DFC returned early in ML956:G-Bar, with an unserviceable port engine and landed safely at RAF Woodbridge. The result of the operation was that the top was blown off the dam, but it was not breached. However, Bomber Command visited it with other formations on several later occasions.

Several attacks were also made on oil and industrial targets at Soest, Mannheim, Osnabrück, Schwerte, Köln and Duisburg. The attack on Duisburg on 11 December is remembered by Grenville Eaton:

In this 'carpet bombing' raid, I led a formation [in ML995:R with F/L Dougie Burke DFC] of twelve bomber Mosquito B. MkXVIs, with an Oboe Mosquito in reserve, for the simultaneous release of 4,000lb 'cookies'. On the run-in, on the 'beam', flak hit and put out of action my starboard engine. Immediately dropping behind, I feathered the starboard propeller, jettisoned the cookie, and staggered with full throttle, down to 12,000ft, maximum height on one engine, at 150 knots across Germany and Belgium. Clear skies, a few odd bits of cumulus [cloud] here and there, but certainly nowhere to hide if we were spotted by fighter or flak. We skirted around Ostend, still in German hands, and crossed the coast sweating vigorously. We were heading across the North Sea towards the emergency aerodrome in Kent, RAF Manston, as RAF Bourn on one engine was a doubtful proposition. Having no hydraulics (wheels, flaps, etc.), on approaching Manston we requested emergency landing permission, released the wheels-catch and began hand-pumping the wheels down. This caused us to lose height constantly. Twice more I requested an emergency landing, twice more I was told to wait as Spitfires were landing for refuelling, whilst we were down to 6,000ft, then 5,000, then 4,000, then 3,000ft – I could wait no longer. I took her more or less round Ramsgate church steeple, and landed at about 140 knots without permission or flaps, whilst passing from behind through three Spitfires landing in line-abreast. Our wheels locked down just as we crossed the aerodrome boundary, so Dougie told me afterwards. Incidentally, the emergency aerodrome had the most enormous runways for just such emergencies, but it was still a close call.

There was a sad ending to the activities of the 11th, when F/L James Gladstone Brass with F/O Dennis Arthur Field were returning in Mosquito MM152:B from an operation to Bielefeld. At 20.59 hours, the Royal Observer Corps reported that an aircraft had crashed at 20.23 hours, east of Newmarket 'at the practice ground'. Further news arrived at 21.22 hours, when PFF reported an aircraft crashed at Longhole Stud, Ashley Road, 1½ miles outside Newmarket. This was confirmed by 8 Group at 22.00 hours, who noted that the aircraft was 'B/105' and that both crew members had been killed. There were also two craters in the ground. Newmarket was arranging a guard. Subsequently the pilot F/L Brass was laid to rest in Brookwood military cemetery and F/L Field in London Road cemetery in Coventry.

There was nearly a tragic accident again on the 15th, when F/L G. Donald (possibly with F/O Frank T. Watson DFM) in ML919:V swung on take-off for Hannover. The aircraft ran off the runway and wiped the undercarriage away. Fortunately, there were no injuries. Further visits followed to Ulm, Hallendorf and Münster on the 17th and 18th, and on the 22nd the weather was beginning to take its toll when a similar occurrence befell W/C T.G. Jefferson AFC with F/O K.J. Gordon DFC in ML911:U. Having attacked Koblenz, they were attempting to land in foggy conditions on an SBA approach, when they hit the inner marker beacon and crashed near the field. Thankfully, the crew were both uninjured.

CHAPTER 19

Battle of the Bulge

On 16 December 1944, at 05.30 hours, a massive German break-out began in the Ardennes, from Monschau in the north to Echternach in the south. The Battle of the Bulge was under way. Hitler planned the assault personally, with the objective of taking the port of Antwerp and hampering the Allied assault capabilities on Germany. The initial barrage took Lieutenant General Courtney Hodges's US 1st Army completely by surprise. The initial armoured thrusts seemed inexorable as Field Marshal Walther Model's Army Group 'B' pressed ahead. In the north were General Josef 'Sepp' Dietrich's 6th SS Panzer [Tank] Army, tasked with fighting his way to Antwerp via the Meuse river to the south of Liège. (In 1946, Dietrich was to be accused and imprisoned for 25 years for the cold-blooded murder, assisted by 42 of his SS officer comrades, of 71 GIs, rounded up and machine-gunned to death in a field, following their surrender at the town of Malmédy on the 17th.) Further south was General Hasso Freiherr Von Manteuffel's 5th Panzer Army, ordered to press ahead towards St Vith, whilst supporting Dietrich. Further south still, General Erich Brandenberger's 7th Army was to forge ahead past Houfflaize and Bastogne, towards Dinant. The German assault advanced, in the knowledge that the weather conditions would preclude air reconnaissance or support for the Allies. Facing this onslaught of 275,000 enemy troops, backed up with armour and artillery, were about 83,000 Americans. The US 1st Army were to the north and the US 3rd Army under General 'Blood and Guts' Patton were to the south. By the 22nd, the US 7th Armoured Division had fallen back to St Vith. There was heavy fighting around them and at Bastogne, which were vital communication points.

Following his comments re 9 November, F/L Ronnie Plunkett DFC recalls the raid the next day, on 23 December 1944. It was 'carried out by 27 Lancasters and 3 Mosquitos, against Köln's Gremberg marshalling yards, in an effort to stem the enemy's ability to re-supply its forces involved in the Ardennes battle.' The operation was to be conducted in three waves. An Oboe-equipped Lancaster, backed up by an Oboe Mosquito, would lead each wave. No. 109 Squadron's S/L Robert Anthony Maurice 'Bob' Palmer DFC* (115722) led the first wave, in 582 Squadron's Lancaster MkIII, PB371, 60:V, accompanied by a 109 Squadron Mosquito B.XVI, ML998, HS:B flown by F/O E.C. Carpenter RCAF, with F/O W.T. Lambeth DFM navigating. The second and third waves were led by 105 Squadron crews. The second wave had S/L G.W. Harding DFC with S/L L.W. Millett DFC operating the Oboe on 35 Squadron's Lancaster MkIII, PB367, TL:Z. They were backed up by Mosquito B.XVI, ML981:D-Bar flown by S/L H.A. Almond DFC with F/O C.R.A. Challis DFC. Finally, the third wave was led by F/L R.E. Jordan with F/L R.W. Plunkett, backed up by Mosquito B.IX, ML922:Y flown by S/L Geoffrey W.A. Parker with F/L V.W. Gordon Musgrove.

Ronnie Plunkett recalled: 'On the morning we were up at 10.36 hours. Bob Jordan and I were taken over to Graveley (35 Squadron's base) and joined a normal Lancaster crew who flew Lancaster PB372, TL:X and took off for the target at 10.38 hours. The outward journey was mainly uneventful but we did see two Lancasters touch wings and spin in. Several crew members were seen to bale out, but this was over the sea. They may have been picked up with a bit of luck.' The two Lancaster MkIIIs were P/O R.J. Clarke's PB678, TL:F and F/O G.S. Lawson's PB683, TL:H. Sadly, of the 14 young crew members, there were in fact no survivors. Those who had taken to their parachutes died of exposure before a rescue launch could get to them.

The weather was as forecast with 10,000ft tops to the clouds which blanketed the skies. However, short of the target at 17,000ft the cloud broke and Ronnie Plunkett remembers the result: 'It was a different story out from Cologne, when we were picked up by predicted heavy flak and were kept under constant anti-aircraft fire during the entire Oboe run. The Lancaster flown by S/L Palmer in the formation ahead of us with its crew from 109 Squadron was set on fire for quite some time [two engines, the nose and the bomb bays were alight], but continued on its bombing run and then spun over. For this S/L Palmer was awarded a posthumous VC.' Had Palmer jettisoned his load, the others would have bombed on his release, missing the target altogether. It had been his 110th operation! Their back-up Mosquito was having a tough time of it too. With one engine feathered and the other in flames, F/O Carpenter had four enemy aircraft attacking him as he waited for the leader to bomb. Then he crashed in flames and both occupants perished. Three Lancasters of 582 Squadron also succumbed to a force of enemy fighters comprising a force of FW 190s and Bf 109s. They had come from a total of 250 fighters in the area, hunting USAAF bombers reported nearby. A fourth Lancaster crashed on the way home when over Belgium. Four of the crew survived to be taken prisoner.

The second wave also fared badly. By this time the aircraft had broken formation and were dive-bombing the target. S/L Harding's Lancaster was severely flak-damaged with three of its engines hit. Nevertheless, he managed to bomb the target. Their back-up Mosquito also suffered flak damage to the hydraulics and as a result the bomb doors would not open and so the bombs stayed on board. The third wave was by now nearing the aiming point and Ronnie Plunkett noted:

> The intention of this raid was that we would all bomb when the leader did, but unfortunately we were not able to do so. The run was unfortunately spoiled by one particular aircraft formating too closely [F/L A.E. Johnson's ME337, TL:A], so Bob Jordan could not accurately stay on the beam and there was no chance of me getting a release signal while this was so. We were therefore forced to release by jettisoning over Cologne. The other aircraft were forced to bomb visually. During the Oboe run we were hit seven times and set on fire. The wireless op and the mid-upper [gunner] tackled the fire and successfully extinguished it. Our Lancaster then lost an engine and to get out of the flak, Bob Jordan dived the aircraft and pulled out at 4,000ft. We then had time to notice that one of the crew [the flight engineer] had taken an injury to his forehead, but fortunately it was not serious and this was bandaged up. On the return trip we were pleasantly surprised to find an allied fighter formating on us back to the Channel, where we got rid of a 1,000lb MC – jettisoned 'safe' (bombs hung up) at 6,000ft. The rear turret was in a bit of a mess, and the pilots also announced that the hydraulics were hit, so we came in at [RAF] Manston and made a successful crash-landing. The landing at Manston was a shaky do. The pilot ordered crash positions, as the aircraft was on fire amidships. We were not sure the undercarriage would come down and lock because the kite was previously damaged by flak. However, I personally took up the crash position behind the main spar, having quite a bit of experience on Wellingtons under similar circumstances. The wheels did come down, but unfortunately the aircraft did not want to stop and saw the full length of the runway until we settled in nicely on the 50ft ground at the end. We evacuated the Lancaster pretty quickly and put a bit of distance between it and the crew. I don't know what had to be done to it, as we returned to our base at RAF Bourn by train.

The return by train was not immediate however, as Ronnie noted: 'With regard to the airman who received the head wound that day, it thankfully did not turn out to be very serious, although it bled a lot. Once we got down at Manston, we had him cleaned up well, and got a

S/L Geoffrey Parker sitting at a desk proudly displays his DFC and PFF badge beneath his pilot's wings. Note the vintage telephone on the desk to his left. (Via Geoffrey Parker)

few pints on the head of it.' Landing five minutes ahead of them, at 14.40 hours had been S/L Harding who had also safely, though precariously, made it back to RAF Manston.

The second and third wave Mosquitos soon arrived over RAF Bourn. First in was S/L Geoffrey Parker who landed on runway 252 at 14.13 hours. At 14.24 hours, when he was preparing to exit, he saw that S/L Almond had managed to land his Mosquito. It had come in with a full complement of bombs still on board, on one engine, and without the use of an undercarriage. ML981, GB:D-Bar was ploughing its way relentlessly along the grassy part at the side of the runway and, to Parker's horror, was heading straight for him. Miraculously, they avoided collision and the bombs did not detonate as the aircraft skidded along on its belly to a halt. The crew then emerged safely, somewhat shaken but mercifully still intact, but their aircraft was damaged beyond repair.

Later that same afternoon, four others visited Sieburg. At the same time, another four Mosquitos went to Limburg, to lead 48 Mosquitos of the Light Night Striking Force to bomb the railway yards. One of the 105 Squadron C-Flight Mosquitos, ML902:C-Bar, was flown by F/L Trevor Walmsley, with F/O E. 'Ted' Povey DFM. Trevor Walmsley recalls their return from Limburg:

Fog was still covering England and most of the continent, so we were told to put down anywhere a hole in the fog showed us a runway. RAF Bourn was fog-bound when we got back, so we punted around looking for a temporary hole, finally landing at Upwood. So did everybody else. What a shambles – Mossies coming in from all directions before the fog closed in again. One of our pilots, landing, overtook a Spitfire taking off on the same runway. How nobody got killed I'll never know – talk about air misses! Debriefing was conducted by a very old Intelligence Officer – must have been about forty, just like a headmaster: 'Squadron?', '105', 'Pilot?', 'Walmsley', 'Navigator?', 'Povey', 'Aircraft?', 'Barred Charlie', 'Purpose of operation?', 'Marking for the LNSF', 'Target?' – now, up to that last question, we knew the answers, but the last one got us. Remember, we used to get a map reference for Waiting Point and Target and didn't necessarily know the name, and we'd had five briefings, all for different targets [before the RAF settled on Limburg]. Ted said 'Cologne'. I said 'No, it was Limburg'. 'No', said Ted, 'that was the other day.'

The Headmaster started to freeze up: 'Do you mean to say', like we'd written on the lavatory wall, 'that you've been marking a target for a bombing operation and don't even know where you've been?' Silence and get ready to bend over, then Ted says 'Got a map?' 'There's one on the wall behind me', said the Head. It was about the size of a football pitch, but we were tired. Ted sauntered over – he was never rattled – traced his finger down in the general direction of Germany, and gave up. So I said, 'This was an Oboe operation so all you need put is "Coped", so we're off.' I got an Oboe debriefing from the other six crews who'd found the hole, and located the scrambler telephone. In a room full of people who knew nothing about Oboe, I gave Tommy Horton back at Bourn our state of the art: 'A-Able [ML973:A-Bar – F/L J.W. Birt with F/L J.D.B.V. Reffitt DFC] Cat OK, Mouse OK. Coped. Barred Freddie [LR503:F-Bar – F/L P.J. Wheeler with F/L C.H. Crown DFC] Cat OK, Mouse u/s. Non-Cope.' And so on. The room quietened to hear this strange language and I felt like chucking in a few more animals, just for fun. I apologized for getting Tommy out of bed and he said he'd send transport to get us back. Then we went for an ops breakfast. A permanent station, with a posh dining room – they even had knives and forks – not like Bourn.

Transport arrived, seven crews, fourteen of us got on board at 4 o'clock in the morning. After about 6 miles, the truck ran out of petrol. We walked. It was one of those warm, foggy nights, with a bright moon, so we strolled through the Cambridgeshire villages singing Christmas carols. We ran out of carols, and just as we started on 'Our home presents a dismal picture' to the tune of 'Deutschland Über Alles' a village bobby appeared out of a side lane, on his bike. He saw us – fourteen paratroopers, complete with flying helmets, Mae Wests, flying boots and revolvers, all singing the German national anthem. The last we saw of him, he was heading for Glasgow! We began to flag, so we sat down in the middle of the road, on a little bridge. Soon an American Army convoy came rumbling out of the fog. 'We waved them down, got on the sides of the wagons and were off. We passed a soldier and a WRAC, busy doing their 'Commando exercises' on the grass verge and admired their concentration; not once did their manoeuvres cease as they were encouraged and advised by Path Finder Force and the United States Air Force. They dropped us at Caxton Gibbett, and we staggered the couple of miles or so to Bourn and bed.

The weather soon deteriorated severely. Walmsley remembered the conditions for Christmas: 'Clearing snow from the runways – ice – but most of all fog. Fog was so bad that, in Oboe, we worked a system whereby the primary attempted to take off, whilst his reserve sat in the aircraft in the pan. If the primary failed to get away, the reserve took over. Take-off was novel. You lined the aircraft up on the one, maybe two visible lights on the runway, set the gyro on zero, opened the throttles and, with head firmly in the cockpit, kept the gyro steady and prayed.'

Dennis Bolesworth also remembered the severe conditions and the inherent dangers: 'On take-off at some 80 mph we had a violent swing to port, over the snow-covered grass heading straight for the watchtower. The inmates all dived for cover knowing what we were carrying [a 4,000lb bomb] as we tobogganed over the snow, to pull up half a wingspan short of catastrophe and taxied back for a fresh start.'

Walmsley continued: 'Christmas Day found scarcely any crews on the squadron. They'd landed all over the UK and Europe, wherever they could find a hole. Ted and I, together with a particular friend who had better be nameless, had been invited to Christmas dinner at a farm. Our friend had, for the past few months, been telling their Land Army girl about the heroic deeds of Path Finder Force. By about 3 o'clock the farmer was asleep. We were very comfortable and our friend, suffering from operational fatigue and an excess of "sherbet", confusing the farmer's wife for the Land Army girl, took her on his knee and tried to seduce her. She was well into her seventies and about six stone wet through. She thought it was Christmas – we knew it was!'

The crossroads at St Vith are marked for 294 aircraft as Bomber Command enter the Battle of the Bulge in the Ardennes. Photograph taken at 22,000ft on 26 December 1944 from F/L Cyril Muller's Mosquito B.IX, MM237, GB:Q. (Via Cyril Muller)

However, despite the distractions of the festive season, further direct support to the Allied troops came on Boxing Day, as the weather had cleared. A controlled Musical Parramatta was launched on snow-covered St Vith. No. 105 Squadron sent out six Mosquitos, only three of which (S/L A.W. 'Tony' Farrell AFC with F/L Reffitt in ML938:H, F/L C.F. Muller DFM with F/L P. Hall DFC in MM237:Q and F/L Peter Sleight with F/L Moher in PF385:K) found and marked the primary target; the St Vith crossroads. A total of 294 aircraft bombed, leaving such devastation that the crossroads were raised to an impassable heap of rubble. All Mosquitos had to land at RAF Graveley on return due to the severe winter weather. The next day Rheydt's marshalling yards were marked by four of 105's Mosquitos to further disrupt General Field Marshal Gerd von Rundstedt's armies in the Ardennes.

The year concluded with the marking of rail targets between the 28th and 29th at Opladen, Bonn, München, Koblenz, and oil targets such as Schloven and Troisdorf. Houfflaise was marked in the early hours of the 31st, for 154 Lancasters, which bombed the German supply bottleneck in the valley. The last operation of the year was to Mannheim, from where F/L Donald, with F/O Watson, returned in MM225:V. Their port engine had been hit when they had met a hail of flak. At 21.30 hours they successfully belly-landed and safely ground to a halt at RAF Manston in Kent.

So 1944 had come to a close. It had been a year of much change and a vast increase in the number of operational sorties, with much experimentation and extension of Oboe's capabilities. The Allied armies were making great strides across Europe and the end of the war was in sight, but the Ardennes battle had still to be won and the Rhein had still to be crossed.

CHAPTER 20

The End in Sight

January 1945 was to see the continued bombing of oil and communications targets. There was a worrying start to the month, however, as on the 2nd, F/L G. Donald and his navigator F/O Frank Taylor Watson went missing from an operation to Castrop-Rauxel in PF431:K-Bar. Speculation abounded about their loss having been due to night-fighters as they disappeared from the ground station's screen over a flak-free area. It was later learned that they had come down at the German town of Wilsum, approximately 20km north-east of Nordhorn. The pilot had been taken PoW, but F/O Watson, who had on a previous occasion been shot down and evaded capture, had been killed. His body was laid to rest in the Reichswald Forest war cemetery.

Further support for the Ardennes battle was given on the 5th, when Houfflaise was marked for an attack by 93 Lancasters of 5 Group. On the 12th, there was an interesting incident when snow was badly hampering operations again. The Gelsenkircher Bergwerks AG at Bochum and a target at Oer-Erkenschwick, 45km west of Hamm, were the centre of attention for two flights of four Mossies. F/O J.L. de Beer with F/L B. Tierney were rolling for take-off in MM226:R, when it swung and crashed into a pile of snow which had been swept up and left at the side of the runway. The Mosquito caught fire and was damaged so badly that it was not used on operations again. Fortunately, the crew survived the crash and were soon back on the Battle Order. Wally Fennell's previously mentioned recollections about armourers come to mind in a comment in the ORB: 'The crew were not hurt, and probably the Engineering Officer had the most exciting time, watching the armourers digging the mud off the cookie to get at the pistol. They did not treat it with the respect he thought it deserved.'

Operations continued, and on the 13th six 105 Squadron Mosquitos marked railway yards at Saarbrücken for 158 Lancasters. Due to the bad weather back at base, all Mosquitos landed at RAF Manston. However, the next day, on the return trip to RAF Bourn, F/L Walmsley with navigator F/O Povey were in Mosquito ML902:C-Bar when it swung on take-off. The crew survived when the undercarriage collapsed under the strain and 'Barred Charlie' ended its days, damaged beyond repair.

On the 14th, Saarbrücken's marshalling yards were again marked, this time for 100 Halifaxes. A Master Bomber controlled the attack, which was successful. There were four Mosquitos airborne for the operation, led by W/C Somerville in ML923:Z. In the event, only Wheeler with Brown in ML999:B-Bar 'coped'. One crew, due to go on leave that afternoon after the operation, was Tidy and Barr. They received their leave early, when their starboard engine on ML922:Y packed up due to flak damage, necessitating a crash-landing at an aerodrome at Evère, near Brussels. The aircraft was so severely damaged that it was left there for the duration. Operations continued with 'spoof' marking of Mannheim on the 16th and training targets the next day at Rüthen, approximately 30km south-west of Paderborn. The Brückhausen AG benzol plant at Duisburg was marked on the 22nd for 362 Lancasters, on the last area bombing raid of the war on Duisburg. On the 28th tragedy struck again as F/L George Lowson Smith McHardy DFC and navigator F/O George Robert Peebles Duncan in ML923:Z 'failed to return' from an operation to mark Stuttgart's marshalling yards. Both airmen were laid to rest, initially at the American cemetery in the French town of Grand Failly, from where they were transferred to France's Choloy war cemetery.

F/L Tom P. Lawrenson DFC (right with moustache) and F/L 'Dud' W. Allen DFC, RNZAF relax in front of C-Flight's Mosquito B.IX, LR503, 'F-Bar' for Freddie at RAF Bourn in April 1945. The aircraft was to complete a record 213 operations and was soon to embark on a disastrous war bond-raising trip to Canada. (Via Tom Lawrenson/Cliff Streeter)

By now, at the end of January, the Ardennes battle was over, and the Allies had beaten their enemy. Sadly, 8,497 Americans had been killed, with 46,000 wounded and 21,000 missing or captured. The Germans had lost 12,652 dead, with 57,000 wounded and 50,000 captured in the process.

MkII Oboe stations had now been installed all over the continent at Molsheim, La Roche, Florennes, Commercy, Rips and Tilburg, with operational control via 8 Group PFF, which would facilitate deeper Oboe penetrations on the continent, but 'copes' would reach an all-time low of 50 per cent for February. On 1 February, Duisburg, Ludwigshaven and Mainz were visited and F/O Tom P. Lawrenson with F/O Dudley W. Allen in ML924:C-Bar, accompanied by F/L F.A. Taylor with P/O F.S. Copestake DFM in MM241:H, carried out a 'spoof' on Mannheim, where they dropped one red TI on a Gee release, and then carried on to Stuttgart to do an Oboe run, dropping one 500lb MC bomb and another on Gee.

On the 4th, F/L D.M. Smith with Sgt K.R. Aspden had a bad time of it, when they ran short of fuel returning from a 'last resort' attack on Würtzburg in MM151:J. They feathered one engine and made a single-engined landing in Belgium on the aerodrome at Knokke-le-Zoute. They crashed very badly and overshot when the other engine cut out. Both were injured and hospitalized.

An attack on the 7th was considered most successful when only one Mosquito out of five 'coped' when marking Kleve, and three of ten 'coped' when marking Goch. The attack was the prelude to an advance by Canadian troops of their 1st Army under Lieutenant-General Henry Crerar, for Operation Veritable which opened at 05.00 hours on the 8th. This was the first of Montgomery's thrusts in preparation for crossing the Rhein and would drive south-east from the

Nijmegen area, between the Rhein and the Maas rivers, through the Reichwald Forest, to reach the Rhein south of Emmerich.

During the month the squadron visited many well-known targets, as well as some new ones such as Wiesbaden, Bonn, Misburg, Frankfurt-am-Main, Worms and Pforzheim. On the 13th F/L Ruck DFC and F/L Gordon DFC survived when they returned early from an attack on Nürnberg when an electrical fault in RV298:B-Bar filled the cockpit with smoke and threatened fire. On the 22nd, when Erfurt was visited by two Mossies, S/L R. Burrell and F/O J. McCulloch dropped 'last resort' in PF442:X. Shortage of fuel nearly claimed another crew, when S/L I.L.T. Ackroyd DFC and his navigator F/O E.F. Casey DFC baled out on the way back. The pilot landed on a hotel roof, and spent, as the record states, 'an alarming five minutes and did many feats of climbing and jumping more in keeping with either Douglas Fairbanks or a cat burglar'. The aircraft, RV298:B-Bar, smashed into the ground south-east of Brugge, leaving a huge crater as testimony to its arrival.

Many promotions were also announced during the month and Temporary Path Finder certificates and golden eagle PFF badges awarded, as well as awards such as a DSO to W/C F.R. Bird and DFCs to others. In March another four DSOs were issued. The CO was promoted and became G/C Slim Somerville DSO, DFC, AFC and other DSOs were awarded to W/C T.G. Jefferson AFC, S/L Jack V. Watts DFC, and S/L H.A. Almond DFC.

As it was thought that it contained German troops and vehicles, the area around Wesel was the subject of a sustained effort by 32 of the squadron's aircraft during the 6th and the early hours of the 7th. No. 109 Squadron also participated. This was followed by an attack by three formations of 'non-musical' Mosquitos in the afternoon, led by 3 Oboe primaries and 3 reserves. Sky marking in the 10/10ths cloud conditions was considered too dangerous, as Allied troops were in the vicinity, and so the Oboe Mosquitos were briefed to attack the German armour. The attack only stopped for 30 minutes throughout the evening. The official record postulated the following: 'It has been suggested that this was to let the Germans come out of their funk-holes, stretch themselves and perform the necessities of nature. Whether or not this was [Bomber] Command's reason for the break, no doubt the Germans took full advantage of it.' Of the following 26 'non-musical' Mosquitos, 22 dropped four 500lb or one 4,000lb bomb each. During the operation, there was an early return for W/O W. Riordan with F/Sgt J.D. O'Connell in PF442:X as they had fuel trouble on their starboard engine. W/C Tommy W. Horton DFC RNZAF with F/L W. Jones DFC had a similar problem in ML924:C-Bar. They had taken off at 19.07 hours and returned on one engine. The aircraft crashed on landing. The crew were safe, but the Mosquito never flew again.

Again on the evening 6 March, S/L R. Burrell and F/O J. McCulloch had an interesting experience in MM134:P when, having taken off at 18.35 hours, severe icing on the port engine required their early return. They landed back at 19.35 hours but were not going to be beaten. Instead of turning in for the night, they took another Mosquito, MM237:Q this time, and were airborne by 21.22 hours heading back to Wesel. Having dropped their load on target, they were returning without navigational aids, and were in the process of talking to the ground station. They had just advised that they were at a certain position of crossing the English coast when suddenly, a 'friendly' British night-fighter decided that they must be a Luftwaffe menace. The night-fighter then proceeded to open fire, setting the Mosquito's port engine on fire and succeeding in shooting it down just south of Frayling Abbey in Norfolk. Fortunately, the crew managed to get out in time and came down on their parachutes. McCulloch was slightly injured as a result of the jump but Burrell received shrapnel injuries to his leg. The crew were nevertheless fortunate to have survived; no doubt Fighter Command had some red faces and some explaining to do thereafter.

No. 105 Squadron at RAF Bourn: March 1945. Back row (left to right): F/L W.H.B. Pritchard; F/L J.C.H. de Lisle; W/O W. Riordan; F/O D.C. Boa; F/O E.F. Casey; W/O P.C. Davies; F/L B. Tierney; F/O K.S. McPherson; F/L P. Sleight; F/L W.A.C. Bowen; F/L J.P.M. Greening; Sgt R.J. Brown; P/O G.D. O'Connell; F/O J. McCulloch; F/L J.L. de Beer; F/L W. Jones; F/L P. Enderby; F/L T.C. Walmsley. Third row: F/L V.W.G. Musgrove; F/L J.A. Ruck; F/L F.T. Halpin; P/O F.W. Deedman; F/L B.J. Wheeler; F/L D. Tidy; P/O F.N. Briggs; F/L W.G. Manifold; F/L R.F. Lewis; F/L G.H. Barr; F/L J.W. Birt; F/L N.H. Kirby; F/L J.P. Molony; Sgt B.J. Fry; F/Sgt G.W. Vance; F/L K.J. Gordon; F/L V.E. Stuchbery; F/O G.W. Edwards; P/O A.Y. Lickley. Second row: F/S J.H. Spicer; F/O J.G. Hicklin; F/L P.F. Hoare; F/O J.F.O.C. de Lori; F/O D.R. Allen; F/L P.L. Whitaker; F/L T.W. Moppett; F/O S.D. Telford; F/O A.D. Bolesworth; F/L D.C. James; P/O F.S. Copestake; F/L L.J. Buckley; F/L F.A. Taylor; F/O A.H. Hammond; F/L E. Povey; F/L J.C. Sampson; F/L C.H. Brown; F/L P.J. Slingsby; F/L J.N. Owen; F/L T.P. Lawrenson. Front row: F/L J.D.B.V. Reffitt; S/L R.E. Jordan; F/L C.F. Muller; F/L Hare (Adj); S/L G.F. Caldwell; S/L J.F.C. Gallacher; S/L W. Baker; S/L G.W.A. Parker; S/L J. Comar; S/L T.L. Hildrew; W/C T.W. Horton; G/C K.J. Somerville (CO); W/C T.G. Jefferson; S/L G.W. Harding; S/L J.D.G. Bishop; S/L H. Almond; S/L I.L.T. Ackroyd; S/L N.F. Hildyard; S/L A.W. Farrell; S/L L.W. Millett; F/L R.A. Strachan; F/O A. McK. Wood; F/L R.W. Plunkett; F/L E.L.D. Drake. (Via A.W. Farrell/R. Plunkett)

On an operation to Witten on the 19th, there was a tragic loss. F/L Leonard Frank Douglas King and his blond-haired navigator F/L Douglas Pollock Tough were lost when their Mosquito, MM170:D-Bar, failed to return. Dennis Bolesworth recalls: 'It was their first op. I told him [King] he was a chump at that stage of the war to volunteer for another tour, and he was only with us for a matter of several weeks before going missing. They never appeared on the controller's screen at Trimmingham, on the Norfolk coast, when called in. What happened to them no one seems to know. King was an ex-fighter [Spitfire] pilot who had been instructing on a BAT flight and was, as were most of the pilots on 105, able to fly on an accurate beam. Tough was on his first tour as he had been navigation instructing in Canada since getting his wings. How Tough got accepted as a navigator I don't know, as all on 105 were 2nd tour men. Whether they lost their way, I don't know, but navigating on a Mossie at night from a Gee chart folded on the knee at 300 mph was a different ball game from instructing students with a chart on a table in daylight.' Both officers are commemorated on the memorial at Runnymede.

Münster, Kassel, Hannover, Hagen, Essen, Dortmund, Wuppertal, Dahlbruch, Bremen, Bielefeld, Homberg, Zweibrücken, Bottrop, Misburg, Erfurt, Mannheim, Nürnberg, Hanau, Rheine, Langendreer, Dorsten, Duben, Hildesheim, Bochum, Paderborn, Sterkrade, Gladbach, Northeim, Harburg, Nördlingen and Hamburg were all visited during the month. The number of sorties rose to 328 with a much-improved 73.5 per cent of 'copes', due to the ground stations having had time to calibrate their equipment on the continental stations.

Because of all the intense activity, several crews were now becoming 'tour-expired' and departed on 'rest'. However, not all movements were departures, as one 'old hand' who was freed by the Allied advance, P/O Paul Addinsell, shot down back on 16 July 1942 on an operation to Wilhelmshaven, had returned to England.

April began with signs of the Allied advance becoming more apparent as crews were asked to mark targets such as Magdeburg and Lüneburg on the 2nd, near which units of the US 9th Army were to reach the River Elbe on the 12th. On the 4th, an unfortunate accident killed another well-respected 2nd tour crew member. F/L Patrick Enderby DFC, who normally flew with F/L N.H. Kirby DFC and bar, was flying in MM134:P. Ron Channon remembers the incident: 'F/L Enderby took off [alone] on a test flight, after his Mosquito had had an engine change. The [port] engine gave out on take-off and it crashed into the farmyard barn on the Bourn road. Of course we were quickly on the scene on our bicycles, as was the crash tender, but the aircraft caught fire and he was killed. I think a fitter was going to go with him on the test, but as he did not have a parachute, and as he would not go all the way back to the parachute section to get one, he saved his own life.' F/L Enderby was buried in Horncastle cemetery.

By the 8th, Berlin was within Oboe range and received regular visits during the month as the crews clambered for the chance to get a Berlin entry in their logbooks. Of an operation 10 days later, Dennis Bolesworth recalls:

A blurred, hazy memory comes to mind of the 'hangover op' to Heligoland on 18th April 1945 – a daylight job. This started on the afternoon of the 17th, as we had arranged a 'sports day' with our sister squadron, 109. These took place at various intervals at alternate bases and this one was our turn. It was meant to be a 'piss-up to end all piss-ups' as the war was coming to a close and a stand-down was obtained from Group for the 17th and 18th. Sundry barrels of amber nectar were purchased and set up in the concert hall a few days before. The snooker, darts, tiddly-winks, draughts and domino teams came over at tea time. The real criterion was a good night and a large capacity.

After dinner, I went to the hall and things were warming up, so I popped back to the billet and changed into the worst battle-dress and shoes I could find, and set off for the fray, rolling

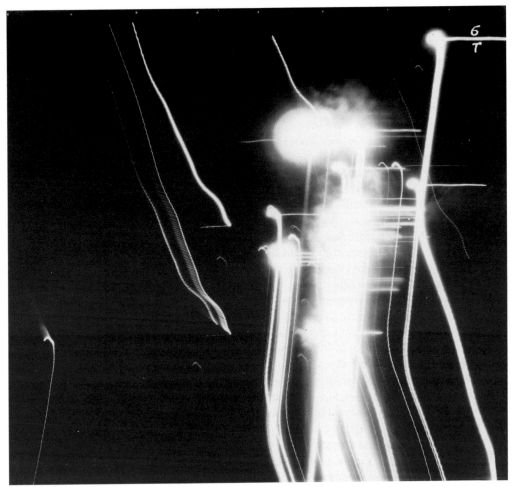

Two red and two red long-burning Target Indicators dropped to mark Potsdam on the night of 14/15 April 1945 from F/L Cyril Muller's Mosquito B.IX, RV322, GB:Q. (Via Cyril Muller)

my trousers above the ankles. It was a warm evening and the drinkers had overflowed on to a grass bank alongside, in various stages of undress. The well ran dry between 1 a.m. and 2 a.m. and 109 mounted their steeds and set off for home. The last thing that I remember was a F/O Met. [meteorological] bod standing on the front of the stage, trying to sing a lewd song with all and sundry throwing pints at him – what a waste as the floor was almost ankle deep. The next day, he was seen in the showers dressed in his 'best blue' with soap and a nail brush, trying to remove the beer stains. If only he had waited a few weeks, it would have saved him the trouble, as he was tossed into the river at Grantchester after a VE-day thrash at the local, for all the 'duff gen' that he had fed us. Standing up to his waist in water, he only needed a crown, some seaweed, and a pitchfork to make a good Neptune.

We had hardly got our heads down when we were awakened by the batman with some tea and shaving water at 6 a.m., stating that breakfast was at 8 and briefing at 9. We told him that it was a stand-down and to get lost. Then he turned up with an SP [Service Policeman] with the same story, who was told in no uncertain terms where he could go, with comments as to his parentage added. Next came the CO and the Flight CO with the terse order: 'Be there or else!' Breakfast was mostly strong, black coffee, and a bunch of red, bleary-eyed bods nursing hangovers turned up.

When we saw that the markers were 4,000lb bombs, never used before [for marking], we knew that it was a hoax by the Flight CO in revenge for the spiking of his car the night before. A rush was made for the calendar to see whether or not it was April 1st. We were then told that we were to drop these [4,000lb bombs] into the North Sea, 50 miles due north of the island, to make a mark for the heavies to turn on and run down the island. I think that if the breathalyser had been about, most of the pilots wouldn't have been allowed to drive a Mini, let alone a Mossie! Take-off was without incident and the only thing I recall of the leg out to the call-in point, was that we had the two triangular flaps on the canopy open to let in some cool air.

One or two of the primary navigators were sick in the cockpit, having first removed their oxygen masks. The pilots handed over to their secondaries, waggling their wings and banking round behind them in a tight married man's formation some 300 yards away. The secondary pilots had to wake up their navs and tell them that they were now primaries and to get cracking. The bombs were duly dropped on Oboe. We did a circuit to watch the huge cascade of mud and water lifted into the air, far greater than that caused by a depth charge, leaving a circle of black, frothing water 300yds in diameter which could be seen several miles away. The heavies turned on this to go down the length of the island, like yachts rounding a mark during a race. We put the nose down and sped for home, the secondaries dumping their bombs in the North Sea as it was dangerous to try to land with them on board. I can't remember the debriefing, which must have been terse as we didn't come within 50 miles of a target, but it counted as an op. After a quick meal it was off to bed until dinner, but not many pints were pulled in the bar afterwards.

Not all of the Mosquitos marked the sea however, as the ORB explains: 'Ten–fifteen of our aircraft marked successfully, three reserves not required. Marking throughout was accurate, though the heavy concentration of bombs on the various A/Ps [aiming points] quickly obliterated the markers. Photographs taken less than two hours after the attack show numerous fires throughout the island and a large oil fire in the Naval Base. The whole island appears to be thoroughly cratered and nearly all buildings destroyed in the central area. Most of the Naval installations have been wiped out or badly damaged, and the runway on the airfield ceases to be a runway. Nearly all the adjacent buildings have been destroyed.'

On the 24th, Munro bombs were dropped on the PoW camps at Ingoldstadt, Laufen, Oschatz, Lüneburg and Neubrandenburg, disgorging leaflets advising Allied prisoners of what to do on the run-up to liberation. The camp at Neubrandenburg was also marked for three Lancasters carrying medical supplies.

On the 25th, the biggest prize of all appeared to be available: the chance to bomb Hitler's lair at Berchtesgaden. Eight Mosquitos with eager crews were airborne, as were others from 109 Squadron, but around lunchtime all were returning having been let down by the fact that the Oboe 'beam' was blocked by the mountains at such long range, despite the fact that they were flying at 39,000ft! Nevertheless, the 359 Lancasters dropped their loads including 617 Squadron's 16 Lancasters loaded with 12,000lb 'Tallboy' bombs. Unfortunately none of the High Command was in residence at the time, but the Berghof, where Neville Chamberlain had met Hitler before Munich, the SS barracks, and dwellings belonging to Göring and Martin Bormann (Hitler's private secretary) were razed to the ground. On 29 April, Bormann was

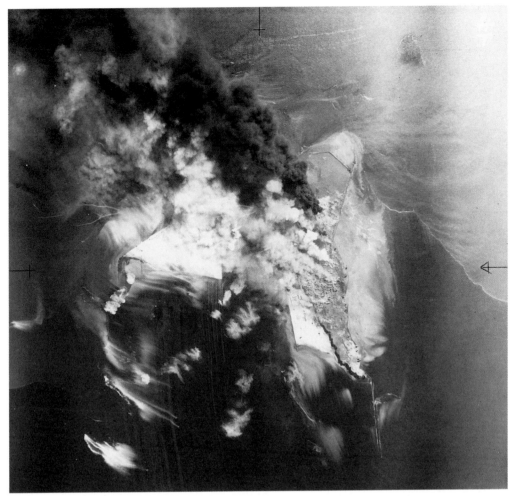

Ten Mosquitos successfully marked the town, airfield and naval basin on the island of Helgoland (Heligoland) for 969 aircraft. Here the naval basin is belching smoke from the attack. Photograph taken at 32,000ft on 18 April 1945 from F/L Cyril Muller's Mosquito B.IX, LR498, GB:Y. (Via Cyril Muller)

witness to the wedding of Hitler and Eva Braun. The next day in the Führer-bunker Hitler shot himself and Eva Braun took poison. Both their bodies were subsequently taken to the Chancellery gardens, where they were put in a trough. Petrol was then poured over them and they were set alight. The Führer was no more.

Bomber Command then followed a humane pursuit as Dennis Bolesworth recalls: 'During the last days of April and the beginning of May 1945, an operation codenamed Manna was performed, dropping about 7,000 tons of food and clothing for the Dutch. From 29,000ft we had to drop a marker on to selected aerodromes, on the intersection of the runways. The heavies at roof-top height dropped the food and clothes. It amazed them to suddenly see a red cascade burn on the intersection, dropped by a plane that they couldn't see with the naked eye.' Between 1 and 8 May, many sorties were made to The Hague, Ypenburg, Valkenburg, Rotterdam and Gouda. The Manna missions were very well received, as Peter Sleight recalled: 'I have recently

On Victory in Europe or VE-Day, 8 May 1945, at RAF Bourn, a happy group take part in the 'groceries to Holland' operation, code-named MANNA. They were off to the Hague Racecource, Ypenberg and Rotterdam to mark for supply food drops by Lancasters. They are (left to right) F/L K.J. Gordon DFC; F/L R.H. Potts; F/L J.C.H. de Lisle DFC; F/O Jean F.O.C. Delori; F/L J.R. Lake DFC, AFC; S/L Tony W. Farrell DFC, AFC; G/C Keith Somerville DSO, DFC, AFC; S/L J.D.G. Bishop DFC. (Via A.W. Farrell)

visited Amsterdam, and a taxi driver told me that he had never tasted bread so good as that dropped by the RAF in April and May 1945.'

During the mercy missions, on 4 of May at Lüneburg Heath, the Commander of the 21st Army Group, Field Marshal Montgomery, accepted the surrender of the Third Reich's armed forces in Holland, North-West Germany and Denmark. The proceedings were concluded on 7 May at General Eisenhower's HQ in Reims, France, where General Alfred Jodl represented Hitler's successor, Admiral Karl Dönitz, and signed a document unconditionally surrendering all the German armed forces to the Allies. The cessation of hostilities was to be immediate on the Western Front, and the surrender was to be effective from 00.01 hours (GST) on 9 May. Victory in Europe had arrived – the war in Europe, and for 105 Squadron, was over.

There was however a sad ending. On 9 May, F/L J. Morris W. Briggs DSO, DFC, DFM and his navigator F/O John C. Baker DFC and Bar landed with a passenger, de Havilland engineer Edward Jack, in Calgary, Canada, having first put on quite an aerial display to signal their arrival. They had been sent to take a Mosquito to Canada as a showpiece for the 8th Victory Loan Bond drive. The Mosquito they were given was 109 and subsequently 105 Squadron's

F/O S Tom Wingham relaxes between opera-
tions in May 1945. (Via Tom Wingham)

well-loved B.IX, LR503 'F-Bar' for Freddie, which had chalked up more operational sorties than any other Mosquito and survived; 213 in all. S/L Tony Farrell DFC, AFC, remembers the aircraft with affection: ' "F" for Freddie was a MkIX and therefore could not take the 4,000lb bomb. It was warmer than the pressurised MkXVI and performed as well, if not better, although longer in the tooth! It was just one of those lovely quirks that make aircraft "human" and to the best of my knowledge it was the best of the MkIXs we had left.' Just after 16.00 hours on 10 May 1945, 'Freddie' took to the air for a trip to Red Dear and Lethbridge, from where they were to return to Calgary. Unfortunately, they decided to 'beat up' the control tower to thrill a crowd that had turned up to see them off. After two passes at very low level, their luck ran out. On the third pass, the Mosquito failed to pull up in time and struck the top of the tower and a metal pole thereon, used for the release of weather balloons. The port wing sheared off and a piece of the tail-plane as well, before 'Freddie' plunged into the ground and was consumed by flames. Sadly, despite having been thrown clear of the aircraft, both crew members were killed in the accident. They were buried the next day at Burnsland cemetery, Calgary, in its Field of Honour.

Meanwhile, back at RAF Bourn, more Permanent Path Finder badges and certificates were awarded, and postings took place. Two Mosquitos and a Lancaster were modified to start what were to be known as 'Cook's Tours'. Dennis Bolesworth recalls the excitement this caused: 'At the end of the war, [Oboe] sets were removed from the nose of the aircraft, and we took any ground staff on a sight-seeing trip at low level to see the damage. A little rivalry sprang up when it was a WAAF as a passenger, as we had to fit and adjust the straps between her thighs. However, it was agreed to do this alternately. A Lancaster was produced and we were able to do this six at a time.' Each person receiving a 'Cook's Tour' was issued with a map and a summary

F/L J. Morris W. Briggs (right) and his navigator F/O John C. Baker in discussion in front of C-Flight's Mosquito B.IX, LR503, 'F-Bar' for Freddie at RAF Bourn in April 1945. The Mosquito crashed at Calgary airport soon afterwards, killing both Briggs and Baker. (Via Geoffrey Parker)

sheet outlining the salient features of the chosen route, which was differentiated by a route identification colour such as 'red' or 'blue'. An example of this can be seen in Appendix 1.

Many changes were now to take place. On 1 June G/C Slim Somerville was posted to the Rehabilitation Board, and command was taken up by W/C Tommy Horton. 'Cook's Tours', operational exercises, cross-countries, bulls'-eyes and bombing exercises continued, and many more Permanent Path Finder badges and certificates were handed out. There were a couple of aircraft losses, fortunately without loss of life. The first was on 14 June, when S/L N.F. Hildyard DFC managed to write off PF518, GB-D, due to suffering an engine failure when practising SBA and single-engine flying. He crash-landed one mile to the south of RAF Bourn, damaging the aircraft beyond repair, but survived to tell the tale. Three days later he was awarded the DSO. The other incident took place on the 24th, when W/O D.C. Webb was flying ML916, GB-B. His starboard engine failed on the way over the continent on a training flight. He therefore had to divert to the Belgian aerodrome at Brussels–Melsbroek, where on approach he put the undercarriage down too late. On touch-down the wheels had not locked home and the undercarriage collapsed under the aircraft's weight, resulting in another written-off Mosquito. Fortunately, he too lived to tell the tale.

On 29 June, the squadron left RAF Bourn and moved to RAF Upwood. S/L Hildyard DSO, DFC, took over A-Flight and S/L Burrell DFC continued as B-Flight Commander, there being

HEADQUARTERS,
PATH FINDER FORCE,
ROYAL AIR FORCE.
16th July 1944.

To: Flight Lieutenant Parker (115938)

AWARD OF PATH FINDER FORCE BADGE

You have to-day qualified for the award of the Path Finder Force Badge and are entitled to wear the Badge as long as you remain in the Path Finder Force.

2. You will not be entitled to wear the Badge after you leave the Path Finder Force without a further written certificate from me authorising you to do so.

*Air Vice-Marshal, Commanding
Path Finder Force.*

ROYAL AIR FORCE

PATH FINDER FORCE

*Award of
Path Finder Force Badge*

This is to certify that
**ACTING SQUADRON LEADER
A. W. FARRELL. D.F.C., A.F.C. 85281**
having qualified for the award of the Path Finder Force Badge, and having now completed satisfactorily the requisite conditions of operational duty in the Path Finder Force, is hereby

Permanently awarded the Path Finder Force Badge

Issued this **17th** day of **MAY** in the year 19**45**

Air Officer Commanding, Path Finder Force.

'Award of Path Finder Force Badge' certificate to F/L Parker (115938) dated 16 July 1944. (Via Geoffrey Parker)

Path Finder Force certificate of 'Permanent Award of Path Finder Force Badge'. (Via A.W. Farrell)

Mosquito B.XVI, PF518, GB:D with GB:H in background. PF518 was destroyed when, on 14 June 1945, it came in to land on one engine, lost height and belly-landed one mile south-west of RAF Bourn. (Via Tom Wingham)

185

Mosquito B.XVI, PF506, GB:U rests like an elegant ballerina on its propeller tips on the perimeter track, as groundcrews attempt to use a crane to attach a fixing to the tail-wheel to gently lower the unfortunate aircraft to the ground again. (Via Cliff Streeter)

Navigator F/O Jean F.O.C. Delori (left) with pilot S/L Tony W. Farrell and their groundcrew on the port wing of their B.XVI Mosquito in July 1945. (Via A.W. Farrell)

At the tail of their B.XVI Mosquito in July 1945, while the groundcrew attend to the port engine, are (left to right) S/L Tony W. Farrell with Belgian navigator, F/O Jean F.O.C. Delori. (Via A.W. Farrell)

A peaceful view taken from S/L Tony W. Farrell's Box Brownie camera across the starboard engine of 105 Squadron Mosquito B.XVI in August 1945. (Via A.W. Farrell)

no longer any operational need for a C-Flight. On 15 October W/C R.C.M. Collard DSO, DFC, took over command from W/C Tommy Horton who was posted to command 28 ACHU. Thereafter, on 5 November, W/C Collard departed on attachment to the Air Ministry and the next day S/L G.O. Lister took over command. He remained in command until 31 December 1945, when he was succeeded by W/C D.G. Stokes, who assumed command until 105 Squadron was finally disbanded on 1 February 1946. Those left over were then amalgamated with 139 Squadron, before it moved to RAF Hemswell in Lincolnshire.

No. 105 Squadron holds the record of having completed the largest number of operational bombing sorties in Bomber Command, and carried out more sorties than any other Mosquito squadron. They had indeed been a 'crack' squadron.

APPENDICES

I: Cook's Tours

The following document was issued to those going on an aerial tour of Germany:

INTELLIGENCE SECTION RAF STATION, BOURN: MAY 1945

This tour of a large portion of the industrial area of the Third Reich has been arranged for you, who have shared with the flying crews in untiring devotion to duty, to give you some idea of the results obtained by your effort in the general contribution to victory.

The events leading up to the outbreak of war in Europe were spread over some years, and culminated in 1939 with the invasion of Poland, and the first unprovoked and brutal bombing attack on Warsaw. The invasion of Poland resulted in an immediate declaration of war upon the Third Reich by England and France. Rotterdam was later to be attacked by the Luftwaffe, and then followed the attacks upon our own country, first by day, and when they had been defeated in the Battle of Britain, by night.

In the height of Britain's agony, and with an Air Force negligible in size in comparison with that of the Luftwaffe, Mr Churchill promised that the cities of Germany would, one by one, be razed to the ground, but it was not until the Battle of the Ruhr. These attacks increased in size and efficiency until the unconditional surrender of the German armed forces on 8th May this year.

During this long time you were all working hard and were willing to work harder to back up the flying crews. You were, however, given no opportunity of learning just how much you were contributing to the effort and the result of your labours was never apparent to you. Now the opportunity is being given to you, so keep your eyes open, and see the devastation, and you will realize how very truly, by your energy and zeal, retribution has overtaken those who have made life unbearable in the whole of Europe; they have terrorised the weak in the countries they have occupied, and their own political dissenters, they have enforced slave labour, and initiated such diabolical, inhuman, disease-ridden and insanitary torture chambers as those found at Dachau, Buchenwald and Belsen; see this devastation, remember these horrors, and then, thank God you were born British.

The towns you will pass over were, until the Spring of 1943, large industrial areas, and some details are set out in the itinerary attached, and the route is marked on the small-scale map.

Itinerary – Red Route

Leaving base you will cross the English coast at Orford Ness, and reach the continent by way of the island of:

WALCHEREN, a Dutch island on the north bank of the Scheldt Estuary. When Antwerp was taken by British Forces, it was necessary to command the Scheldt Estury before the port could be of use, but it was several weeks before Walcheren was occupied by the Canadians. Bomber Command assisted materially in the reduction of the island, both by breaching the sea wall near Westkapelle and so flooding a large area, and by attacking with success coastal batteries not rendered useless by the flooding. After flying east for some 20 miles, the line of the Scheldt will be seen to starboard, and given good visibility it should be possible to pick out the port of Antwerp, with its cathedral spire. A few miles farther on you will pass over:-

GILZE RIJEN AERODROME, used by the Luftwaffe as a night fighter aerodrome, and attacked many times by Bomber Command and TAF [Tactical Air Force]. Another 45 miles will take you over the River Maas, and shortly after you will reach the small town of:-

GOCH. This town, a key point in the way of the advance of the Second Canadian Army when they struck east and south from the Nijmegen area in February of this year, was attacked successfully by 150 aircraft of Bomber Command on the night of 7/8th of that month, and fell to the Canadians soon after. The Rhine should now be in sight ahead, with:-

WESEL on the far bank. A small agricultural town of some 10,000 inhabitants, it became of supreme importance in the operation by the Canadians mentioned above, for here were a rail bridge and a road bridge over the river, the first upstream from Emmerich 20 miles to the north. As a result, our bombers attacked the place on no less than seven occasions, the final attack, in heavy force, almost eliminating the town, being followed immediately by the crossing of the river at this point by General Montgomery's 21st Army Group, and the capture of the area. The bridges had, of course, previously been destroyed by the enemy. From here the river is followed until we reach the area of the Western Ruhr, and come to:-

HAMBORN, noted for the large Thyssen steel works and Benzol plant, both of which were attacked on several occasions by our aircraft. Hamborn is a suburb of:-

DUISBURG to the south, which has a population of 443,000, and which is the largest inland port in Europe, with extensive docks, and railway yards, collieries and coking plants, and numerous heavy industries of military importance. The town was a target for Bomber Command on several occasions, and, although the area is very scattered, effective damage was done to the various industries centred there. Turning west you pass over:-

OBERHAUSEN, with a large marshalling yard, and come to:-

ESSEN, famous as the home of the Krupps Armament Works. The greater town has a population of over one million people, comparable in size with Birmingham, and it is believed, that the Krupps concern alone employed at least 175,000 workers in 1942. The scene of the second thousand-bomber raid, and of 22 other attacks by the RAF, in addition to the 2 by the USAAF, production was effectively curtailed, and finally in February of this year, entirely stopped.

GELSENKIRCHEN appears, probably to port, almost at once, and is of chief importance as a centre of the synthetic oil industry, the several plants there being severely damaged on several occasions. Numerous collieries and coking plants, and several heavy industries are also grouped here. The next town is:-

CASTROP-RAUXEL, also a little port of track. Here too, the chief industry is the manufacture of synthetic oil, and here again the production of this highly important commodity was periodically reduced or stopped by the action of our aircraft. The last of the large Ruhr towns you will see is:-

DORTMUND, with a population of 550,000, or a little larger than Sheffield, and noted as a centre of heavy industry and engineering works. The well known Dortmund–Ems canal can be seen beginning its run immediately west of the town, and running north-north-west. Targets in the town have been the object of attack on sixteen occasions by large forces of heavy aircraft, and on twelve occasions by the Americans, and the damage is widespread. Course will now be changed to slightly north, and after passing over Kamen on track, you will come to:-

HAMM, with its extensive marshalling yards, and railway junction, which have been the target for so many attacks by Bomber Command, and, latterly, by the USAAF. For the next 40 miles there is little of importance and you will more or less follow the railway to:-

BIELEFELD, where you can see the viaduct breached by aircraft of this Command with the aid of some of its larger bombs. Another 15 miles will bring you to:-

HERFORD, a small town of 40,000 inhabitants, containing various small engineering works. Isolated damage has been caused by small numbers of Mosquitos. A few miles farther on at:-

BAD OEYNHAUSEN, another damaged viaduct may be noticed. You will now turn almost due east again after travelling some fifty miles during which you should pass Hameln (Hamlin of 'The Pied Piper' fame). On your starboard you will reach:-

HILDESHEIM, which, in view of its importance as a railway junction was attacked last winter by a force of 230 heavy aircraft of Bomber Command, causing very severe damage throughout the town. From here you will head due north for 20 miles, and pass over:-

MISBURG, where there is an important oil refinery which has been built on the western edge of an extensive oil field. This refinery was completely out of action as a result of various RAF attacks, in particular, 260 aircraft in March this year.

HANOVER, about five miles due west of Misburg will be the next town you will pass over. With a population of nearly half a million, Hanover is a highly industrialised city, and one of the chief commercial and administrative centres of Northern Germany. The main industries are engineering, rubber works and armaments, with a number of other large scale industrial works. Both RAF and American bombers have attacked targets here many times, and there is severe damage, mainly in the southern half of the town. The next run is to:-

OSNABRÜCK, about seventy miles due west. A town of 100,000 inhabitants, it is a vital railway centre where the main line from Holland to Berlin crosses the line going from the Ruhr to Bremen and Hamburg. The main industries are iron and steel rolling mills, whilst the less important concerns include several engineering works, and a large cotton spinning and weaving mill, as well as a paper factory. Both heavy aircraft and Mosquitos have caused severe devastation, particularly in the northern part of the town. The next town you will pass over is:-

MÜNSTER, about 27 miles south-west of Osnabrück. This is the chief town and administrative centre of Westphalia. There are a variety of industries, none of outstanding importance, but the six heavy attacks by Bomber Command and 13 by the Americans were due to its importance as a railway junction. The Dortmund–Ems canal passes north to south through the town. The route then goes almost due west again to:-

EMMERICH, on the Rhine, a small town where, when the 21st Army Group crossed the Rhine further south, the Germans fought hard to prevent its advance towards the north and north-east.

CLEVE, which you will pass a little further on across the Rhine to the south-west and Emmerich were attacked by heavy forces of our bombers in October last at a time when both towns were full of enemy troops and armour, and for the same reason Cleve was attacked again in February of this year, with devastating results. After Cleve, you pass over the northern part of the:-

REICHSWALD FOREST, where the enemy stored ammunition and motor transport and which was the scene of heavy fighting by the Canadians in their advance from:-

NIJMEGEN, on the River Maas. This will be remembered as being the scene of the attempted thrust to the north-east, leading to the bitter fighting around Arnhem, a venture which, had it succeeded, may have shortened the war by some weeks. From here you fly to:-

THE HAGUE, passing Rotterdam some 10 miles to your port. The Hague is the capital of the Netherlands, and it is just north-east of the city from where many of the V-2s which reached this country were launched. You will make landfall over England over Orford Ness, and arrive at base, having completed a round trip of 840 nautical miles.

Itinerary – Blue Route

After leaving base you will cross the English coast at DUNGENESS and then cross the Channel to the French coast passing over:-

CAP GRIS NEZ. Here the heavy coastal batteries were attacked by our aircraft with great success. The route then carries you to:-

WIZERNES. This is a large storage site for flying bombs and components, and was officially dealt with by Bomber Command during June and July 1944. You now go on to:-

ST VITH, about 150 miles from the French coast and have passed over the north section of the Ardennes. You are now about to cross the German frontier about 5 miles on track. St Vith was attacked by Bomber Command on Boxing Day 1944 in support of our armies, who were engaged in stemming the last German offensive campaign. Then on to:-

KAISERSLAUTERN, a town of 70,000 inhabitants with large marshalling yards and railway workshops, and a most important distribution centre. Heavily attacked by Bomber Command and USAAF on several occasions. From here we go to:-

KARLSRUHE. Having just crossed the Rhine. This town with a population of 100,000 was an important distribution centre for supplying Italy between April 1944 and February 1945 to destroy transport facilities and war material. Now flying northwards along the Rhine you come to:-

SPEYER, with its Messerschmitt factory and population of some 28,000 inhabitants, and then to :-

MANNHEIM, a very important manufacturing and industrial centre with a population of about 430,000, lying on the east bank of the Rhine and on the west bank is Ludwigshaven with a population of

150,000 and the largest IG Farben chemical works will be soon sighted along the river. Both these large industrial war centres have frequently been attacked with results which will be apparent. Still heading northward down the Rhine you come to:-

WORMS, lying on the west bank of the river. An important railway centre and a population of 52,000 people, engaged normally in the leather trade. This town was attacked as late as 21 February 1945 and later on a bridgehead was established by the American forces. Crossing over the Rhine some 20 miles north-east lying surrounded by beautifully wooded country is:-

DARMSTADT, with a population of 110,000 engaged mostly in chemical and explosive manufacture. And some engineering shops with commodious marshalling yard. A major attack was made on this town in September 1944. The next town heading north-east over picturesque forest land is:-

HANAU, a small but important railway centre for transit to Rhine areas – Berlin and Munich for Italian transport. This war communication centre was attacked in January and March 1945. Now heading to the west you will see the River Main going west until it brings you to:-

FRANKFURT-ON-MAIN, with the River Rhine right ahead and the bend as seen on your map, clearly defined. Frankfurt is an old and important financial and administrative centre with about 600,000 inhabitants. It is an important distribution centre and a source of great pride to the German people. The town of HOECHST can be seen just along the river ahead. This is a large chemical works of IG Farben. The town of Frankfurt is familiar to you as a regular target. Now on to:-

MAINZ, with its inland harbour, large railway centre, military installations and 145,000 inhabitants. Heavily attacked by Bomber Command in February of this year. Now on to:-

BINGEN, with a population of 22,000 and on the bend of the Rhine lying on the southern bank. Important for its marshalling yards, repair facilities and distribution. This town only suffered during the latter part of the hostilities and now going north you come to:-

KOBLENZ, with a population of 86,000 and the Rhine and Moselle river junction. A very important rail and river traffic centre and was heavily attacked before General Patton crossed the Moselle. Now on to:-

REMAGEN, where the first crossing of the Rhine was made by General 'Blood and Guts' Patton and the American troops on the original German bridge which was left intact, later to be damaged and abandoned after the Allied engineers had constructed new bridges. A small town but for us a main springboard for the final invasion of the late Third Reich. The next town of:-

BONN is a large university town of 100,000 inhabitants and containing chemical and engineering works and much industrial and experimental work. It has received five heavy attacks, and now you will come to:-

COLOGNE, the main railway centre in the Rhineland with a population of approximately 1,000,000 inhabitants and an industrial centre of primary importance. Look at this once beautiful city on the Rhine, now a lasting memorial to the memory of Hitler and all he stood for. Now due west you will come to:-

DUREN, once a stubborn point of resistance to our offensive on Cologne with a population of 44,000 disappointed Herrenvolk and just look at the town now and go on to:-

AACHEN, with a population of 164,000 inhabitants, a main railway centre, mining centre, with engineering works, marshalling yards, repair shops and a big reputation on German history. It certainly has had its turn too. So on we go to:-

DUNKIRK, where the British Army made their glorious retreat to the jubilation and mockery of the Nazis. The remnant of a disappointed but valiant army was among the boys who on D-Day less than one year ago returned to the continent and went forward without faltering to their avowed objective the UNCONDITIONAL SURRENDER of the German Armies and the final liberation of all the remaining German occupied territories.

The Nazi gang are being rounded up one by one, and their punishment will follow. Some have already, in their desperation, committed suicide, in some cases having already murdered their families. Inevitably some of these war-soaked Herrenvolk will escape, always with the idea in their heads of creating a Fourth Reich. IT IS UP TO YOU AND YOUR CHILDREN TO SEE THAT THE PRUSSIAN MONSTER NEVER AGAIN RAISES ITS HEAD. BE LIKE THE ELEPHANT – NEVER FORGET.

II: Commanding Officers

Note: Decorations are valid as at the date of completion of post.

W/C P.H.A. Simmons DFC
1 October 1941 – 1 August 1942

W/C H.I. Edwards VC, DSO, DFC
1 August 1942 – 10 February 1943

W/C G.P. Longfield (Killed in Action)
10 February 1943 – 26 February 1943

W/C J. de Lacy Wooldridge DFC*, DFM, AE
17 March 1943 – 25 June 1943

G/C H.J. Cundall DFC, AFC
25 June 1943 – 25 September 1944

G/C K.J. Somerville DSO, DFC, AFC
25 September 1944 – 1 June 1945

W/C T.W. Horton DSO, DFC
1 June 1944 – 15 October 1945

W/C R.C.M. Collard DSO, DFC
15 October 1945 – 5 November 1945

S/L G.O. Lister
6 November 1945 – 31 December 1945

W/C D.G. Stokes
31 December 1945 – 1 February 1946

III: Aircraft

Mosquitos used by 105 Squadron

All aircraft are listed by their manufacturer's serial number. The wartime squadron coding for 105 Squadron was GB. Where known, the aircraft's single coding identification letter is detailed after the colon. In the event of an aircraft having more than one code letter during it's squadron service, all letters used are listed in chronological order. The first date each aircraft was flown operationally is listed beside the serial number. A code suffixed by '-Bar' indicates operation as a C-Flight aircraft while adopting that particular code.

Following use by 105 Squadron, the fate of each aircraft is detailed, although in many cases the ultimate fate of those passed to other units are not listed here. Failed to return is abbreviated as FTR. The use of asterisks* indicates aircraft is not listed in the ORB as having flown operationally in wartime with 105 Squadron, but which is understood to have been on its charge. If the asterisk precedes a code, this indicates that the letter following the asterisk is a peacetime allocated letter, e.g., PF464:C/*U was coded C in wartime and recoded as U at some subsequent point in peacetime. ---------- Indicates no operational use with 105 Squadron.

W SERIES

PR/ Bomber Conversion type as
B. MkIV Series i:
W4064:C, 31.05.42, FTR: 31.05.42 – Irish Sea returning from Köln; W4065:N, 31.05.42, FTR: 19.08.42 – High-level attack on Bremen; W4066:A, 25.06.42, To 8 OTU; W4068:B, 01.06.42, FTR: 01.06.42 – High-level attack on Köln; W4069:M, 31.05.42, FTR: 16.07.42 – Attacking Wilhelmshaven ship yards; W4070:C, 18.06.42, FTR: 27.08.42 – Vagesac power station, Köln; W4071:L, 31.05.42, To 1655 MCU; W4072:D/W, 31.05.42, To 1655 MCU.

F. MkII Conversion to Dual Control Trainer
W4075:T , To 1655 MCU.

DK SERIES

B. Mk. IV Series ii

DK288:F, 01.09.42, To 1655 MTU; DK291:Q, 21.07.42, To 139 Squadron; DK292:B, 20.06.42, To 1655 MTU; DK293:*, ----------, To 618 Squadron for 'Highball' duties; DK294:F, 20.06.42, FTR: 02.07.42 – Low-level bombing of Flensburg; DK295:P, 02.07.42, FTR: 28.07.42 – Essen; DK296:G, 11.07.42, To 305 Flying Training Unit; DK297:O, 11.07.42, FTR: 25.08.42 – Brauweiler Switching Station, Köln; DK298:H, 02.07.42, FTR: 02.07.42 – Low-level bombing of Flensburg; DK299:S, 02.07.42, FTR: 11.07.42 – Low-level bombing of Flensburg; DK300:F, 11.07.42, To 109 Squadron; DK301:H , 21.07.42, FTR: 08.12.42 – Crashed forced landing Abbey Farm; DK302:D, 16.07.42, To 139 Squadron; DK303:V, 22.07.42, FTR: 29.08.42 – Shot down in sea off Dungeness; DK308:J, 25.07.42, FTR: 01.08.42 – Missing after take-off for Bremen; DK309:S, 04.08.42, FTR: 15.08.42 – High-level Mainz; DK312:K/U, 28.07.42, DBR: 01.08.42 – Crashed: overshoot, Horsham St Faith; DK313:M/E, 01.08.42, To 139 Squadron; DK316:J, 10.08.42, FTR: 30.10.42 – Cloud-cover attack on Lingen; DK317:K, 12.08.42, FTR: 11.10.42 – Dusk attack on Hanover; DK322:P, 02.09.42, FTR: 06.09.42 – High-level attack – Frankfurt-on-Main; DK323:N, 29.08.42, FTR: 29.08.42 – Crashed at Lympne; DK325:S , 27.08.42, FTR: 25.09.42 – Oslo – shot down by fighter; DK326:M, 09.09.42, FTR: 19.09.42 – Berlin – shot down by fighters; DK328:V, 02.09.42, FTR: 07.11.42 – Shipping in Gironde river; DK330:N, 06.09.42, To 139 Squadron; DK336:P, 16.09.42, FTR: 27.01.43 – Burmeister & Wain, Copenhagen; DK337:N , 14.09.42, To 139 Squadron; DK338:O, 16.09.42, FTR: 01.05.43 – Eindhoven: Crashed after take-off; DK339:C, 16.09.42, FTR: 09.10.42 – Dawn attack on Duisburg.

Oboe Equipped

B. MkIV Series ii

DK 333:HS-F, 09.07.43. Borrowed from 109 Squadron / To 192 Squadron.

DZ SERIES

B. MkIV Series ii

DZ311:Y, 23.01.43, FTR: 23.01.43 – Railways: Oldenburg–Osnabrück; DZ312:U, 01.10.42, To 1655 MTU; DZ313:E, 20.10.42, FTR: 20.10.42 – Cloud-cover attack on Hannover; DZ314:F, 02.10.42, FTR: 08.12.42 – Low-level on Den Helder docks; DZ315:L, 01.10.42, FTR: 09.01.43 – Engine sheds at Rouen; DZ318:*, ----------, To 1655 MTU; DZ320:Y, 11.10.42, FTR: 13.11.42 – Attack on *Neumark* in Flushing; DZ340:X, 06.10.42, DBR: 30.10.42 – Crashed on return from Leeuwarden; DZ341:A , 06.10.42, FTR: 11.10.42 – Dusk attack on Hannover; DZ343:Z, 21.10.42, FTR: 23.10.42 – Low-level on Hengelo; DZ348:K, 23.10.42, To 139 Squadron; DZ349:A, 20.10.42, To 305 Flying Training Unit; DZ351:B/L, 23.10.42, To 139 Squadron; DZ353:E, 23.10.42, To 139 Squadron; DZ354:C, 27.10.42, FTR: 12.12.43 – Essen as DZ354:D; DZ355:M, 25.10.42, To 618 Squadron for 'Highball' duties; DZ360:A, 13.11.42, FTR: 22.12.42 – Shot down by flak near Dunkirk; DZ361:C, 13.11.42, FTR: 13.11.42 – Attack on *Neumark* in Flushing; DZ365:V, 13.11.42, FTR: 26.02.43 – Rennes: collided with DZ413:K; DZ367:J, 16.11.42, FTR: 30.01.43 – Berlin; DZ369:B*, ----------, FTR: 28.11.42 – Crashed landing at Molesworth; DZ370:Z, 16.11.42, To 139 Squadron; DZ371:*, ----------, To 139 Squadron; DZ372:C, 06.12.42, DBR: 02.03.43 – Crashed landing at Marham; DZ373:*, ----------, To 139 Squadron; DZ374:X, 06.12.42, To 1655 MTU /105 Squadron /1655MTU; DZ378:K, 14.12.42, To Technical Training Command as 3509M; DZ379:H, 08.12.42, To 139 Squadron; DZ407:R, 22.12.42, FTR: 27.01.43 – Burmeister & Wain; Copenhagen; DZ408:F/H, 29.12.42, FTR: 20.01.44 – Rath: control lost then abandoned; DZ413:K, 02.10.42, FTR: 26.02.43 – Rennes: collided with DZ365:V; DZ414:E/O, 20.04.43, FPU attached 109 / 105 / 139 Squadron; DZ415:A, 09.01.43, To 627 Squadron; DZ416:Q, 13.01.43, FTR: 28.03.43 – Liège: Shot down by fighter; DZ420:*, ----------, To 139 Squadron; DZ458:J, 12.02.43, To 139 Squadron; DZ460:W, 12.02.43, FTR: 08.03.43 – Low-level on railways at Lingen; DZ461:G, 12.02.43, To 139 Squadron; DZ462:S, 12.02.43, To 627 Squadron; DZ467:P, 15.02.43, FTR: 27.05.43 – Low-level on Zeiss works at Jena; DZ468:E, 15.02.43, To 139 Squadron; DZ472:Z, 15.02.43, FTR: 27.02 43 – Lost wing and crashed near Marham; DZ474:X, 15.02.43, FTR: 19.02.43 – Crashed on overshoot at Debden; DZ483:R, 27.03.43, DBR: 27.05.43 – Jena: crashed at base on return; DZ489:B, 26.02.43, DBR: 18.11.43 – Aachen: crashed landing as DZ489:D; DZ492:K, 20.03.43, To 109 Squadron; DZ518:A, 04.03.43, To 618 Squadron for 'Highball' duties; DZ519:U, 27.03.43, To 139 Squadron; DZ520:* , ----------, To 618 Squadron for 'Highball' duties; DZ521:V, 03.04.43, To 139 Squadron; DZ522:W, 27.03.43, FTR: 28.03.43 – Liège: Shot down by fighters; DZ536:Z, 28.03.43, FTR: 11.04.43 – Hengelo: Shot down at Bentheim; DZ548:D, 04.05.43, FTR: 05.02.44 – Collided as DZ548:J with a B-17G; DZ589:C, 13.06.43, To 1655 MTU; DZ591:O, 16.05.43, FTR: 22.10.43 – Knapsack power station as DZ591:K; DZ595:C, 17.05.43, To 1655 MTU when Oboe-equipped.

Oboe-equipped Conversions

B. MkIV Series ii
DZ408:H, 29.12.42, FTR: 20.01.44 – Rath: Crashed near Kings Lynn; DZ548:J, 04.05.43, FTR: 05.02.44 – Collided with USAAF Boeing B-17G; DZ591:K, 16.05.43, FTR: 22.10.43 – Knapsack power station, Köln; DZ595:H, 17.05.43, FTR: 26.08.43 – Undercarriage collapsed at Foulsham.

Oboe-equipped

B. MkIV Series ii
DZ317:HS-R, 22.08.43, Borrowed from 109 Squadron / To 1655 MTU; DZ354:D, 27.10.42, FTR: 12.12.43 – Essen; DZ429:B , 28.11.43, To 1655 MTU; DZ433:HS-J, 14.01.44, Borrowed from 109 Squadron / To 1655 MTU; DZ441:D, 30.08.43, To 140 Wing; DZ485:HS-W, 09.07.43, Borrowed from 109 Squadron / To 1655 MTU; DZ489:D, 26.02.43, DBR: 18.11.43 – Aachen: crashed landing at Marham; DZ550:A, 25.07.43, To 1655 MTU; DZ587:B, 25.07.43, FTR: 05.11.43 – Bochum: crashed on return, Hardwick; DZ589:C, 13.06.43, To 1655 MTU.

LR SERIES

B. MkIX
LR475:*, ----------, To 139 Squadron; LR476:T, 01.01.44, FTR: 22.03.44 – Deelen A/F: blew up on landing; LR477:B, 22.11.43, FTR: 23.11.43 – Knapsack: crashed in circuit ; LR496:N/K, 01.04.44, FTR: 27.04.44 – Training: swung on landing; LR497:A, 06.04.44, To 627 Squadron; LR498:W/Y, 22.01.45, Struck off Air Ministry charge on 15.05.46; LR500:B, 29.03.44, Struck off Air Ministry charge on 26.05.45; LR503:C/F-Bar, 13.03.44, FTR: 10.05.45 – Crashed on display at Calgary; LR504:C/H, 13.03.44, To 109 Squadron; LR506:E, 13.07.43, FTR: 29.09.43 – Bochum: Crashed West Raynham; LR507:F, 12.07.44, Struck off Air Ministry charge on 15.05.46; LR508:G/F/G, 25.07.43, To 109 Squadron; LR510:N, 26.09.43, To 109 Squadron; LR511:R, 26.09.43, To 109 Squadron; LR512:O, 26.09.43, To Bombing Development Unit; LR513:H-Bar/U, 07.10.44, To 109 Squadron.

ML SERIES

B. MkIX
ML896:P, 20.10.43, To Middle East; ML897:*, ----------, To 1409 Flight; ML898:*, ----------, To Telecommunications Flying Unit; ML902:S/C-Bar, 26.09.43, DBR: 14.01.45 – Crashed on take-off at Manston; ML904:T, 20.10.43, FTR: 15.11.43 – Düsseldorf; ML911:U, 05.11.43, FTR: 22.12.44 – Collided with beacon at Bourn; ML913:E, 22.10.43, FTR: 06.07.44 – Schloven; ML914:K/N/C, 10.12.43, To 627 Squadron; ML915:*, ——, To 109 Squadron; ML916:L/P/B, 12.11.43, DBR: 24.07.45 – Crashed on landing, Melsbroek; ML917:C-Bar, 21.04.44, To 1409 Flight; ML919:V, 18.10.43, FTR: 15.12.44 – Hannover: crashed on take-off; ML920:W/D, 18.10.43, Struck off Air Ministry charge on 17.05.46; ML921:X, 08.11.43, DBR: 09.04.44 – Crashed on take-off from Bourn; ML922:Y, 04.11.43, Struck off Air Ministry charge on 07.06.46; ML923:Z, 09.11.43, FTR: 29.01.45 – Stuttgart; ML924:C-Bar, 01.02.45, DBR: 06.03.45 – Berlin crashed on landing, Bourn.

B. MkXVI

ML934:D, 26.03.44, To 139 Squadron; ML935:*, ----------, To 692 Squadron; ML936:E-Bar/G, 06.04.44, To 1409 Flight / 105 Squadron / Fleet Air Arm; ML938:D/H/A, 02.03.44, To 16 OTU; ML956:G-Bar , 12.10.44, To Admiralty on 10.07.47; ML958:*, ----------, To 109 Squadron; ML962:*, ----------, To 109 Squadron; ML964:J, 21.03.44, FTR: 07.07.44 – Caen: shot down by fighter; ML967:*, ----------, To 109 Squadron; ML968:*, ----------, To 692 Squadron; ML970:D, 26.04.45, To 692 Squadron; ML971:*, ---------, To 692 Squadron; ML973:A-Bar/C-Bar/A-Bar , 18.04.44, To Fleet Air Arm; ML974:B-Bar/S, 18.04.44, To 16 OTU; ML978:C-Bar, 20.04.44, FTR: 13.05.44 – Châteaudun: crashed returning; ML981:D-Bar/C-Bar/D-Bar, 07.05.44, DBR: 23.12.44 – Köln: crashed on landing, Bourn; ML982:E-Bar, 29.04.44, To 109 Squadron; ML983:F-Bar/K-Bar/J-Bar/Y/F-Bar, 29.04.44, To 16 OTU; ML986:P/G-Bar, 26.09.43, DBF: 04.10.44 – Heilbronn: crashed on landing; ML987:C-Bar, 20.05.44, FTR: 14.07.44 – Schloven: crashed returning; ML989:F-Bar, 06.09.44, To 109 Squadron; ML991:*, ----------, To 109 Squadron; ML992:U/A-Bar , 28.12.44, To 109 / 105: Struck off charge on 07.06.46; ML993:H-Bar, 04.06.44, FTR: 19.10.44 – Düsseldorf: crashed on take-off: ML995: R/Q; 26.05.44, To Admiralty on 14.08.47; ML996:K, 06.06.44, FTR: 06.10.44 – Dortmund; ML997:*, ----------, To 109 Squadron; ML999:J-Bar/B-Bar/F/K-Bar, 05.06.44, Sold as scrap on 08.07.48.

MM SERIES

PR. MkIX

MM229:?, ----------, To 1409 Flight.

B. MkIX

MM237:M/Q, 23.12.43, FTR: 06.03.45 – Wesel: shot down by night fighter; MM241:H, 28.01.45, To 109 Squadron.

B. MkXVI

MM112:*, ----------, To 109 Squadron; MM116:*, ----------, To 571 Squadron; MM117:R, 05.03.45, To 109 Squadron; MM119:*, ----------, To 571 Squadron; MM120:*, ----------, To 571 Squadron; MM121:*, ----------, To 571 Squadron; MM134:E/P , 07.07.44, DBF: 04.04.45 – Engine test: crashed on take-off; MM135:*, ----------, To 692 Squadron; MM136:*, ----------, To 571 Squadron; MM137:*, ----------, To 692 Squadron; MM139:*, ----------, To 692 Squadron; MM151:J, 12.07.44, FTR: 04.02.45 – Würtzburg: crash-landed Knokke; MM152:C-Bar/B-Bar/B, 17.07.44, FTR: 11.12.44 – Bielefeld: crashed, Newmarket; MM154:*, ----------, To 109 Squadron; MM170:D/D-Bar, 10.10.44, FTR: 18.03.45 – Witten; MM171:* K, ----------, Struck off Air Ministry charge on 01.07.46; MM172:*, ----------, To 692 Squadron; MM177:*, ----------, To 109 / 105 to Admiralty on 09.05.4; MM178:*, ----------, To 109 Squadron; MM191:A-Bar/J-Bar, 23.10.44, To Fleet Air Arm; MM192:*, ----------, To 128 Squadron; MM193:*, ----------, To 109 / 105 to Admiralty on 13.08.47; MM199:*, ----------, To 128 Squadron; MM202:*, ----------, To 128 Squadron; MM205:* G, ----------, Sold as scrap on 22.08.49; MM222:*, ----------, FTR: 06.11.45 – crashed from take-off, Upwood; MM224:*, ----------, To 692 Squadron; MM225:V, 21.12.44, FTR: 31.12.44 – Mannheim: crashed, Manston; MM226:R, 18.12.44, DBF: 12.01.45 – Swung taking off in snow, Bourn.

PF SERIES

B. MkXVI

PF382:*, ----------, To 109 Squadron; PF385:A/K , 05.10.44, To General Aircraft Limited; PF388:*, ----------, To 692 Squadron; PF396:*, ----------, To 109 Squadron; PF407:J-Bar/V, 15.11.44, To Central Bomber Establishment; PF410:*, ----------, To 128 Squadron; PF411:*, ----------, To 128 Squadron; PF414:*, ----------, To 692 Squadron; PF431:K-Bar, 24.12.44, FTR: 02.01.45 – Castrop-Rauxel; PF434:W, 23.04.45, Struck off Air Ministry charge on 07.02.46; PF435:*, ----------, To 109 Squadron; PF437:*, ----------, To 128 Squadron; PF439:*, ----------, To Central Bomber Establishment; PF442:X, 04.02.45, To Central Bomber Establishment; PF443:*, ----------, To 128 Squadron; PF446:*, ----------, To Central Bomber

Establishment; PF452:B-Bar/*V, 28.02.45, To 109 Squadron; PF454:W, 07.03.45, Struck off Air Ministry charge on 18.09.50; PF458:*, ----------, To 128 Squadron; PF460:D-Bar, 04.04.45, To 139 Squadron; PF464:C/* U, 03.04.45, Sold as scrap on 27.05.49; PF467:D-Bar, 23.04.45, To 139 Squadron; PF484:H, 14.04.45, To 16 OTU; PF489:*, ----------, To 608 Squadron; PF491:*, ----------, To Central Bomber Establishment; PF492:*, ----------, To 608 Squadron; PF493:P, 11.04.45, Sold as scrap on 05.09.48; PF497:S, 19.04.45, DBR: 11.12.45 – Crashed on take-off, Upwood; PF505:*, ----------, To 608 Squadron; PF506:* U, ----------, To 139 Squadron; PF511:*, ----------, To 109 / 139 / 105 to 139 Squadron; PF518:* D, ----------, FTR: 14.06.45 – Single engine landing near Bourn; PF521:* T, ----------, Sold as scrap on 22.09.49; PF522:* R, ----------, To Central Bomber Establishment; PF524:* W, ----------, To Central Bomber Establishment; PF540:*, ----------, To 163 Squadron.

RV SERIES

B. Mk XVI
RV298:W/B, 01.01.45, FTR: 22.02.45 – No fuel/abandonned near Brugge; RV299:*, ----------, Sold as scrap on 26.05.49; RV303:J, 01.02.45, To Central Flying Establishment; RV304:H-Bar , 31.01.45, To 139 Squadron; RV308:J, 11.04.45, To Admiralty on 13.08.47; RV309:*, ----------, To 571 Squadron; RV310:*, ----------, To 692 Squadron; RV312:*, ----------, To 180 Squadron; RV316:*, ----------, To 109 Squadron; RV317:*, ----------, To 578 Squadron; RV322:Q, 30.03.45, Sold as scrap on 22.08.49; RV326:*, ----------, To 571 Squadron; RV362:*, ----------, To 571 squadron.

IV: Roll of Honour

105 Squadron Mosquito Crews

Date	Aircraft	Rank	Initials	Name	Award/ Service	Serial
31.05.42	W4064:C	P/O	W.D.	Kennard		101549
		P/O	E.R.	Johnson		108041
11.07.42	DK299:S	F/L	G.P.	Hughes	MiD, RCAF	J.4819
		F/O	T.A.	Gabe		65556
28.07.42	DK295:P	F/O	F.W.	Weekes	RAAF	Aus.402176
		P/O	F.A.	Hurley		47905
01.08.42	DK308:J	P/O	P.W.	Kerry		104576
15.08.42	DK309:S	F/O	G.W.	Downe	RAAF	Aus.400463
		P/O	A.W.	Groves	DFM	109063
19.08.42	W4065:N	F/Sgt	C.D.	Kelly	RAAF	Aus.404658
27.08.42	W4070:C	S/L	R.N.	Collins	DFC	39713
		P/O	W.	May		116969
29.08.42	DK303:V	Sgt	C.	Atkinson		1254703
06.09.42	DK322:P	Sgt	H.E.	Evans		943115

Date	Aircraft	Rank	Initials	Name	Award/ Service	Serial
19.09.42	DK326:M	S/L	N.H.E.	Messervy	DFC	40057
		P/O	F.	Holland		130725
25.09.42	DK325:S	F/Sgt	G.K.	Carter		1283561
		Sgt	W.S.	Young		1344278
09.10.42	DK339:C	W/O	C.R.K.	Bools	MiD	564555
		Sgt	G.W.	Jackson		1054492
20.10.42	DZ313:E	F/Sgt	L.W.	Deeth		1264627
		W/O	F.E.M.	Hicks		523113
23.10.42	DZ343:Z	S/L	J.C.	Simpson	MiD	36147
		F/L	C.B.	Walter		44227
30.10.42	DK316:J	Sgt	E.L.	Simon		1381056
		Sgt	T.W.	Balmforth		655642
13.11.42	DZ320:Y	F/O	C.A.	Graham	RAAF	401623
		F/O	R.F.L.	Anderson	RCAF	J.10415
13.11.42	DZ361:C	F/Sgt	N.	Booth		1376648
		Sgt	F.A.	Turner		983303
28.11.42	DZ369:B	Sgt	J.W.	Egan		1070497
22.12.42	DZ360:A	Sgt	J.E.	Cloutier	RCAF	R.97434
		Sgt	A.C.	Foxley		811126
09.01.43	DZ315:L	W/O	A.R.	Noseda	DFC, RAAF	Aus.406029
		Sgt	J.W.	Urquhart		1348237
23.01.43	DZ311:Y	F/O	L.J.	Skinner		110849
		Sgt	F.H.	Saunders		1286414
27.01.43	DZ407:R	Sgt	J.G.	Dawson		1315442
		Sgt	R.H.	Cox		1254141
26.02.43	DZ365:V	W/C	G.P.	Longfield		27229
		F/L	R.F.	Millns		115317
26.02.43	DZ413:K	F/O	S.G.	Kimmel	RCAF	J.9561
		F/O	H.N.	Kirkland	RCAF	J.10427
27.02.43	DZ472:Z	P/O	G.W.	McCormick	RAAF	Aus.408661
		W/C	J.W.	Deacon		25042
28.03.43	DZ416:Q	F/O	J.G.	Bruce	DFM	124216
		F/O	R.L.	Reily		119261

Date	Aircraft	Rank	Initials	Name	Award/Service	Serial
28.03.43	DZ522:W	Sgt	G.K.	Leighton		1232161
		Sgt	T.N.	Chadwick		1537059
11.04.43	DZ536:Z	F/O	D.	Polgase	RNZAF	NZ.415714
		Sgt	L.C.	Lampen		1311504
01.05.43	DK338:O	F/O	O.W.	Thompson	DFM, RNZAF	NZ.401791
		F/O	W.J.	Horne	DFC	133536
27.05.43	DZ467:P	P/O	R.	Massie		48894
		Sgt	G.P.	Lister		1064071
27.05.43	DZ483:R	F/O	A.J.	Rea	DFM	132174
		P/O	K.S.	Bush		136704
29.09.43	LR506:E	Lt	F.M.	Fisher	DFC	?
		P/O	L.	Hogan	DFM	158337
22.10.43	DZ591:O	F/L	G.	Sweeney	DFC, RAAF	404555
		F/L	W.G.	Wood		128447
05.11.43	DZ587:B	F/L	J.	Gordon	DFC	86721
		F/O	R.G.	Hayes	DFC	120087
23.11.43	LR477:B	P/O	E.	Wade	BEM	145656
		F/O	A.G.	Fleet		142563
12.12.43	DZ354:D	F/O	B.F.	Reynolds		118712
		F/O	J.D.	Phillips		138829
05.02.44	DZ548:J	F/L	J.F.	Slatter		87660
		F/O	P.O.	Hedges		145109
22.03.44	LR476:T	F/L	C.F.	Boxall		69472
09.04.44	ML921:X	F/L	R.B.	Smith	DFC, RAAF	Aus.402757
10.04.44	ML921:X	F/L	P.E.	Cadman	DFC	145333
13.05.44	ML978: C-Bar	F/L	N.	Clayes	DFC	47351
		F/O	F.E.	Deighton		155114
06.07.44	ML913:E	F/L	G.K.	Whiffen		81668
		F/O	D.K.	Williams	DFC	155999
07.07.44	ML964:J	S/L	W.W.	Blessing	DSO, DFC, RAAF	404648
10.07.44	ML919:V	P/O	J.E.	Fox	DFC	177086

Date	Aircraft	Rank	Initials	Name	Award/ Service	Serial
06.10.44	ML996:K	F/L	J.E.	Brook		116765
		Sgt	W.W.	Bowden		1170874
19.10.44	ML993: H-Bar	F/O	L.P.	Whipp		173314
		P/O	C.	Bertenshaw		158336
11.12.44	MM152:B	F/L	J.G.	Brass	RCAF	J.10499
		F/O	D.A.	Field		155125
02.01.45	PF431: K-Bar	F/O	F.T.	Watson	DFM	159930
28.01.45	ML923:Z	F/L	G.L.S.	McHardy	DFC	138688
		F/O	G.R.P.	Duncan		157337
19.03.45	MM170: D-Bar	F/L	L.F.D.	King		42612
		F/L	D.P.	Tough		123616
04.04.45	MM134:P	F/L	P.	Enderby	DFC	126587

V: Line Shoots

It was customary on overhearing an exaggerated statement or tale, possibly in the mess and issued when under the influence or otherwise, for the statement to be recorded and witnessed for posterity in the mess 'Line Book'. Many recordings were personalized humour, only to be understood by those who were involved at the time; however some were fairly obviously humorous exaggerations about flying skills, the winning of decorations, etc. The following 'lines' from 105 and 139 Squadron aircrew were recorded in the Line Book at RAF Marham:

21.7.42 – P/O Fry discussing operational landings: 'We got down nicely the other night, and as I finished taxiing to the Watch Office, Major (navigator) piped up "Come on Fry, pull your finger out and b—well get down!!??"'

P/O Bill Farquharson in the ante-room on the night of the staff dance: 'Gee! I did a wizard landing today. I didn't know I was down until I stopped.'

Bill Blessing describing a 'do' to an amazed audience of listeners, casually remarked: 'Of course we weren't hit at all by the flak-wallahs but unluckily we stopped a 5" shell from somewhere or other.'

2.12.42 – Stated by P/O (Tubby) Cairns in 105 Navigation Office: 'The only reason I have flown with Wing Commanders ever since war began is because I happen to be the wireless king!'

Said to F/O Miller that West Raynham aerodrome had a bumpy surface and was bad for landing, F/O Miller replied: 'As a matter of fact, when I landed there, I didn't see any of the aerodrome at all.'

27.1.43 – W/C Longfield, when speaking of the Path Finders' additional flying badge, remarked: 'I have been flying so long that wings are sprouting from my shoulders.'

30.1.43 – At breakfast 05.00 hours, before first daylight on Berlin, F/L Gordon: 'Night take-offs don't scare me – when I started flying they only had gas light.'

4.3.43 – At 10.30 hours in the ante-room, talking of gongs [medals] S/L Berggren stated: 'I skip those things. I did so many trips on my first tour, I got beyond it!' Ten minutes later after discussing his experiences with W/C Shand 'Were you ever upside down in cloud with nothing on the clock? [Air Speed Indicator]' Answer: 'Yes. Who told you?'

2.3.43 – Talking about DFCs & bars in the ante-room in the evening, F/O Wickham: 'What do you do after the third bar, that's what's worrying me.'

F/L Gordon (10/10 drunk), after being forcibly prevented from setting a 'stolen' piano on fire, was heard to say: 'It isn't the first time I have had a piano on my Mess Bill in the morning.'

10.3.43 – P/O Thompson RNZAF in the ante-room: 'Yesterday the flak was so thick that I couldn't see the aircraft in front of me.' The observer, P/O Hoare, added 'We couldn't even see over the wing tips.'

6.4.43 – 11.10 hours, 105 ante-room. S/L Ralston complained: 'Some Junior Officer has pinched my 6th log book and put his name on it.'

14.5.43 – In the Interrogation Room after a Met. Recco. P/O (Scruffy) Wright DFC 'We were flying so low this morning that we could easily have been torpedoed!'

14.5.43 – F/O Hayes DFC, 105 Squadron, remarks: 'Why listen to the news – we made it!'

S/L Channer DFC, speaking of having a dual aircraft attached to his squadron: 'Of course it wasn't necessary to have one in the old Blenheim days. So long as the pilot knew how to take off, it didn't matter whether he could land it or not!'

28.6.43 – At the 139 & 1483 farewell party. F/L Patterson DFC said: 'I have saved England by my example, and will, I trust, save Europe by my exertions.'

16.7.43 – F/L Humphrey: 'I can't read these beacons – they're too slow.'

7.8.43 – F/L Fisher: 'When I've had this moustache for four weeks I'll have to put it in bobby-pins so I can eat!'

10.9.43 – The day he got his gong. When F/L Westerman was about to sew on his ribbon, someone remarked that his wing was a trifle low. 'I know,' he remarked modestly, 'I hadn't figured on getting a gong just yet!'

23.11.43 – S/L Channer, overheard in the ante-room at 16.00 hours: 'You know, old boy, I always prefer operating in Mark IVs.' On being asked why, he replied, 'Well, old boy, they're much cheaper to run!'

16.2.44 – W/C Ralston, 21.30 hours in the ante-room: 'The snag is, when you become notability, everybody knows you, but you can't remember them.'

17.2.44 – F/L Humphrey: 'I can never understand it. Sometimes one wakes up in the morning and feels 'Boy oh Boy! Just the day for an op. . . .'

22.3.44 – F/O Howard: 'With regard to birth I am completely ignorant but in the matter of conception I am a MASTER.'

Bibliography

1. PRIMARY SOURCES

a. PUBLIC RECORD OFFICE, KEW, LONDON

AIR14/ 2555:	RAF Station Bourn – Flying Control Log: 3/1943 – 4/1944
AIR14/ 2556:	RAF Station Bourn – Flying Control Log: 4/1944 – 7/1944
AIR14/ 2557:	RAF Station Bourn – Flying Control Log: 7/1944 – 9/1944
AIR14/ 2558:	RAF Station Bourn – Flying Control Log: 9/1944 – 11/1944
AIR14/ 2559:	RAF Station Bourn – Flying Control Log: 11/1944 – 3/1945
AIR14/ 2560:	RAF Station Bourn – Flying Control Log: 3/1945 – 7/1945
AIR14/ 2719:	1655 Mosquito Training Unit: 4/1943 – 9/1944
AIR14/ 3018:	Oboe Ground Stations: 4/1944 – 1945
AIR14/ 3365:	Bomber Command Summary of Operations
AIR 27/ 826:	105 Squadron Operations Record Book
AIR 27/ 827:	105 Squadron Operations Record Book
AIR 27/ 828:	105 Squadron Operations Record Book
AIR 27/ 830:	105 Squadron Operations Record Book (Appendices)
AIR 27/ 960:	139 Squadron Operations Record Book
AIR 28/ 94:	RAF Station – Bourn
AIR 28/ 287:	RAF Station – Foulsham
AIR 28/ 288:	RAF Station – Foulsham (Appendices)
AIR 28/ 322:	RAF Station – Graveley
AIR 28/ 325:	RAF Station – Graveley (Appendices)
AIR 28/ 386:	RAF Station – Horsham St Faith
AIR 28/ 517:	RAF Station – Marham
AIR 28/ 869:	RAF Station – Upwood
AIR 29/ 613:	1655 Mosquito Training Unit
AIR 50/ 207:	Combat Reports
F300 – F309:	GRO War Deaths RAF All Ranks: 1939 – 1948

b. COMMONWEALTH WAR GRAVES COMMISSION

http://yard.ccta.gov.uk/cwgc/register.nsf

c. PRIVATE SOURCES

Interviews and correspondence with former aircrews and groundcrews listed in the acknowledgements section of this book.
Memoirs of S/L Charles Patterson DSO, DFC, RAF (Ret'd)
Student to Stalag: Memoirs of Robin P. Thomas DFC, RAF (Ret'd), RIBA.

2. SECONDARY SOURCES

a. BOOKS

Bennett, CB, CBE, DSO, Air Vice-Marshal D.C.T., *Path Finder* (Goodall Publications, 1988)
Bishop, Edward, *Mosquito: The Wooden Wonder* (Airlife, 1990)

Boiten, Theo, *NachtJagd; The Night Fighter versus Bomber War over the Third Reich 1939–45* (Crowood Press, 1997)

Bowman, Martin W., *Low Level from Swanton* (Air Research Publications, 1995)

Bowman, Martin W., *The Men Who Flew the Mosquito* (Patrick Stephens, 1995)

Bowman, Martin W., *De Havilland Mosquito* (Crowood Press, 1997)

Bowyer, Chaz, *Bomber Barons* (Book Club Associates, 1983)

Bowyer, Chaz, *Mosquito at War* (Ian Allan, 1973)

Bowyer, Chaz, *Mosquito Squadrons of the Royal Air Force* (Ian Allan, 1984)

Bowyer, Michael J.F., *2 Group RAF: A Complete History, 1936–1945* (Faber & Faber, 1974)

Bowyer, Michael J.F., *Action Stations 1. Military Airfields of East Anglia* (PSL, 1990)

Bowyer, M.J.F. and Philpott, Brian, *Classic Aircraft No.7: Their History and How to Model Them* (PSL, 1980)

Bowyer, M.J.F. and Rawlings, John D. R., *Squadron Codes 1937–56* (PSL, 1979)

Burgess, Alan, *The Longest Tunnel: The True Story of the Great Escape* (Bloomsbury, 1990)

Corser, Squadron Leader W., *Airfield Focus No. 18* (GMS)

Chorley, W.R., *Royal Air Force Bomber Command Losses of the Second World War*: Vol. 3: *1942* (Midland Counties Publications, 1994)

Chorley, W.R., *Royal Air Force Bomber Command Losses of the Second World War*: Vol. 4: *1943* (Midland Counties Publications, 1996)

Chorley, W.R., *Royal Air Force Bomber Command Losses of the Second World War*: Vol. 5: *1944* (Midland Counties Publications, 1997)

Chorley, W.R., *Royal Air Force Bomber Command Losses of the Second World War*: Vol. 6: *1945* (Midland Counties Publications, 1998)

Delve, Ken, *RAF Marham: The Operational History* (PSL, 1995)

Green, William, *Famous Bombers of the Second World War* (Macdonald, 1959)

Green, William, *Famous Fighters of the Second World War* (MacDonald, 1960)

Halley, James J., *Royal Air Force Aircraft: W1000 to W9999* (Air-Britain, 1983)

Halley, James J., *Royal Air Force Aircraft: DA100 to DZ999* (Air-Britain, 1987)

Halley, James J., *Royal Air Force Aircraft: LA100 to LZ999* (Air-Britain, 1991)

Halley, James J., *Royal Air Force Aircraft: MA100 to MZ999* (Air-Britain, 1991)

Halley, James J., *Royal Air Force Aircraft: PA100 to RZ999* (Air-Britain, 1992)

Halley, James J., *The Squadrons of the Royal Air Force* (Air-Britain, 1980)

Hamlin, John F., *The Royal Air Force in Cambridgeshire*: Part 4 (John F. Hamlin, 1990)

Hamlin, John F., *Supplement to The Royal Air Force in Cambridgeshire*: Part 4 (John F. Hamlin, 1990)

Hardy, M. J., *The de Havilland Mosquito* (David and Charles, 1997)

Hardy, M. J., *The de Havilland Mosquito Super Profile* (Haynes, 1984)

Hastings, Max, *Bomber Command* (Michael Joseph, 1987)

Hinsley, F. H., *British Intelligence in the Second World War* (HMSO, 1994)

Holliday, J., *Mosquito: The Wooden Wonder Aircraft of World War II* (Doubleday, 1970)

Howe, Stuart, *The de Havilland Mosquito: An Illustrated History* (Aston Publications, 1992)

Howe, Stuart, *Mosquito Portfolio* (Ian Allan, 1984)

Jefford, MBE, RAF, Wing Commander C.G., *RAF Squadrons* (Airlife, 1988)

Johnson, J.E. 'Johnnie' and Lucas, P.B. 'Laddie', *Courage in the Skies: Great Air Battles from the Somme to Desert Storm* (Stanley Paul, 1992)

McKee, Alexander, *The Mosquito Log* (Souvenir Press, 1988)

Maas, Jon van der and Neeven, Aad, *Zonder Waarschuwing; Feiten en achtergronden over de luchtaanvallen op Haarlem 1940–1945* (De Vrieseborch Haarlem, 1995)

Maynard, John, *Bennett and the Path Finders* (Arms & Armour, 1996)

Messenger, Charles, *Crucial Battles of World War 2: Cologne – The First 1000-Bomber Raid* (Ian Allan, 1982)

Mondey, David, *Concise Guide to British Aircraft of World War II* (Temple Press, 1984)

Musgrove, Gordon, *Path Finder Force – A History of 8 Group* (McDonald & Jane, 1976)

Middlebrook, Martin and Everitt, Chris, *The Bomber Command War Diaries – An Operational Reference Book 1939–1945* (Midland Publishing, 1996)

Profile Publications, *The de Havilland Mosquito Mks I – IV*, No. 52 (Profile Publications, 1965)

Ransom, Derek, *Battle-Axe: A History of 105 Squadron RAF* (Air-Britain, 1967)

Richards, Denis, *Royal Air Force 1939–1945* Vol. I: *The Fight at Odds* (HMSO, 1953)

Richards, Denis and Saunders, Hillary St George, *Royal Air Force 1939–1945* Vol. II: *The Fight Avails* (HMSO, 1954)

Salmaggi, Cesare and Pallavisini, Alfredo, *2194 Days of War* (Winward, 1977)

Saunders, Hillary St George, *Royal Air Force 1939–1945* Vol. III: *The Fight Is Won* (HMSO, 1954)

Sharp, C. Martin and Bowyer, Michael J.F., *Mosquito* (Faber, 1971)

Shores, Christopher, *Duel for the Sky* (Blandford Press, 1985)

Simons, Graham M., *Mosquito: The Original Multi-role Aircraft* (Arms & Armour, 1990)

Smith, David J., *De Havilland Mosquito Crash Log* (Midland Counties, 1976)

Smith, Graham, *Norfolk Airfields in the Second World War* (Countryside Books, 1996)

Smith, J. R. and Kay, Anthony, *German Aircraft of The Second World War* (Putman, 1978)

Snyder, Louis L., *Encyclopedia of the Third Reich* (Wordsworth Editions, 1976)

Turner, John Frayn, *British Aircraft of World War II* (Book Club Associates, 1977)

Watts DSO, DFC*, CD, Jack, *Nickels and Nightingales* (General Store Publishing House, Canada, 1995)

Wooldridge DFC and bar, DFM, J. de L., *Low Attack* (Sampson Low 1943; Crécy, 1993, ISBN 0-947554-31-9)

Mosquito in Action Part 1 (no.127)- (Squadron/Signal, 1992)

Mosquito in Action Part 2 (no.139)- (Squadron/Signal, 1993)

b.   MAGAZINES

The Aeroplane

Index

Because this book describes the Mosquito era of 105 Squadron, references to both appear on nearly every page. Therefore, these references have not been included in the index.